HAROLD ARLEN

Happy with the Blues

A page of "jots" in Harold Arlen's manuscript. Each check indicates a separate song idea, or in the composer's phrase, "melodic springboards to be developed into songs."

HAROLD ARLEN
Happy with the Blues

by EDWARD JABLONSKI

New introduction and
supplementary song list
by the author

A DA CAPO PAPERBACK

Library of Congress Cataloging-in-Publication Data

Jablonski, Edward.
  Harold Arlen, happy with the blues.

  (A Da Capo paperback)
  Reprint. Originally published: 1st ed. Garden City,
N.Y.: Doubleday, 1961.
    1. Arlen, Harold, 1905–   . 2. Composers — United
States — Biography. I. Title. II. Title: Happy with the
blues.
ML410.A76J3   1986   780′.92′4 [B]   86-11667
ISBN 0-306-80274-0 (pbk.)

This Da Capo Press paperback edition of *Harold Arlen: Happy with the Blues*
is an unabridged republication of the edition published in New York in 1961,
here updated with a new introduction and a supplementary list of works by the
author. It is reprinted by arrangement with Doubleday & Co.

Published by Da Capo Press, Inc.
A Subsidiary of Plenum Publishing Corporation
233 Spring Street
New York, N.Y. 10013

INTRODUCTION TO THE DA CAPO EDITION

Since the first edition of this book, Harold Arlen's reputation has grown immeasurably even as his output has slowed to a halt. He is now generally acknowledged as one of the giants of popular song. A sketch here of his accomplishments in recent decades will simply add some details to a record firmly established and a legacy that is one of the greatest in American music.

Several factors precipitated Arlen's withdrawal from composition since 1960: the debacles of *Saratoga* and *Blue Opera*, which encouraged him to scrutinize more carefully any books submitted for proposed musicals; personal tragedy; and frustration as nothing came his way that seemed worth doing.

There was a brief flurry when he was approached by British producers who wanted him to provide the music for a cartoon adaptation of Dicken's Pickwick Club sketches. It was a project filled with promise: Christopher Fry would do the adaptation, Ronald Searle the drawings, and Ira Gershwin the lyrics. But like so many good ideas—and bad—the cartoon died a-borning. Arlen was disappointed for he looked forward to working with Gershwin again and the comparative serenity of Beverly Hills.

Early in 1961 Anya and Harold Arlen did take a house in Beverly Hills, however, to work on another musical cartoon. The lyricist was Yip Harburg and the voice for which they would be writing was that of their friend Judy Garland. Produced by UPA, prestigious creators of innovative and creative cartoons, among them *Gerald McBoing-Boing* and the *Mister Magoo* series, the feature, treating the affairs of felines, was rather archly entitled *Gay Purr-ee*.

Arlen settled in comfortably in their rented house and established a typical, for him, routine. "I'd be on the golf course by around 7:30, be finished by around 11:30, then come home; Annie would be up by then," he recalls. "Yipper would show up around three, with a bottle of schnapps under his arm. He'd take a couple of sips, then fall asleep (Yipper was a night person). After his nap we'd work on the songs."

And so the summer of 1961 was spent in California tranquility. The Arlens saw the Gershwins and such old friends as Harry Warren and Ted Koehler. Work went well and a full score was conceived for *Gay Purr-ee*, ranging through the folk-like "Little Drops of Rain," the moody "Paris is a Lonely Town" (which Arlen believes is graced with one of Harburg's finest lyrics), an unusual waltz, "Take My Hand, Paree," and a couple of trenchant comic songs, "The Horse Won't Talk" and "The Money Cat." When the Arlens returned to New York in mid-October of 1961, he could leave the calm of Beverly Hills with a sense of accomplishment.

Gay Purr-ee was released in time for the Christmas season of 1962. By the summer Arlen had received the sound track recordings and wrote to a friend that "my special pleasure at the moment is the 'Gay Purr-ee' track. Judy is a treasure and one's musical creation could not be in better hands. She does a superb job and while the rest of the cast and numbers come off excellently, she alone shines.

"Nothing new as far as material for the theatre or movies, but ever hopeful, we go on."

August 1962 was a busy time and Arlen, an inveterate television news devotee, commented on current events in a wry quatrain: "The air is full as you know with launching rocket, lunar ferry, orbit space ship, NASA, Van Allen belt, African Veldt.

> Gone—the sane season
> Gone—the age of reliance
> Gone—man's reason
> We're up to our ass in science."

With no film or show in the offing, Arlen accumulated jots or taped "possibilities" for future use. He also began a collaboration with lyricist Dory Langdon (then married to conductor-pianist André Previn). Over a period of about three years they turned out several interesting songs, two of which resulted in important recordings: "The Morning After" (Eileen Farrell) and "So Long, Big Time!" (Tony Bennett, with the composer conducting the orchestra).

Yip Harburg, ever eager to be doing something, especially with Arlen, frequently came around. They did their last song for Judy Garland, the title song for her final film, *I Could Go on Singing*. A year later, Harburg, inspired by the Rachel Carson book, provided Arlen with a strong lyric for the song, "The Silent Spring," which is not so much a commentary on the hazards of environmental poisoning as it is Harburg's reading of the political climate in the country at the time—the fear, dissent, alienation between groups and factions because of the Vietnam experience. Not a typical "popular" tune, nor a blatant political tract, it is merely a fine, affecting song.

In 1964 a new songwriting partnership began in a novel manner. Arlen encountered Martin Charnin, musical theatre performer (he had appeared in the original production of *West Side Story*) turned lyricist in the offices of Harwin Music Corporation. The lyricist slipped a piece of paper into the composer's pocket; written on it was a single line: "I could be good for you." Amused and charmed by Charnin's whimsy, Arlen agreed to write the music for a song with that title, producing a characteristic, pulsating setting. This began a flood of song.

"That's a Fine Kind of Freedom" followed and was recorded by the composer himself for Columbia Records in an album entitled "Harold Sings Arlen (with friend). The "friend" was Barbra Streisand, fresh from her triumphs in *Funny Girl*.

Evidently the collaboration worked well for both writers, so they turned their attention to a full scale musical, set in Japan, entitled *Softly*. Although over a period of about a year they turned out close to thirty songs (and many rejects), the show never came off, primarily because of book problems. Writer Hugh Wheeler revised his script, trying several endings, but the project finally died.

Around this time Arlen experienced more serious anxieties. Anya Arlen had been evincing signs of illness, initially considered an indication of emotional stress. But she refused to see a doctor, and not until much later was it discovered that she suffered from a brain tumor. After her death on March 9, 1970, Arlen, in deep depression, lost all interest in his work, which had before sustained him in difficult times. He became reclusive and spent his time watching television in his apartment; he rarely went out except to visit his brother Jerry and his wife, Rita. He occasionally saw a few close friends, among them Wilva and Robert Breen.

It was Breen who ended this withdrawal, albeit only temporarily, by introducing Arlen to a young avant-garde dramatist, Leonard Melfi. Blessed with a wild sense of humor (and hair to match, which led to Arlen's nicknaming him "Curley") as well as a deep respect—close to awe—for the composer, Melfi worked with Arlen on a short television musical, *Clippity Clop and Clementine*. The plot revolves around a Central Park horse-drawn carriage driver. One of its most haunting songs, "I Had a Love Once," characterized by a rich, swaying, chordal accompaniment under the melody, is one of Arlen's masterpieces.

Arlen completed his work in 1973, but Melfi has not completed the libretto and the songs remain unheard. It was the last sustained effort for Arlen.

His concerned, forceful friend Yip Harburg consistently tried to inspire Arlen to work again. He hoped to get the composer to write two new tunes for a projected revival of *Bloomer Girl*, but Arlen simply was not interested. Harburg did, however, persuade him to complete two songs in 1976, "Looks Like the End of a Beautiful Friendship" and "Promise Me Not to Love Me." When it became obvious that the composer was not in the mood for work, Harburg planned to include this latter song in the *Bloomer Girl* revival.

But this, tragically, did not materialize. While driving in Hollywood, Harburg suffered a heart attack and died on March 5, 1981. For a tribute to Harburg, organized by ASCAP, Arlen composed a simple eulogy: "We all lost a great contributor to our popular song, one of the rare poets of our profession. I personally lost a good and faithful friend in Yipper. His wit, his playfulness with words, his brilliance, produced a torrent of lyrics. We truly collaborated in every sense of the word. I miss him, we all miss him. There was only one Yipper."

                              ❄   ❄   ❄

In recent decades, Harold Arlen has achieved the recognition and appreciation that his many admirers felt he deserved: *Twentieth Century*, a television program with Walter Cronkite as host, devoted two complete Sunday shows to the composer, his songs, and some of his collaborators. In March 1965 *Cue* magazine presented a star-studded salute at Lincoln Center's Philharmonic Hall; among the performers were Eileen Farrell, Sammy Davis, Jr., Bert Lahr, pianists Stan Freeman, Cy Walter, and Lisa Kirk. He was one of the charter inductees in the Songwriters Hall of Fame founded by the National Academy of Popular Music; and in 1973 he received the Handel Medal, New York City's highest award to its distinguished citizens, from his good friend, then-mayor John V. Lindsay.

In October, 1979, the Theatre Hall of Fame (housed in the Uris Theatre) inducted him along with other distinguished contributors to the American musical scene: Leonard Bernstein, Abe Burrows, Alan Jay Lerner, Frederick Loewe, the late Frank Loesser, and the turn-of-the-century team (Ned) Harrigan and (Tony) Hart.

The American Society of Composers, Authors and Publishers (ASCAP), on whose Board of Directors Arlen had served for several years, saluted his "extraordinary talent" and his "enormous contributions to the musical enjoyment of people all over the world," with a generously proportioned and handsomely composed birthday greeting—his 75th—in the *New York Times* on February 15, 1980 This gesture on the part of his colleagues deeply touched the composer, who had spent the day quietly at home, much of the time on the telephone with happy birthday wishers.

Another highlight of recent years was a celebration by his fellow songwriters, publishers, and entertainers presented by the National Academy of Popular Music on March 15, 1982. This musical tribute featured a medley of Arlen songs performed by Dinah Shore (who had made her film debut singing his *Up in Arms* in 1943); salutes by Marvin Hamlisch, Charles Strouse, Julie Styne, and Burton Lane, who, with his wife Lynn, was the motive force behind the occasion; and an ensemble finale of "Over the Rainbow." At the finish, a committee composed of Carol Channing, Larry Kert, Barbara Cook, and others came off stage to present Arlen with the Academy's "Johnny Mercer Award." As he stood to acknowledge the ovation (not easy for him because of a weakness in his legs), Arlen clearly was touched by the tribute, but he topped off his feelings with an audible murmur to a friend next to him that the statuette was "a poor likeness of Johnny."

The next day the plaque took its place on the wall of his workroom den, along with the other awards that have accumulated over the years, from his "Over the Rainbow" Academy Award to a recent one—for the same song—as a Country and Western hit!

His good friend Irving Berlin calls frequently with a new joke, or to bring Arlen's attention to a worthy television show of political or cultural interest—or one which is featuring Arlen songs. This friendship is extraordinary—salutary and enriching. Arlen, it might be noted, greatly admires the master songwriter and frequently addresses him as "Mr. B."

Another sustained friendship was that with Ira Gershwin, although the lyricist's California residence precluded frequent visitation. For years it was their habit to bet modestly on the big Bowl games on New Year's Day. Gershwin, if his home state were playing, invariably chose California; if not, Arlen took his choice of teams. For years in a row, Arlen chose the winning team. Gershwin would send off his check (the amount varying according to a whimsical handicapping system) with a delightful letter. Virtually an entire wall in one of the smaller rooms in the Arlen apartment on Central Park West is covered with these framed letters and checks—to the dismay of Gershwin's accountant.

Rarely, but on occasion, Arlen sits at the piano for a few moments; he talks about getting back to work if he could find the right lyricist. He ponders the various projects that regularly arise, ranging from requests for interviews through nightclub acts and revues built around his songs, ambitious song anthologies and revivals. All of this serves to remind him that those unassuming melodies that came out of the blue, evolving from jots and "possibilities," have found a permanent place of honor in America and all over the world's rainbow.

—EDWARD JABLONSKI
New York City
July, 1983

* * * *

Harold Arlen's last years were courageously miserable; during the last decade he was afflicted with degenerative Parkinson's disease. Confined to his apartment, he stopped most activities, saw fewer people. Then, in 1983, he lost his long time friend, Ira Gershwin.

Despite his disability (at times he was unable to stand or walk and required round-the-clock nurses), he was pleased to learn of a new Arlen revue, or that a club singer was featuring his songs. He was especially pleased with the superb *Harold Arlen Songbook*, a collection of seventy-six songs meticulously and affectionately edited by David Bickman and published late in 1985.

The anthology was particularly well-timed, coming as it did shortly after he was released from the hospital after surgery. Surviving that in his condition was virtually a miracle; tragically, however, it was found that he was suffering from cancer. After returning to his home he enjoyed several weeks of feeling somewhat (a relative term) better. In this period he was alert enough and had the strength to enjoy two fine recorded collections of his songs: Maxine Sullivan singing *The Great Songs from the Cotton Club* produced by Ken Bloom, Bill Rudman and Keith Ingham; Bloom and Rudman visited Arlen to present him one of the first copies.

The second album featured Judy Kaye singing his art song grouping, the *Americanegro Suite* and songs primarily from his show and film scores, produced by Stuart Triff. He heard a rough version of it on cassette for his 81st birthday, February 15, 1986. He was clearly pleased for he frequently sang along with Judy Kaye, tapped out the beat and applauded and praised the performances. This was the last Harold Arlen recording he was to hear and one which gave him much joy.

On April 23, 1986, he died peacefully in the early afternoon; his family and two friends were with him. His long ordeal, which had begun with the death of Anya Arlen sixteen years before, was over at last. Soon the air filled with his music from Banff, Canada, to Sydney, Australia. At the services for him, his friend Burton Lane delivered a beautiful eulogy; Ellin and Irving Berlin sent a lovely bouquet.

On Friday, the twenty-fifth, he was buried beside Anya in Hartsdale, New York. Days later the New York *Times* reported many calls about curious phenomena that day in New Jersey: rainbows. "All the rainbow reporters," Ron Alexander wrote, "mentioned two facts: that they hadn't seen a rainbow in a long, long time and that April 25th was also the day Harold Arlen was buried."

—EDWARD JABLONSKI
New York City
May, 1986

By Edward Jablonski and Lawrence D. Stewart

THE GERSHWIN YEARS

FOR MY PARENTS
AND ESPECIALLY FOR ANYA AND "DAD"

Art is a compromise between what we want to achieve and what circumstances allow us to achieve.

RALPH VAUGHAN WILLIAMS

I have been told that standardized mass-production is excellent for motor-cars; it is sometimes fairly effective for detective-stories. But it is iniquitous for human beings and art.

GUSTAV HOLST

Contents

List of Illustrations

Preface

Biographies are not written, they are compiled. At least it is true of this one. Without the help of literally dozens of people, without their information—and yes, misinformation—the writer's task would have been an impossible one. It is indeed a compliment to Harold Arlen, and an indication of the esteem in which he is held by all his collaborators, associates, and friends, that so much time was given me as I interviewed them time and again. And those few whose paths just somehow did not cross mine were most generous with their time by writing unusually long and valuable letters.

Of the individuals who gave time to me that they might have spent at their own work I must thank the composer's brother Jerry Arlen, Fred Astaire, Robert Russell Bennett, Irving Berlin, Harry Belafonte, Robert Breen, A. L. Berman, Ray Bolger, Mr. and Mrs. Earl Crane, Joseph Daffron, Lou Davis, Agnes de Mille, Robert Emmett Dolan, Roger Edens, Dr. Miguel G. Elias, Hannah Epstein, Arthur Freed, Judy Garland, Stanley Green, Myrna Greenfield, Lennie Hayton, Lena Horne, Ralph Harris, Moss Hart, Dan Healy, Samuel E. Hyman, Mrs. Ray Hyman, Andre Kostelanetz, Robert Kotlowitz, Goddard Lieberson, Peter Matz, Hugh Martin, Asher Markson, Rodger McHugh, John McGowan, Ethel Merman, E. H. Morris, Abe Olman, Cole Porter, Richard Rodgers, Leo Reisman, Kay Swift, Marie Schaaf, Dr. Maurice W. Schachtel, Carl Van Vechten (for various assists), Robert Wachsman, and Harry Warren.

Harold Arlen's collaborators were a rich source of information, not only because of the facts at their command, but also because each contributed his own special view of the composer; while these were all remarkably different, all the lyricists had in common a genuine affection for the composer and a deep respect for his work. Thanks then are due to Ralph Blane, Truman Capote, Dorothy Fields, Ira Gershwin, E. Y. Harburg, Ted Koehler, Johnny Mercer, Leo Robin and Jack Yellen, not only for their help so generously given, but also for permission to quote from some of their lyrics.

To the American Society of Composers, Authors and Publishers must go acknowledgment for its always-willing assistance in research, not only for accurate information, but also for rare photographs generously lent. I received valuable aid from Mr. Louis L. Gitin of the Buffalo Board of Education, as I did also from the Buffalo Chamber of Commerce (S. M. Ziccardi), from Miss Alice Pickup of the Buffalo Historical Society, and Mr. Ramsi P. Tick of the Buffalo Philharmonic Orchestra, all of whom graciously contributed even more than was requested.

To the publishers owning the copyrights on the lyrics and music I must gratefully acknowledge their permission to quote from songs appearing in the text: to Music Publishers Holding Corporation for excerpts from "Quartet Erotica" and "Beautifying The City," by Ira Gershwin and E. Y. Harburg, unpublished lyrics from *Life Begins at 8:40;* to Chappell & Co., Inc., for the couplet from "Eliza Crossing the Ice" by E. Y. Harburg, from *Bloomer Girl,* for the quotations from Ted Koehler's lyrics from the *Americanegro Suite,* and Johnny Mercer's lyrics from "Legalize My Name," "A Woman's Prerogative," and "I Wonder What Became of Me?"—all from *St. Louis Woman.* To Edwin H. Morris & Co., I owe thanks for the use of the lyrics by Harold Arlen and Ralph Blane to "It's Deductible," and "Twenty Seven Elm Street," from *Down among the Sheltering Palms,* and Ira Gershwin's "The Man That Got Away" from *A Star Is Born;* also "Don't Rock The Boat, Dear," lyrics by Harold Arlen and Ralph Blane (from *My Blue Heaven*); and "I Never Has Seen Snow," lyrics by Truman Capote and Harold Arlen, from

House of Flowers; the quatrain by E. Y. Harburg from *Jamaica's* "Napoleon"; and the excerpt from Johnny Mercer's lyric to "Have You Heard?" from *Saratoga.* Mr. Mercer graciously allowed the use of his unpublished lyric "Hangin' On to You," from *The Sky's the Limit,* the songs of which were published by E. H. Morris. All copyrights on songs from *A Star Is Born, My Blue Heaven, Down among the Sheltering Palms, House of Flowers, Jamaica,* and *Saratoga* are published by Harwin Music Corporation with Edwin H. Morris & Co., serving as sole selling agents.

Publishers of books, also, have been kind: Little, Brown & Company must be credited with the quotations from its books by Agnes de Mille, *Dance to the Piper* and *And Promenade Home.* From Ira Gershwin's *Lyrics on Several Occasions* I have quoted a brief passage he devoted to Harold Arlen; this invaluable book was published by Alfred A. Knopf. The quotations from R. Vaughan Williams and Gustav Holst are from *Heirs and Rebels,* sensitively edited by Ursula Vaughan Williams and Imogen Holst, and published by Oxford University Press.

I am personally indebted to *Theater Arts* magazine, *Playbill, The Theater* for permission to quote, or at least to lift, ideas from articles by me that originally appeared in these publications. Also, to William K. Zinsser and to *Harper's* magazine, I owe my thanks for brief quotes taken from Mr. Zinsser's fine article, "Harold Arlen, the Secret Music Maker."

Everyone mentioned has been co-operative and helpful in the extreme, but I do have particularly special thanks to give to my editor, Kenneth McCormick, who saw this book through with a minimum of fuss and a maximum of dispatch; to Cyrus Rogers, for meticulous copy editing and for encouragement that began even before there was any copy; to William Sweigart, who did a great deal of the precise research and who made it all selflessly available, I am most grateful; not only was he always encouraging, but he made available to me anything I required from his virtually complete collection of sheet music and recordings. To Alfred A.

Simon and Leonid Hambro I must bow for their interest and willingness to play the music of Harold Arlen for me and to discuss it after. Mr. Simon played me dozens of songs with rare understanding, and Mr. Hambro played exciting renditions of the difficult *Hero Ballet,* and the recent *Ode,* for which he displayed his usual affinity. Lawrence D. Stewart supplied me with valuable facts, ideas, and suggestions.

I doubt that I can fully express the unique debt I owe to Anya and Harold Arlen. They have been more than understanding throughout the entire writing of this book; and they have given me more time than any biographer could have hoped for. I'm certain that my intrusions interfered with their private lives. The composer generously went through the manuscript to guard against factual errors; he has not tampered with any of my views or opinions. What errors or misjudgments remain, even omissions, must be attributed to the author.

Anya Arlen must be voted the most gracious hostess in New York, especially as a writer developed the habit of dropping around at unusual times; how she managed to seem at all times unobtrusive and yet able to appear with sandwiches and glasses of milk at the right moment will no doubt remain a great mystery. Her suggestions and good memory were always most helpful, but more important were her sweetness and understanding.

I cannot thank my wife Edith for "typing from the messy manuscript." She had no time for that. But she has an even greater task—and that was and is to keep David, Carla, and Emily amused, occupied, or, if necessary, absent while "Daddy worked." It was a subtle and ever-gentle encouragement that was more appreciated than it seemed. As for David, Carla, and Emily—without their delightful and irresistible presence this book might have been finished a month sooner.

E.J.

New York, June 1960

"... they're playing my song ..."

Some seasons ago a popular game among song fanciers and
followers of musical comedy was one in which the name of
Harold Arlen, then appearing quite regularly on television,
was coupled with the titles of an astonishing number of songs
he had written.

The "And Then He Wrote" game—an extension of the television treatment he never failed to receive—proved to be a
decided revelation even to those who were not unfamiliar
with the composer. Everyone knows that Jerome Kern composed "Ol' Man River," that George Gershwin created "The
Man I Love," that Irving Berlin wrote, among others, "White
Christmas." But few realized that one man, Harold Arlen,
composed such diversified songs as "I Love a Parade," "I've
Got the World on a String," "I Gotta Right to Sing the Blues,"
"Stormy Weather," "Between the Devil and the Deep Blue
Sea," "Let's Fall in Love," "That Old Black Magic," "Happi-
ness Is a Thing Called Joe," "Evelina," "Ac-cent-tchu-ate the
Positive," "Over the Rainbow," and "Come Rain or Come
Shine," to skim over the most popular. This impressive out-
put earned Arlen the doubtful distinction of being "the most
sung, yet least sung-about popular composer."

As with most well-turned phrases this one was not completely true, of course—especially among his colleagues. Arlen
has also been called "the composer's composer," another half-
truth, for this would hardly account for the immense popularity of so many of his songs. But it is an interesting idea.
When asked for his opinion, the elusive, extremely modest
dean of American popular song writers Irving Berlin was

delighted to speak of his relationship with Harold Arlen. "As a person," Berlin said, "I have a deep respect for Harold. He has the courage to keep going despite great odds. As for his talent—he's just loaded with it! His songs are always in good taste. I don't think it fair that some people type him as a blues writer. He has written some of the most beautiful ballads we have. Harold's musical talent obviously stems from his father, who was a great cantor. But Harold also knows the value of a good lyric and what to do with it. In a nutshell, no one has written better songs than Harold Arlen."

Richard Rodgers first met Harold Arlen in the latter Twenties. "At the time, he was a little advanced for me, but I caught on pretty soon to his unusual harmonic structure and form. I realized he was the greatest new talent in years. Larry—Hart—thought he was great. Harold has a real valid talent, it is his own, and completely original."

Cole Porter considers Arlen "a distinguished personality in music and I have admired him for years."

These tributes could be multiplied, for some of Harold Arlen's greatest admirers are other song writers. As professionals they can appreciate the technique as well as aesthetics of a well-constructed, effective, song. All are also men of outspoken integrity and would hardly say anything they did not honestly feel. As professionals, however, they would hardly react as would the layman—who has, after all, sung Harold Arlen's songs for three decades.

Though his name is mentioned regularly with all the other great contributors to American popular music, Arlen has also been mentioned in the company of Stephen Foster. Defining Harold Arlen's historical niche in American music becomes simpler with the introduction of Foster's name.

Arlen's art—and it is art—is rooted, as is Foster's, in American folk music; yet it is not a purist's folk music in the sense that it has sprung from the traditional music of the people. In Europe, where Arlen's music is more often related to Foster's than to Arlen's musical-comedy contemporaries, there is a deeper consciousness of those qualities that constitute enduring song, because Europeans are more aware of folk songs than are Americans. Lacking the long traditional history of European cultures, American folklore is more urbanized and has taken on more sophisticated characteristics than are generally associated with the folk.

The only true American folk music readily identified as purely American is jazz, the blues, ragtime, and the other contributions by the American Negro, but so is the music of Broadway and Tin Pan Alley. The two musics have exchanged influences and have even enriched American art music.

Although he has composed in a "blues" style, Harold Arlen is not strictly "Happy with the Blues." Nothing annoys him more than being typed. The fact is that the blues as a musical form—with its implied structure and harmony—is minimal in the total output of Harold Arlen. A further fact is: of all the composers of stature, and in whose company he belongs by virtue of his rich achievement, Harold Arlen may well be the most versatile. And, significantly, he has developed this versatility without sacrificing personal style.

Though Arlen is happy with the blues he has written— "Blues in the Night," for example—he has written songs of simple purity containing absolutely no references to the blues in mood or musical characteristics: "Over the Rainbow," "Let's Fall in Love," "My Shining Hour," "Sing My Heart," "Right as the Rain." This is not a point to labor, but it does emphasize that Arlen's full contribution has yet to be fully appreciated.

If he himself has not received that personal recognition he deserves, Harold Arlen has witnessed many a pleasing song success. Possibly his position is best illustrated by an experience he had during a Manhattan cross-town taxi ride. After he had settled in the seat, he found himself confronted by a classic situation. The cabby was whistling "Stormy Weather," an Arlen standard dating back to the Thirties. It was an opportunity for experiment that the composer could not ignore.

"Do you know who wrote that song?" he asked the driver.

"Sure—Irving Berlin."

"Wrong," Arlen informed him, "but I'll give you two more guesses."

The cabby thought hard, and at times audibly if not understandably explaining that the name of the composer was on the tip of his tongue but he just couldn't come up with it. Arlen prompted him: "Richard Rodgers?"

"That's the name I was thinking of," the cabby admitted, "But he's not the one."

"How about Cole Porter?"

"That's who!"

"No, you're wrong again," Arlen told him. "I wrote the song."

The cab darted across an intersection before the driver, still thinking, finally asked, "Who are you?"

"Harold Arlen."

At this the cabby turned around in his seat and asked, "Who?"

HAROLD ARLEN

CHAPTER 1

Buffalo Rhythm

Buffalo, New York, is more than five hundred miles from Louisville, Kentucky, and young Samuel Arluck wondered on that day in April 1904 why he had made the trip. For, unless he could conjure up a wife in a moment, the entire trip from Louisville might have been made for nothing.

He had fallen into the predicament quite innocently. Visitors from Buffalo had heard him sing in a Louisville choir and were so affected by the beauty of his voice and the dignity of his mien that when they returned to Buffalo they told members of the Clinton Street synagogue of this splendid young singer who would make a marvelous *chazzan* (cantor) for the congregation. They were both enthusiastic and persuasive, for here now was the young man himself, thinking fast.

The twenty-four-year-old singer had filled all qualifications to everyone's satisfaction: he sang with a fine, rich voice, deported himself with great assurance and poise, and evidenced an unusual affinity for improvisation.

When the elders informed him that the position carried one further stipulation—a wife—and then asked Samuel Arluck if he was married, he merely added one further improvisation to the morning's vocalizing and answered, "Yes." The job was his.

He had only to return to Louisville to bid his family good-by, settle up whatever matters required settling, and, of course, get married. His own father, Moses Arluck (or Erlich—meaning "honorable"—in its more authentic pronunciation) has been described as "a disciplinarian, old-fashioned in the matter of social amenities and social behavior, strict in the

values of integrity and human conduct." He was also "pas-
sionately devoted to the value of education; was, himself,
multi-lingual, well-read in history, geography, and the classics."

Moses Arluck had come to America around 1885, to find
a place for himself, his wife, and three children. Because many
of his friends from around Vilna, Poland, had settled in Louisville, Moses Arluck decided upon this same lovely city on the
banks of the Ohio River as the new home for his family.
His grandson, Samuel E. Hyman, recalls Moses Arluck as
"a tall man, of military, aristocratic bearing with a closely
trimmed golden-grey beard (along the lines of the later
Freud) . . . His home and his practices were orthodox Jewish.
He was, until his death in 1915, the paid secretary of the
B'Nai Jacob Congregation and held like positions for several
social, cultural, and athletic organizations, such as the Young
Men's Hebrew Association.

"Whether or not there was in the family any European
cantorial background, I do not know; there was, always,
excited interest in things cantorial and in the cantorial tradition. You might say the entire family were passionate music
listeners."

Both Samuel's brother and sister sang. Like his father,
Samuel was a fine scholar and received, besides the traditional
religious education, a further, secular education in "the historic George W. Morris School," where "he more or less excelled in his studies."

As he had been disciplined into a passion for integrity, it
devolved upon the newly appointed, but yet incomplete, cantor
to keep his innocent improvisation from becoming a lie.

The city of Cincinnati, Ohio, lies some hundred thirty-five
miles north and east, on the Ohio River, from Louisville.
Just how Samuel Arluck managed to get there is no doubt
best explained by the river, a pleasant avenue of travel. That
he got there is certain, for in Cincinnati lived petite and pretty
Celia Orlin. Just how they met is now a not very important
mystery, but they did, and when Arluck gave the congregation
members his positive answer, the "wife" he had in mind was

Celia Orlin. On his application for the marriage license Samuel Arluck gave as his occupation "Minister," his father's name as simply "M. Arluck," and his mother's, "Ida Danischewsky."

The twenty-two-year-old Celia Orlin gave as her occupation "Saleslady," her father's name: Mottl Orlin, and curiously, and significantly perhaps, her mother's name: Mollie Musician.

On April 15, 1904, Samuel Arluck and Celia Orlin were married by the Rabbi J. G. Lesser in the home of the bride, at 829 Barr Street. The resourceful young cantor had his bride, and the Clinton Street *shul* had its cantor.

The Arlucks took a modest house at 389 Clinton Street, not far from the synagogue, which, in turn, was located near downtown Buffalo. In 1904 Buffalo was a bustling lake town of well over 300,000 population. The principal industries were grain, steel, meat packing, and shipping.

The Jewish population was small. In 1910, when Buffalo's population had grown to more than 400,000, the Jewish community numbered only about 6500. The Arlucks chose to live in the Jewish neighborhood within a mile's walk from Niagara Square, the heart of Buffalo.

On February 15, 1905, Celia Arluck was delivered of twins. One, weighing seven pounds, died the following day; the other, weighing but four pounds, was named Hyman. A second son, Julius, was born seven years later, on November 11, 1912. By this time Samuel Arluck, now thirty-two and a celebrated cantor who "had the kind of voice that made the women shed plenty of tears," had moved into a better position as cantor of the Pine Street synagogue. One of his duties was directing the choir, in which could be heard the affecting soprano of his elder son, Hyman, now seven. In order to be seen, as well as heard, Hyman had to stand on a chair. Though he loved to sing, he was, unlike his father, extremely shy, and almost spoiled his first solo by choking midway in song. Cantor Arluck, as always, was equal to the crisis: a gentle step on the toe of his first-born was enough to evaporate

stage fright, and the services continued without further incident.

Music, because of the father's work, was important in the
Arluck home, by now located in Pratt Street, in a quiet
middle-class neighborhood. The Arlucks shared a two-family
house with a Negro family living on the first floor. Though
the home "was filled with music all the time," there was very
little popular music, for Cantor Arluck's tastes ran to Italian
opera. His record collection contained, besides traditional
Hebraic melodies, recordings by Caruso, and John McCormack.
Cantor Josef Rosenblatt's recordings were in the Arluck collection, and for a time it seemed likely that Cantor Arluck
would team up with the famed cantor for a concert tour,
but he decided against it because he did not want to leave
his family.

The Arluck home was a focal point for all visiting Jewish
dignitaries, particularly cantors who admired their colleague's
work. A Hebrew scholar, Samuel Arluck, visited the synagogue
twice a day. In his capacity as cantor he sang during services,
sometimes traditional music, other times original melodies
to fit already-existing texts. The cantor, too, would officiate
at weddings, funerals, and other solemn ceremonies of a
religious nature.

Hyman Arluck too was being trained in traditional ways;
while they were still living on Clinton Street, he began to
study Hebrew with a Rabbi Bloch. The rabbi was so strict
in his religious views that he never attended services because others who did violated the Talmudic laws by driving
to the synagogue. Rabbi Bloch stayed home, read the Torah,
and instructed his pupils in the law.

The Arluck home was hardly that strict, though Celia
Arluck adhered to the orthodox beliefs. The atmosphere was
one given over to warmth and love, with a strong, respected
father at the head, and a gentle, affectionate mother to inject
the humor to counterbalance the sometimes stern dignity of
the father. She could also intervene in the father-son crises that
might come up, and would.

Though not musical, Celia has been described as "a highly poetic woman—everything she said had a ring of poetry in it"; she was responsible for the introduction of a piano into the house on Pratt Street.

It was Celia's belief, and hope, that though her sons were not mandatorily expected to follow in their father's profession, Hyman might begin to prepare himself for the kind of work that would enable him to keep his own hours, and thus would also keep the Sabbath. To Celia Arluck the teaching of music seemed a solution. A Miss Faller, who lived nearby, was a piano teacher and with her Hyman Arluck began studying at about the age of nine. After the usual preliminaries Hyman outgrew Miss Faller and was considered promising enough to continue with Arnold Cornelissen, the leading local teacher, who was also a conductor (at the time Hyman studied with him, of the Buffalo String Orchestral Society), organist, and composer.

For each study session with Cornelissen, Hyman would pack his music into a fine leather brief case his father had given him and ride through Buffalo via streetcar and bus to his teacher's home. But like most piano students of nine or ten, he had no love of practice and soon learned to keep a precautionary eye out for the image of his mother reflected in the window glass as a signal to begin musical activity. Though the Chopin *Études*, favored by Cornelissen in their studies, were beautiful, there were other musical adventures to entice the embryo pianist. At the age of twelve he came upon a piano rag number, "Indianola," the first popular composition he had ever attempted to play. Something about its syncopation and unconventional harmonies stirred him and captured his imagination. He began to collect jazz records, which sounded strangely out of place emanating from the Victrola accustomed to Caruso, McCormack, and Cantor Rosenblatt. And whenever a jazz band came to Buffalo, Hyman Arluck managed to hear it.

Restless and searching as he was, Hyman began to reflect his musical interests in a lack of interest in regular schoolwork. At P. S. 32 he had begun to have some troubles, particularly in arithmetic, but with the help of his father he managed to get through. He kept in good musical trim in school by playing in the school orchestra and singing for school entertainments in the auditorium filled with proud parents. There were other stirrings within him, for he took to waiting on a corner for a girl in his class "I thought I was in love with. We'd meet, have our lunch, take a walk, then go back to school." He joined in the kissing games, too—"about ten or twelve boys and girls; we'd go into a darkened room. You barely got to kiss her cheek—and we were happy." He even carried books for his first love, as he walked her home. Always the gentleman, he never failed to walk on the side of the sidewalk nearer the street.

Hutchinson Central High School, which was a long walk from home, and which he entered in 1920, was a more imposing problem, for here he was confronted with English, Latin, math, history, and physical education. The last proved within his grasp, for though slender and light, Hyman managed to be a good swimmer, play a good game of basketball, and to do some pretty impressive high jumping. The other subjects were another kind of hurdle, and though he managed to make it through the first semester, by the second, in 1921, he decided to drop out of Hutchinson High, where he was not impressing anyone with his scholarship. He had even taken to playing the piano in bands around town.

Although his mother took his decision with her usual resigned sweetness, his father raised strong objections. He even called in a friend to talk to his son. Because of Hyman's interest in music, Cantor Arluck called upon Jack Yellen, a Buffalo boy who had made good in New York as a song writer. Yellen's father had been a close friend of the Arlucks, and Yellen, about thirty at the time, who had been sports editor on the Buffalo *Courier* before deserting Buffalo for Tin Pan Alley, was considered most successful. He was also a college graduate, and Cantor Arluck felt that he would be ideal to plead the cause of education with his rapidly defecting son.

Yellen commuted between New York and Buffalo on week-ends; on one Cantor Arluck called him: "I want you to speak to my boy, Chyiam."

"What about?" Yellen asked.

"He won't go to school. I want you to speak to him."

"Well, *Chazzan,* send him over."

"He came over," Yellen relates, "a nice-looking boy of about sixteen. At the time he was playing at 'Minnie's,' a roadhouse of no good reputation. 'What do you expect to be?,' I asked him. He laughed and said, 'A musician.' So I said, 'Fine, play something for me.' He did, something of his own and whatever it was, it was a pretty good indication that he was his father's son. He would never be the doctor or lawyer that his father wanted him to be.

"Afterwards, I called his father and the first thing I said was, 'It's all your own fault, he's going to be a musician.'"

To pacify his parents somewhat, Hyman halfheartedly continued his schooling by having himself transferred to Technical High School, a vocational school where he studied, among other things, "astronomy, made chairs, and worked in the carpenter shop."

His restlessness and searching took an innocent though substantial turn one Friday night in his fifteenth year. It began conventionally with the traditional family celebration of the advent of the Sabbath. Celia lighted the two candles at sundown, while reciting the lovely ritual:

> *Come let us welcome the Sabbath.*
> *May its radiance illumine our hearts*
> *As we kindle these tapers.*
> *Light is the symbol of the divine.*
> *The Lord is my light and my salvation.*
> *Light is the symbol of the divine in man.*
> *The spirit of man is the light of the Lord.*

After the lighting of the candles the *Kiddish,* a recitation in praise of God, is spoken over a cup of wine. The Friday-night meal, too, perpetuated centuries of symbolic tradition with the two plaited loaves of bread. As the sons were later to recall, "love and warmth," security, and orderliness permeated the observance of these old rituals.

Still, the Arluck home was not unrelentingly religious. Samuel would return to the synagogue, Julius would be sent off to bed, and Hyman, like all fifteen-year-olds in all cities in America, would repair out of doors to "the corner." While the Sabbath was a holy day, it did not preclude the ordinary pleasures of life, and to Hyman Arluck on this specific Sabbath evening it meant a visit to the corner poolroom. Here he met a friend excitedly talking revolt from parental authority; he held forth, too, on adventure in faraway places, the sea. Swept along by his friend's oratory, and especially the promise of adventure, Hyman found himself following him to the docks of Buffalo. As a bustling lake port, Buffalo was a good town for young men seeking work aboard ship and the two slightly-less-than-able-bodied seamen shipped out that night.

They were, in keeping with the cruel traditions of the sea, assigned to the ship's galley, where, before the voyage had made many knots into Lake Erie, Hyman's revolutionary companion had succumbed to fumes, a choppy lake, and a land-lubber's case of *mal de mer*. It fell then to Hyman to do his friend's work.

The next night, when the ship docked in Detroit, both boys had had surfeit of the sea; they jumped ship. Adrift in a strange port, they were before long assailed by hunger, the desperation of which drove Hyman to the stealing of a roll for their meal—a far cry from his mother's rich fare served, though tearfully, on Pratt Street that night.

Further desperation drove them to stow away on a train. With a little help from a sympathetic, though corruptible, railroad employee they managed to get into a sleeping car and under a lower berth. There, frightened, hungry, cramped, and apparently extremely quiet, they remained all the way to Cleveland, without disturbing the woman who slept in the berth over their heads. Once in Cleveland, Hyman led his by now-chastened traveling companion to the home of a cousin, who called the distraught Arlucks, and arrangements were made for the boys' return to Buffalo, where they had caused the usual distress and received the usual forgiveness.

Hyman's brief adventure, however, in no way resolved his academic problem. As an educator observed, after enumerating the subjects Hyman took, "from the low academic results I would safely say the subjects took him."

In later years the unwilling student could look back on those months in 1921 in which he was confronting decisions to be made with the hesitating uncertainty of youth. "Something was stirring in me, then," he recalls. "I didn't know what it was, but it kept me troubled for a while." Already clothes-conscious, he found much to admire in his cousin Eddie Orlin's silk shirts, the last word in smart dress. Since the quarter-a-week allowance he received from his father did not take silk shirts into consideration, Hyman got a job in a rubber factory. It was hard work, but it enabled him to get a fine silk shirt. Young Hyman could be described as pretty natty; he even pressed his own bell-bottomed trousers himself, to be certain of the proper razor edge.

Eventually the cantor's son found pleasanter employment as a butcher boy in the Gaiety, a burlesque theater. With one eye out for possible customers and the other on the stage, he managed to absorb some of the routines of the Billy Watson's Beef Trust Company, which he adapted to his own use for local amateur-night competitions, drafting as a partner his friend Hymie Sandler.

Hyman took a job as a pianist in a movie house; he was practically the leader of the small pit band. He kept an eye on the screen and signaled to the other members of the band whenever the movie called for a change of mood in the music. The fast music, that which usually accompanied an Indian attack, or some other such ominous situation, was called a "hurry." For a love scene the cinema patrons heard the same "hurry" in a slow tempo. To cue in the orchestra, Hyman would flash a light on the piano—and there were lights on the music stands of two other instruments—for a change of "hurry." It was work he greatly enjoyed, and particularly loved flashing the lights.

Later he moved to another job in another movie house, a more splendid one, in fact, that planned to feature the organ. It was one of the first, if not the first, in Buffalo. This was so exciting an event that even Cantor Arluck stayed up all night to watch the installation of the instrument in the theater. That he had never studied the organ did not disconcert Hyman; no one seemed to notice the absence of the bass notes (these were manipulated by the feet) from his playing. "I loved to walk up the aisle after I'd finished my playing, or to sweep off the bench to take a bow."

While still supplying the "hurries" in the other movie house Hyman and band also played for a vaudeville troupe that shared the bill with the screen fare. Among the vaudevillians was a singer, pink and round and lovely, who captured the boy pianist's heart. "She was a little above burlesque, I would say. And she reeked of the most glorious perfume—cheap perfume, maybe—but it was wonderful! What a thrill when she took me around backstage and introduced me." There were deep stirrings indeed, and new worlds were opening. Hyman Arluck began to associate the making of music with entertainment, glamour, even love (at least, that's what he thought it was).

His show-business experience eventually led to the formation of Hyman Arluck's band, The Snappy Trio. With Hymie Sandler on the drums and Ted Meyers on violin, fifteen-year-old Hyman completed the personnel of The Snappy Trio, in which he sang, played the piano, besides devising the arrangements. Even though all members of the trio were teen-agers, they had little trouble getting work in Buffalo's red-light-district cabarets, not too distant from their homes, along Pearl and Franklin streets. The manager of one of these spots hired them because their leader not only could play a pretty jazzy piano, he also doubled on the clarinet. The bargain-hunting manager took some satisfaction out of paying for three musicians and actually getting four. His musical sophistication, not to mention his ear, was untutored enough not to notice that the leader of The Snappy Trio actually played a kazoo he had put into the clarinet's mouthpiece. There was, however, no actual payment from the management for the group's services; on the bandstand they had placed a good-sized can invitingly labeled "Sugar," as an inducement to the patrons for contributions. These somehow mounted up and the young band leader found that he was earning "good money." This affluence was conspicuously consumed with the purchase of dashingly sporty clothes and a Model T Ford, the first and, for a time, the only one in the neighborhood. This success symbol may have stirred the neighbors' admiration, but to the Arlucks the Ford was a vehicle of the devil that carried their first-born home each morning around eight, when others, working at less racy occupations, were just leaving for their jobs.

Besides playing with the trio and vocalizing Hyman was expected to serve as an accompanist for any patron whose soul, filled with song, wished to share it with all. Such un-trained voices required constant key transposition, but the young pianist found this impossible, which lack he covered at the beginning of each song with an extravagant flourish that took in practically all eighty-eight keys of the piano, after which he invariably returned to the published key of the song; the performers, meanwhile, none the wiser.

The band's book reflected the leader's own musical tastes with emphasis on early-jazz-age compositions such as "Ag-gravatin' Papa," "Lovin' Sam (The Sheik of Alabam')," and "Louisville Lou (The Vampin' Lady)"—the last two with lyrics by Jack Yellen.

The Snappy Trio used the Arluck living room as a rehearsal hall. Brother Julius, now seven, was fascinated by the hot licks, and especially by the playing of Ted Meyers, who, true to the traditions of fiddlers, wore his hair spectacularly long. It may have been the haircut as much as the music that attracted Julius; when it came time for him to begin the study of music he chose the violin as his instrument. Frequently he would slip into the practice room while The Snappy Trio had left to take a break, pick up an instrument and would get music out of it. When the trio expanded into the five-man Southbound Shufflers, Julius had additional instruments to choose from while the band was out, including the saxophone, which he managed to master pretty well merely by watching and tootling while the owner was busy elsewhere.

A summer on the Crystal Beach lake boat *Canadiana*, as a candy butcher, gave Hyman entrée with his band for the following year, when he booked the Southbound Shufflers for a season on the *Canadiana*. In the summer of 1924 the band was playing at nearby Lake Shore Manor.

The young band leader based his arrangements on those of his musical heroes, the Original Memphis Five. This was a quasi-jazz band comprised of Phil Napoleon on trumpet, Jimmy Lytell, clarinet, Miff Mole, trombone, Frank Signorelli, piano, and Jack Roth, pounding the drums. Purists would hardly call it a true jazz band, though on occasions the group did play "hot." To Hyman Arluck, however, such hairsplitting distinctions meant nothing, for he was attracted to the ragged ensemble playing and the often imaginative solo work. His hero worship reached the point that he made another excursion out of Buffalo this time to Brooklyn, and with the knowledge and over the protests of his parents, in the company of similarly oriented friends in an automobile of uncertain reliability.

Another early hero was pianist Arthur Schutt, exponent of a subdued though intricate piano style, bordering on jazz. Whatever it might be accurately labeled, to the aspiring musician it represented a break away from the stereotyped, steady-tempoed, monotonous performances of the average band. Hyman wanted his Southbound Shufflers to sound like the jazz bands then coming into favor. He also gleaned a great deal out of listening to "race records," the special discs made for the Negro trade, of Ethel Waters and Bessie Smith. It was the free, improvisational style he could hear in these recordings that Arluck studied and imitated.

He recalls a local hero, too, a pianist who played in a Chinese restaurant. "I used to go up there when I was a kid, with a date, if I could afford it. The pianist—I don't remember his name—had the ugliest hands I had ever seen: the nails were very short, about half the size of the normal nail, and the fingertips were literally pushed over the ends of the nails. I childishly thought this had something to do with his brilliant piano pounding."

When asked what he remembered best about his South-bound Shufflers days on the lake boats, he laughingly replied, "My ego." It was during this time that he took a crack at song writing; then nineteen, he collaborated with a family friend, Hyman Cheiffetz, in May 1924, on "My Gal, My Pal," which was copyrighted by the composers as "My Gal, Won't You Please Come Back to Me?" The lyrics were by Cheiffetz and the composer's name is given as Harold Arluck. Later in the same year they collaborated again but with equal lack of success. Looking back today, the composer feels that "no one would ever have known from the early songs that I would have, could have, become a composer. Maybe there was something discernible of what might come in my arrangements, or my singing, but not in 'My Gal, My Pal.' This is the kind of song we get today in letters."

Still the new song writers had sufficient faith in their work to pay for the making up of miniature piano rolls, with the lyrics imprinted, which they plugged by giving out on the lake boats; but nothing happened with the song.

Harold Arluck, the pianist, singer, arranger, did much better, however. He was invited to join a smart local band, The Yankee Six, a group very popular on the collegiate dance circuit. Since there were four owners—Harold Tapson, Jack McLoughlin, Dick George and Jules Piller—the employees were outnumbered two to one. As one half of the employees, Harold Arluck continued as he had with his own bands, to arrange, sing, and play the piano. Before long the band grew into an eleven-man group, now calling themselves The Buffalodians, one of the best and most popular around Buffalo. Besides playing college and society dates, the band played in Geyer's ballroom-restaurant in downtown Buffalo in the theater district. It was while playing here that Harold Arluck met an eccentric young dancer from Boston named Ray Bolger. The dancer, who had broken vaudeville records in Buffalo (seventeen weeks at the Hippodrome), was particularly taken with the very modern arrangements played by The Buffalodians. The arrangements were, of course, jazz-inspired, and even though none of the members of the band was a jazz musician, they were good enough readers to be able to play what their arranger wrote out for them, jazz "breaks" and all. As a member of the celebrated Buffalodians the twenty-year-old son of the cantor was averaging from $75 to $110 a week.

American music in 1924–25 was in a kind of ferment that excited young musicians. Popular music, having received a strong transfusion from jazz quarters and also from such fine musicians as Victor Herbert and Jerome Kern, began to flower as an art form. Irving Berlin, a largely self-taught song writer, brought to his writing an honest, earthy quality that appealed immediately to the singing man in the street. The younger George Gershwin, taking his inspiration from both Berlin and Kern, soon asserted his own musical personality and brought a fresh new definition to American music and even went further to endow it with an unexpected respectability by casting it into the larger forms of "classical" music.

When he worked in Murray Whiteman's Music Shop in the spring of 1920, Harold Arluck, as well as other musicians, was struck by the originality of a song then sweeping the country, "Swanee." In it Gershwin dared use the chord of the diminished seventh as a cadence or end of the song (the now common "good evening, friends" close). It was a startling departure that was soon taken up by all self-styled "advanced" pianists, initiating a rash of diminishing sevenths on keyboards throughout the land. A Buffalo pianist, returning from a New York visit, brought "Swanee" and its unorthodox ending home. It was Hyman Arluck's introduction to the music of George Gershwin.

As soon as the first recording of the *Rhapsody in Blue*

was available in Buffalo, some years later, Dick George, also a
pianist with The Buffalodians, made an arrangement of it for
two pianos and orchestra that he, Arluck, and The Buffalodians
played with great success around Buffalo.

It was also a good showpiece, and a popular one, for the
band to feature when they went on tour. The tour was to
begin in Cleveland, after which the band hoped to arrive, eventually, in New York.

While their musician son was on the move with The Buffalodians, the Arlucks moved also, to Syracuse, where Samuel
Arluck took a position as cantor in the beautiful Temple Adath
Yeshurun. Three blocks away from Syracuse University, atop
a gently sloping hill, the temple would be filled with the rich
lyric tenor of Cantor Samuel Arluck for the next twenty years.

In 1924, when the move was made, Julius was a boy of
twelve and already good enough a violinist to serve as accompanist for his father when the latter sang over the Syracuse
radio station. The cantor made frequent appearances on the
station during his long stay in Syracuse, and, after his eldest
son became the celebrated Harold Arlen, delighted the congregation of Temple Adath Yeshurun by weaving such melodies as "Over the Rainbow" and "Come Rain or Come Shine"
into the services.

Samuel was his son's most trusted critic, and the latter never
felt comfortable about anything he did until his father had
expressed some opinion on it. More than any other influence he
might have had, the composer feels that he owes his greatest
debt to his father, "the greatest theme-and-variations man I've
ever known"; his father's singing style, his way with melodic
phrases, his ability to improvise hauntingly beautiful melodies,
Arlen feels, were inherited. Or at least he lived with it long
enough to have absorbed it.

CHAPTER 2

Get Happy

In Cleveland, where The Buffalodians began their tour playing in a restaurant, they made an impressive beginning leading a long stay. The restaurant was located in the heart of the city; also making its beginning, though on the outskirts of town, was a new band led by Guy Lombardo.

Late in 1925 the band was booked into Pittsburgh, after which they came to New York to play the Palace Theater and then Gallagher's Monte Carlo, a blazing night spot on Fifty-second Street between Broadway and Seventh Avenue. Like all the night clubs that counted, the Monte Carlo was a downstairs club. Coincidentally, the one-man floor show at the Monte Carlo was the young dancer Ray Bolger, with whom Arluck renewed his friendship. They struck it off well enough to decide to team up and take an apartment together, which they did on West Fifty-seventh Street in a rooming house between Ninth and Tenth Avenues.

Often they would sit up well into the morning talking and making plans. Bolger found Arluck's arrangements far in advance of anything he heard, and even hinted that he would like him to make his song and dance arrangements. Most of all he noted the shyness and gentleness of the musician, "the wistful feeling in anything he did, in his conversation, when he mentioned his father, or talked about what he was going to do. His ambition, however, was not a driving force, but something very sympathetic and sweet. And his wonderful sense of humor—it was never an insult kind of humor, but a teasing kind. He used to joke about my eccentricities—and Harold and I had wonderful laughs about that."

On the many nights the musician and the dancer did not sleep it was because the former worked hard on his arrangements while the latter tried to sleep. Yet Bolger warmly speaks of that period in his life. "We were—and are—very fond of each other, and we never bothered one another. He was a fine roommate."

Although arranging, playing, and singing were taking practically all his time, Harold Arluck collaborated with Dick George on what was to be his first published music, *Minor Gaff* (*Blues Fantasy*). Published by the Triangle Music Publishing Company, the piece was a solo piano number, and bore the name of Harold Arluck; before long he would apply the sound, if not the spelling, of the end of his mother's maiden name, and the transformation would be complete: Hyman Arluck would become Harold Arlen. He had become annoyed with the telephone reception of his name. It was not a common name, and he had to waste what seemed to him a lot of time repeating it. By softening the ending he found that he was greeted less frequently with "What's that name?"

Composing did not interest him greatly; he was bent on a singing career. Arranging and piano playing were considered means to an end. He earned extra money by working up arrangements for other bands, too. While The Buffalodians were berthed at the Monte Carlo, Fletcher Henderson's band could be heard at Roseland. Henderson liked Arlen's way with a number and asked him to do some arrangements for him. Among them was "Dynamite," one of Henderson's most successful numbers. Arlen had not only written the orchestrations, he had even inserted what sounded like an improvised jazz solo for trumpeter Joe Smith.

For the summer of 1926 The Buffalodians moved to Gallagher's place in Far Rockaway on Long Island. It was here that Harold Arlen had his second, and last, fist fight. The first was in Buffalo when he was still a boy. It was a typical kid fight and ended after the first punch, a lucky one Arlen had managed to land first on the nose of his opponent. The sight of blood and the anguished crying of his former opponent

immediately took all the belligerence out of Arlen, who, arm
around the crying boy, took him to his mother for first aid.

The Far Rockaway battle erupted one night when Jack
McLoughlin, then leader of the Buffalodians, was in an
argumentative mood and had shifted his hostilities to Arlen,
whose popularity as arranger and pianist might easily have
been misconstrued by McLoughlin as a threat to his position
as leader. And as a vocalist Arlen had attracted attention, not
only with his unique singing style, but also with his sense of
humor, which took the form of clowning in some of the numbers. These overshadowing tendencies might have bothered
McLoughlin; then, too, there might easily have been a bit
of Prohibition spirits consumed. Whatever the reason or reasons, Arlen found himself trying to placate the implacable
McLoughlin. Always a hater of friction, tension, and argument, Arlen tried to talk and joke his way out of the situation,
but it soon became evident that this would not work.

Arlen was a slight young man, McLoughlin a burly one;
there was nothing for Arlen to do, in light of his peaceful
tendencies, and with the fact that he did not have weight
on his side and had been a good track man—he ran.

The argument unfolded in a chase through the streets
of Far Rockaway, with Arlen holding his own for a time,
though he eventually became exhausted and decided to face
fate. He turned around, at the same time putting out a protec-
tive hand, well, fist—and the obliging, momentum-swept Mc-
Loughlin ran into it, knocking himself out cold.

The peace was made shortly after, but McLoughlin left
the band and Arlen took it over, having won the position in
more or less fair combat. It was the last battle he ever
fought.

His singing style was beginning to get attention. The mid-
Twenties saw the advent of the crooners, and Arlen's singing
fitted into that category. But with a difference: some of the
musical ideas he had learned in his father's choir, and some
he had picked up from his father's singing; there was even
some hint of the singing of the blues artists; the rest was

personal invention. One night he was talked into singing at the Silver Slipper, popular with musicians, and chose as his song "I'm Comin' Virginia." Just as he finished, the cornettist, Bix Beiderbecke danced by with the lovely Bee Palmer in his arms and called out, "That's great, kid!"

Another appreciator was band leader Arnold Johnson, who owned what was practically a band syndicate. He furnished the music for the extremely popular radio program *The Majestic Hour*, played for dancing at the Park Central Hotel, and was signed to play in the pit of the *George White Scandals*. Johnson, Bolger recalls, was particularly impressed with the "new sound" that Arlen was able to put into his orchestrations. But if Johnson wanted Arlen the arranger, he had to take Arlen the singer. So it was that Harold Arlen became a member of the Arnold Johnson band. He turned out arrangements, and for their stint at the Park Central even worked up a little act in which he sang.

The *Scandals* assignment was even better, and closer to his goal. He did a couple of arrangements for "American Tune" and "I'm on the Crest of a Wave." He sang the latter song during the entr'act. The revue opened on July 2, 1928, and some months later, after it had closed, one of the luminaries of that edition, Frances Williams, moved to the stage of the Palace, "courtesy of George White," according to the program. Accompanying her "at The Music Boxes" were duo-pianists Leo Feiner and Harold Arlen.

For Arlen, however, the grind was becoming too much, and what he really hoped to do, sing, was only incidental to the work he was doing. Toward the end of 1928, practically in the middle of an arrangement, he called Arnold Johnson and told him that he had had enough. He then struck out on his own as a single act in vaudeville. He went into *Maytime Melodies*, a revue headed by Ted Healy. Arlen's act consisted of songs at the piano. He even defied Ziegfeld by using as one of the songs, "Makin' Whoopee!" current in Ziegfeld's *Whoopee* at the New Amsterdam. It was an unwritten law then—and it remains so yet, with some exceptions—

that songs from current shows could not be done in vaudeville. The feeling was that such exposure would spoil the song for the theater-goer who heard it in a vaudeville theater, cabaret, or club. But Arlen liked the song and managed to slip it in now and then over the protests of the managers. Another song he sang in his act was "She's Funny That Way."

Arlen was happy in this life, for the arrangement grind had palled. He wanted to be a vocalist and as a single he was finally on his way. His style was distinctive, his popularity was growing, and he was doing what he really liked.

Professional song writing held little interest for him. Still, there was a little stir caused by "The Album of My Dreams," written in February 1929 to the lyrics of Lou Davis, who was a successful salesman (of meat to hotels and restaurants) with a love of and flair for song writing. He and Arlen had met at a party and Davis talked the singer into a collaboration. The song was published and enjoyed some success. It was picked up and recorded by Rudy Vallee; Arlen's first royalty statement of $900 rather startled him, though years later he attributed the success of the Vallee record to the singer's great vogue at the time, and "there was a *good* song on the other side of the record."

Actually "The Album of My Dreams" is a pleasant ballad, one that might easily be summed up as "a nice little song," of no great importance or distinction. It was his second published song, to ignore his published instrumental pieces. The first, "Jungaleena," is one he completely disowns, and rightly. "The Album of My Dreams" has a better-than-average, quite appealing melody, decorated with some harmonies that point to the Arlen to come. The publisher thought enough of it to have two special arrangements made of it, and Abe Lyman's band took it up for a while. It might not have been vintage Arlen, but it wasn't a bad song.

The mild though welcome success of "The Album of My Dreams" was pleasurable but did not divert Arlen from trying to continue his career as a singer. This was given an important and decisive push by no less a musical force than composer

Vincent Youmans, who had heard, and liked, Arlen's singing.

In 1929, when Youmans "discovered" Harold Arlen the singer, the former had several formidable songs to his credit, among them "Oh Me, Oh My, Oh You," written with one Arthur Francis, who later became better known under his real name, Ira Gershwin; "Bambalina," "I Want to Be Happy," "Tea for Two," "I Know That You Know," "Sometimes I'm Happy," and "Hallelujah." In 1928 he wrote the score for *Rainbow,* one of his best, which survived less than thirty performances. Possibly the handling of this show prompted Youmans to do his own producing, which he hoped to do with *Great Day* and for which he had signed Arlen to sing and act in the role of Cokey Joe.

Fine composer though he was, Youmans was a difficult man otherwise. He didn't like to bother with collaboration; he merely sent his lead sheets to the lyricists and left it to the hapless words men to fit words to the melody—and without changes. Because he was a good pianist Arlen was drafted into the job of taking Youmans' tunes to Billy Rose and Edward Eliscu; he then played them for the lyricists. In this way Arlen actually got to know the score of *Great Day* before Youmans. In his role of producer Youmans did not make for smooth sailing, and eventually, as the weeks and months went by, the show became known as *The Great Delay* along Broadway. Work began in the spring, in the summer *Great Day* was making the rounds of the environs in one of its several versions, in July 1929 it did play in Jamaica, Queens, and Harold Arlen was heard singing "Doo Dah Dey" there, as well as in Philadelphia. But alterations went on all the time, as time and money drained away.

Arlen became restive and began looking around for something else to do. Will Marion Cook, who had been hired to direct the Negro chorus for *Great Day*, took a liking to him and tried to help by getting Arlen in to sing for other producers. He managed to arrange an audience with the Shuberts one day. Arlen sang, and sang, and sang, while Jake Shubert, seemingly uninterested, continued with the day's business. He didn't seem to note Arlen's presence till the singer had gone hoarse and stopped singing; only then did Shubert look up, inquiring, "What's the matter?"

This sort of experience—the competitiveness of auditions, the uncertainty, the tensions, the stiletto smile, the up-and-down life of a singer—began to pall on Arlen. The round of auditions that the kindly Cook had arranged for and the work of a constantly changing *Great Day* didn't sit well with him. Perhaps this was not really The Life after all.

Great Day, for which Youmans composed three of his finest songs—the title song, "More Than You Know," and "Without a Song"—finally opened on October 17, 1929, but Harold Arlen and "Doo Dah Dey" were not in it.

One of those chance incidents occurred during the summer rehearsals, one that changed the entire course of Arlen's career. Arriving one day for rehearsal, he learned that the regular pianist, Fletcher Henderson, was ill. Arlen was asked to play for the dancers. During the several inevitable waits he unconsciously toyed with the pickup (the musical phrase, a vamp, that serves as a signal for the dancers that a routine is about to begin). As the rehearsal progressed the pickup emerged more and more as a song fragment, a variant that strayed far enough from the original idea to take on all the proportions of an original song. Will Marion Cook, a composer himself, recognized a potential song in the one-time vamp, and suggested that Arlen make a song of it.

So did Harry Warren, himself a composer of consequence already, though he was working as a song plugger for a music publishing house. Warren and Arlen had met at the Park Central Hotel in 1927; Warren had then written a song, "Away Down South in Heaven," which he hoped the Arnold Johnson band would play. He and Arlen had remained friends, and when Arlen played the new song idea Warren felt that it was "pretty jazzy—I know just the guy to write this up."

The "guy" was the lyricist Ted Koehler, then living in Brooklyn, and like Warren, associated with Remick's. Warren arranged the introductions, and Koehler liked the tune also, decided to do a lyric. On July 31, 1929, Arlen and Koehler signed a year's contract with the firm of George and Arthur Piantadosi, a subsidiary of Remick's.

For Arlen this was a new way of life. He didn't even have to go to the publisher's office; all that was required was an occasional song. He did go in, however, so that he and Koehler could work together, for once the first song was finished they worked up some others. Once they interrupted work to gaze out of the window as the *Graf Zeppelin* passed overhead on its way to Lakehurst, New Jersey (this was, incidentally, in August 1929).

Managing the Piantadosi firm was a young (barely twenty-one) man about the music business, Edwin H. Morris, whose age encouraged everyone to call him "Buddy." He had officiated at the signing of the Arlen-Koehler contract, which was, actually, predicated on the strength of the one song that had been developed, in a typical "theme and variations" style, into the song "Get Happy."

With the signing of the Piantadosi contract Arlen's hoped-for career as a singer came to an end. Assured an income of fifty dollars a week, plus whatever, if any, royalties might accrue, he was quite suddenly catapulted into another profession, that of composer. The security afforded by the small though steady income brought an end to the competition of auditions, of working in public ". . . it got me away from that which I had loved, a goal I had set. And yet I suddenly realized that goal had become something my temperament couldn't take."

Simultaneously with the completion of "Get Happy," Ruth Selwyn was planning to produce a revue, and for a time it appeared that the newly formed team would do all the songs for it. Along the line, however, plans were changed, and Mrs. Selwyn decided upon a composite score. Arlen and Koehler managed to get a couple of songs into it; among the other contributors were Kay Swift, the Gershwins, Vincent Youmans, and Rudolf Friml. Sketches were written by Ring Lardner, Eddie Cantor, Anita Loos—again, among others. The choreography was by Busby Berkeley. There were many cooks stirring the pot to be titled *Nine-Fifteen Revue,* which was to star Ruth Etting.

In Boston the show seemed to be shaping up, but as Kay Swift pointed out "Students love everything." To the professionals it soon became obvious that all was not well. Show doctors would travel up from New York and only end up shaking their heads—all the way back to New York. Among those looking in were Earl Carroll, Clara Bow, and singer Harry Richman, the last referring to himself in a deferential third person and expressing the consensus with, "Richman can't do anything for it."

Kay Swift had arranged for the interpolation of the Gershwins' "The World Is Mine" (a song that had been dropped from *Funny Face*), retitled "Toddling Along." The Gershwins were also in Boston with their own show, the second version of *Strike Up the Band* (an obvious hit) and found time to look in on the fortunes (obviously bad) of *The Nine-Fifteen Revue.* The one spot that impressed George Gershwin was the first-act finale, "Get Happy," and he made a point of telling Arlen that it was "the most exciting first-act finale I ever heard."

But what he saw could hardly have impressed him. "The staging," Arlen recalls, "made no sense. It was a beach setting— the cast was in bathing suits—the sun was shining down— and the sand! But rhythmically and orchestrally it was wonderful. It did bring in a definite style, full of what later would be called 'hot licks.'" In the band were such purveyors of hot licks as Benny Goodman, Red Nichols, Joe Venuti, and, formerly of the Original Memphis Five, Frank Signorelli, and Miff Mole: all under the astute direction of Don Voorhees.

The kind of wayward showmanship that filled a stage with sand served to scuttle the production. Kay Swift composed a twelve-minute ballet in a delicate manner, almost impressionistic in style, only to have the entire twelve minutes filled with the rattle of a simulated machine gun, pertinent to the ballet. None of the music could be heard above the sounds of battle.

One of the Swift songs, "High among the Chimney Pots," was never forgotten by Arlen, and Miss Swift, though she barely saw him, recalls how she felt that "there was something fresh about his music."

The Nine-Fifteen Revue opened at the George M. Cohan Theater on February 11, 1930. The performance did not go well; during the course of the evening two girls in the chorus tripped and fell; producer Selwyn left before the final curtain. There were only six more performances before ultimate wisdom set in, and the *Revue* ended.

But for Harold Arlen and Ted Koehler it was the beginning. "Get Happy" became a big hit, and became in Arlen's phrase "a noisy song." It was published with Ruth Etting's photograph on the cover and the legend that she was the "Sweetheart of Columbia Records," but no mention of *The Nine-Fifteen Revue*.

The noise of "Get Happy" was loud enough to attract the attention of Earl Carroll, who contracted Arlen and Koehler to do some songs for the eighth edition of his *Vanities*. The hit of the show was the single interpolation by James Campbell, Reg Connelly, and Ray Noble, "Goodnight, Sweetheart." Most of the score was the work of Jay Gorney (music) and Edgar Y. Harburg (lyrics). Arlen and Koehler contributed a memorable waltz, "One Love," which utilized the opening notes of "My Gal, My Pal," as its main theme—and to which Faith Bacon danced wielding her fans in the first famous fan dance, one of her earliest appearances thus unattired.

Another song was titled "The March of Time," which had a curious history, although not strictly in chronology. Five years after it had been introduced in the *Vanities* of 1930, the song writers were approached by *Time* magazine, then preparing a radio series they hoped to title *The March of Time*, and for which theme music was required. What was needed was an impressive melody, one imposing enough to match the doom-inflected voice of announcer Westbrook Van Voorhis. Agreements were reached and contracts drawn resulting in the use of "The March of Time" as the theme for the radio series beginning in January, 1935. For this the song writers received $125 a week, with an additional $100 in the event of a filmed series. For two years the checks arrived with pleasant regularity and promptness, but when the time did arrive for *The March of Time* to be produced as a film, someone discovered that a few note changes in the Arlen tune resulted in a new theme of the proper dignity and pomp, and with a good saving, for then the regular flow of checks could be turned off.

Thus the fragile form of melody. A. L. Berman, Arlen's legal advisor, who had arranged the transaction to begin with and had always thought of the checks as "found money," did not bring in a tune detective to prove the relationship between the now two "March of Time" themes and the matter dropped. Arlen and Koehler, of course, had other songs to consider and could hardly give concentrated attention to any one tune that had gone astray.

Ted Koehler, in remembering his first meeting with Arlen, has said, "When we met I had been writing for quite a while, but Harold never struck me as being a young fellow trying to be a writer. I felt he was a pro from the start—I mean by that: unlike most young writers who start slow and learn as they go, Harold had it when I met him. As a matter of fact, I think our first song was 'Get Happy' and that was as solid as anything we did later. We seemed to feel and think the same way, therefore were able to work well together."

Arlen was fortunate that he was able to have made his first professional step with so solid a craftsman as Ted Koehler. Eleven years Arlen's senior, Koehler had been active in show business from his eighteenth year. Born in Washington, D.C., in 1894, Koehler moved to Newark, New Jersey, while still a young boy. His father owned a photo-engraving plant in New York to which he commuted daily.

Koehler's father instilled in his son a respect for Old World craftsmanship, a quality the younger Koehler exhibited ever since, whether in his lyrics, drawings, photography, or handiwork around the house.

Along with his early education came the study of the piano,

which, by the time he was in his teens, he could play very well. His style might best be described as improvisational, "barrel-house," in the manner of the white jazz pianists of the time. Koehler worked days in his father's shop, but his evenings were given over to playing the piano in Newark's hot spots. His comings and goings led to a crisis in the Koehler household and an ultimatum: in bed by midnight—or out.

So Koehler went out. Wandering the streets of Newark, literally homeless and without a job, Koehler was not so dejected that he failed to notice a very attractive blonde turn into the lobby of the Sea Shell Theater. The blonde turned out to be the cashier; thus inspired, Koehler asked the manager if he needed a pianist, which he did. So began Ted Koehler's musical career.

Eventually expanding his professional horizons, he left Newark to play the piano in theaters in Brooklyn, Manhattan, Coney Island, and eventually Chicago. There he began writing special material for Chicago singers; he also found a job with the publisher J. W. Stern before switching to the bigger publishing house, Leo Feist. Koehler became the manager of Feist's Chicago office, where he put his mechanical ingenuity to work to devise an organ slide for use in motion picture houses. A new twist on the old nickelodeon slide's, Koehler's organ slide projected messages and song lyrics on the screen while the then-ubiquitous organist thundered out the songs of the day (generally Feist's). The device was introduced by Jesse Crawford at the Chicago Theater, where it proved to be most effective, and successful. Soon its inventor was working practically full time at lettering captions for the advertisements, the song lyrics, usually preceded by such exhortations as:

> *Can You Sing This One? Well, All Right Then!*
> *Give It All You've Got!*

Some of Koehler's energies were devoted to writing songs, too, for such personalities as Rudolph Valentino (momentarily *persona non grata* in the film capital and making a tour of film houses), Sophie Tucker, and Ruth Etting, whom Koehler

had taken out of the chorus and featured at the Marigold
Theater.

Not only was he writing the songs and acts for some of
these entertainers, Koehler also worked on the sets, painted
scenery, and helped with the lighting, which predilections
earned him the nickname—and one that stuck—"Willie Wes-
tinghouse."

Tired of Chicago, Koehler teamed up with Coleman Goetz
for a vaudeville tour. His wanderlust was cured when he met
Elvira Hagen, married, and settled down in Brooklyn. He
went to work again for a publishing house, this time Shapiro,
Bernstein, a firm managed by the Piantadosi brothers. When
they splintered away from the giant firm, the Piantadosis took
Koehler with them. And, once introductions by Harry Warren
were taken care of, and Koehler had heard his new song,
Harold Arlen was brought into the firm also.

Although gentle, retiring, and soft-spoken, Harold Arlen
could, when he sang, open up and let himself go. His singing
of his own songs, and the songs of others, for that matter, is a
stirring experience. Koehler, on the other hand, was always
at a low emotional pitch—at least outwardly; he never got
excited about anything. Even when a song became a great
hit, he accepted it as a matter of course, remained unruffled.
He seemed content to let off steam in his lyrics; once the
words were out of the way, he would find something practical
to occupy himself with, a job that might require a hammer or
a saw rather than a pen.

In their first song Koehler and Arlen fused their individuali-
ties in a type of song they could write as could no others. For
all the sun and sand, "Get Happy" is a kind of spiritual—one
critic even referred to it as "the 'Hallelujah' song"—characterized by an intense rhythmic drive. Like all inevitable creations, its effects are simply achieved.

Take the song's climax, for example. In the music there is
a repeated three-note phrase (on the words "Forget your . . ."
"You better . . ." and "Sing Halle [lujah]"), which begins each
of these three times on the same note. But on the fourth time

it is raised a fourth (from the B flat below C to the E flat above C). The conventional interval would have been a third, but that extra step of one tone generates the deciding tension culminating in the song's exciting climax. After the middle "the release," when the three-note phrase returns, it is again in the original key.

All of this can be seen in the printed sheet music to "Get Happy," or better, heard in an actual performance of the song. It does not, however, truly explain why the song is a good song, or an effective song, nor why it has remained a living song. Analysis discovers the ingenuity only after it has already discovered itself.

Although "Get Happy" was not the only Arlen-Koehler song in *The Nine-Fifteen Revue,* it was the only one that made any noise. It's wide popularity identified its composers as hit writers, and also as creators of "hallelujah" songs.

After their assignment for Earl Carroll, Arlen and Koehler interpolated a couple of numbers into the score for the show at the Silver Slipper. One of the songs written for this cabaret was "Shaking the African," which, while a lot more secular in tone than "Get Happy," also added to the growing reputation of Harold Arlen and Ted Koehler as writers of bluesy rhythm songs, and bluesy rhythm songs were much in demand in the flourishing cabarets. It so happened that many, if not all, of the cabarets during the prohibition years were managed on the interlocking directorate principal: the real owners, the men behind the scenes, of the clubs happened also to operate the Phoenix Cereal Beverage Company in West Twenty-sixth Street. It was the function of the company to supply all the beer for the clubs in the West Side and even as far north as Harlem.

CHAPTER 3

Harlem Holiday

Harry Block did not make it all the way home one night. When he was eventually found, in the elevator of his own apartment building, he was a little bullet-riddled. The story, never proved, that went around was that Harry's home-coming had been arranged as a retaliation for the Plantation Club incident.

The Plantation was a Harlem rival of the Cotton Club. The rivalry went too far when the management of the Plantation persuaded Cab Calloway to bring his orchestra from the Cotton Club to the Plantation. Calloway was one of the major attractions at the Cotton Club with his famous "Minnie the Moocher" routine. As he was an irrepressible night-club-floor personality, purveyor of stentorian "hi-de-hos," and leader of a remarkable orchestra, his leaving the Cotton Club was looked upon as pretty unfair competition.

One night "some of the boys" dropped in on the Plantation Club. Though not of New York's Finest, they worked completely within the philosophy of Captain Patrick McVeigh's edict, when he dealt with the "clips" afflicting his town: "Toss this joint in the street!" This the boys did, all the tables and chairs, reduced to splinters, shattered glasses and bottles, even the bar was deracinated and replanted at the curb. Had there been wallpaper on the Plantation's walls, no doubt that too would have peeled and scattered, but the glass paneling served as well. When the boys finished with the Plantation Club, the street was the healthier place to be. Calloway and band, needless to say, returned to their old stand.

There was something about the manner in which the "Unfair Competition" aspects of the Plantation Club were handled that bespoke the touch of The Master. It soon got around town that Owney Madden just might have arranged for the visit by the boys. It was further rumored, though never publicly, that Madden, along with the now late Harry Block and George DeMange—his friends called him "Big Frenchy"— were the actual owners of the Cotton Club, possibly the finest night club in Harlem. In truth, the club was managed by Herman Stark; the owners rarely interfered with the actual running of the club; supplying the Cereal Beverages was their major concern. "Big Frenchy" was around a good deal, but Madden, always chary of the limelight, was rarely seen. Unlike his peer in Chicago, Al Capone, Owney Madden was free of any egoistic drive for celebrity; he attended to his business, such as it was, and the less fuss the better.

When he was paroled in 1923, coincidentally the year the Cotton Club opened, Madden, former leader of the old Hell's Kitchen Gopher Gang, found himself in a changed world. While he had been in prison, prohibition had been embraced by the American people led by the good-intentioned but fuzzy-minded. Prohibition had not been Owen Victor Madden's idea —he hadn't even voted for it. But he would be a poor business-man, indeed, if he were to allow its exploitation possibilities to slip away untested.

Although the Cotton Club was a prime outlet for "Madden's No. 1," the product of the West Twenty-sixth Street plant, it was also, in the words of Lady Mountbatten, "The Aristo-crat of Harlem." Of course the Cotton Club also furnished drinks more aristocratic than beer, both American and Chinese dishes, and, most aristocratic of all, exciting entertainment.

Originally the unsuccessful Club Deluxe, under the manage-ment of fighter Jack Johnson, the Cotton Club was located at 142nd Street and Lenox Avenue up one flight, over the Douglas Theater. It did not cater to local trade, however. If the prices did not take care of that, other forces would. "There were brutes at the door," Carl Van Vechten has said, "to enforce the Cotton Club's policy which was opposed to mixed parties. Altho sometimes somebody like Bill Robinson or Ethel [Waters] herself could get a table for colored friends."

Devoted neither to the betterment of race relations nor to the advancement of the arts, the Cotton Club was none-theless the place to go in Harlem. There were lesser spots, such as Connie's Inn, the Saratoga Club, The Nest, Small's Paradise, and the Sugar Cane Club—all supplying vintage jazz-age music—but of all the Cotton Club was the true aristocrat. There were two shows a night, the first at midnight and the second around 2 A.M. For entertainment, according to the Cot-ton Club's brochure, there was "the cream of sepia talent, the greatest array of creole stars ever assembled, supported by a chorus of bronze beauties." The bands of Cab Calloway, Duke Ellington, and Jimmy Lunceford played at the Cotton Club. To their vital new music danced such talents as Bill Robinson, Carolynne Snowden, Henri Wessels, and Anise Boyer. And a composer could hardly dream of better voices than those of Aida Ward, Leitha Hill, Ethel Waters, Adelaide Hall, and George Dewey Washington, among other great Negro tal-ents.

During the early Twenties the Cotton Club shows had been produced by Lew Leslie and the songs furnished by Jimmy McHugh and Dorothy Fields. Naturally they were good, as might be expected from such talents, but the Cotton Club shows took on their now famous form after Herman Stark hired Dan Healy to "conceive and produce" the floor shows.

Healy was a young veteran of show business; he could dance, sing, was a quick ad-libbing comedian and a skilled master of ceremonies. On the night of July 16, 1919, when the Eighteenth Amendment went into effect, Healy, who had not so long ago returned from the wars, showed his disdain on the stage of the Majestic by impersonating the now famous Rollin Kirby caricature that was to represent the figure of Prohibi-tion. As he reeled about the stage, Danny Healy, with a bottle sticking out of his hip pocket, symbolized and satirized, "the gaunt, cruel-lipped chap with the funereal get-up, the high hat and the suspiciously boozy nose." Healy had no idea that he would be one of those knights who would do battle with the dragon and windmills he openly challenged that night—and that he would win.

Dan Healy had a typical song-and-dance man's background, in vaudeville as well as appearances in legitimate musicals such as the *Ziegfeld Follies of 1927*, the Rodgers and Hart show *Betsy*, Kalmar and Ruby's *Good Boy*, among many others. Before he came to the Cotton Club, Healy had staged similar shows for the Chateau Madrid, for "Legs" Diamond's *Frolics*, and for shows in clubs in Atlantic City, Philadelphia, and the Silver Slipper in New York. The Silver Slipper belonged to the Owney Madden-"Big Frenchy" cartel also; it was a simple move uptown to the Cotton Club for Danny Healy. In 1926 he took over the production of the club's shows, two a year.

Quick-witted, irrepressible, Dan Healy found the Cotton Club assignment (he did other work at the same time) his cup of scotch. "The chief ingredient was pace, pace, pace!" he will tell you. "The show was generally built around types: the band, an eccentric dancer, a comedian—whoever we had who was also a star. The show ran an hour and a half, sometimes two hours; we'd break it up with a good voice: Aida Ward or Ethel Waters. And we'd have a special singer who gave the customers the expected adult song in Harlem, a girl like Leitha Hill. There was good food too, and a cover charge of $3.00. There was practically every kind of drink. Good booze, too—it was the McCoy."

The "McCoy" was always readily at hand at the Cotton Club, though the prices were steep enough so that only the society and show-business clientele catered to by the club could meet them: a glass of "Pure Orange Juice" cost $1.25, a "Quart of Lemonade" $3.50, American Ginger Ale, Splits (the tiny bottle), $1.00, and Owney's No. 1, on the menu as "Beer, Bottle," also cost a dollar.

Food was no higher than might have been found at other cabarets: the steak sandwich was $1.25; so were deerfoot sausage and scrambled eggs. A lobster cocktail was listed at a dollar, so was a crab-meat cocktail; olives could be had for fifty cents (the menu doesn't state how many). On the Chinese half of the menu soups were uniformly fifty cents, and the prices were higher on this side of the page with the highest being "Moo Goo Guy Pan" at $2.25. However, when the patron got thirsty he was invariably in trouble; even milk cost fifty cents.

Neither Arlen nor Koehler remembers how they became associated with the Cotton Club. The "Get Happy" popularity brought them to the attention of public and professionals alike, and the job they did for the Silver Slipper brought them into the sphere of Owney Madden and company. The combination of Jimmy McHugh and Dorothy Fields formed in 1927 had gone into the writing of the successful *Blackbirds of 1928,* and by 1930, when they did the score for *The International Revue,* they were ready to leave the Cotton Club. Miss Fields was never really happy there and often refused to sign her name to some of the more single-entendre songs she was expected to do.

The Cotton Club needed song writers for its 1930 edition, *Brown Sugar—Sweet but Unrefined,"* to quote Dan Healy's title in full, and Arlen and Koehler were available. Next came the edition called *Rhythmania,* again with Arlen-Koehler songs, the following year, which put the Cotton Club on the musical map. Aida Ward introduced "Between the Devil and the Deep Blue Sea," and Cab Calloway's specialities were "Trickeration" and "Kickin' the Gong Around," which became one of the year's hits, along with "Between the Devil." And for "I Love a Parade" Dan Healy devised a spectacular routine complete with batons and fancy stepping.

Ted Koehler vividly remembers the circumstances inspiring the last song. "Harold lived at the Croydon Hotel [on Eighty-sixth Street at Madison Avenue], which was a pretty good walk from the building where the publishing offices were. Harold liked to walk, I didn't—however, he used to talk me into walking and I remember one day it was a little cold out and to pep me up he started to hum an ad lib marching tune. I guess I started to fall into step and got warmed up."

Along the route of their march Koehler commented and generally complained, and he made suggestions such as "Why don't you join the Army if you love to walk so much?" and others less printable. "However he kept humming and we kept marching. When we got down to Forty-seventh Street, 'I Love a Parade' was almost written."

The year of their first Cotton Club show, 1930, Harold Arlen was officially elected to membership of the American Society of Composers, Authors and Publishers (ASCAP), on September 25, 1930, to be precise. For the next four years he and Koehler turned out songs for two Cotton Club shows a year. For this they received fifty dollars a week and "all the Frivolity Sandwiches (these were juicy steaks) they could eat," as one friend recalls it. Having the Cotton Club as a sounding board for their work more than compensated for the meager salary. Not only were there such stars as Aida Ward, Cab Calloway, and Duke Ellington to introduce the songs, the club's patrons were just as glittering.

The Cotton Club became the hangout for the Mink Set, escaping Park Avenue for the earthier realities of Harlem, but even more important, it was one of the places open late enough so that show people could relax after their own performances. Healy recalls the image of the exquisite Marilyn Miller doing a soft-shoe, or the tearful Helen Morgan singing, or Bert Wheeler clowning. Mayor Jimmy Walker could be found at the Cotton Club, if not at City Hall; financier Otto Kahn was fascinated by the Cotton Club. He had come uptown with producer Vinton Freedley, and Kahn's son, Roger Wolf, who wanted to lead a jazz band and open his own club, both of which, eventually, he did.

"Celebrity Nights" were held on Sunday evenings and not only were the big names in the audience, in Healy's words, "expected to take a turn, they were also expected to pick up their own tabs, too."

Musicians came to hear the bands but somehow never managed to copy their unique styles. Responsible for both the widespread fame of the Cotton Club and its exciting orchestras

was the exploitation afforded by the ubiquitous new mechanical ear, radio. Both CBS and NBC placed their microphones
in the Cotton Club to broadcast its music. One of the announc-
ers was Ted Husing, whose major function was the dropping
of names and introducing the bands. Jazz historians consider
the Duke Ellington broadcasts from the Cotton Club of great
importance to the development of the art.

Opening nights at the club were as exciting, celebrity-
studded, and as important as any Broadway opening. The
newspapers sent their top columnists, Louis Sobol, Ed Sullivan,
and Walter Winchell, to cover the event. Husing delivered his
coverage with the urgency he would give to a sporting event.

In retrospect, in view of the club's management, it is curious
that there were never any real typically Twenties or Thirties
"incidents." Harry Block was confronted in his apartment
building and dispatched in classic style. There was one other
associated incident, however, not in the Cotton Club itself.
Arthur Flegenheimer, who attained fame as "Dutch" Schultz,
had had a falling-out with one of his top executives, Vincent
Coll, appropriately named "Mad Dog." "Dutch" Schultz, who
controlled distribution of "the stuff" in the Bronx, lived on good
terms with Owney Madden, who attended to Manhattan's
needs. Coll, however, struck out with that vicious logic that
earned him his frighteningly accurate sobriquet. Because of
Schultz's relationship with Madden, Coll kidnapped "Big
Frenchy" DeMange, and held him for $35,000 ransom (he had
boasted that he would kidnap Madden's brother-in-law, even
Madden himself, but settled for DeMange). Madden paid but
never forgot. The year Arlen and Koehler did "Between the
Devil and the Deep Blue Sea" and "I Love a Parade" they
were not much aware of the struggle for power. In that year,
1931, Coll descended upon a street in Harlem gunning for
another rival and killed instead a five-year-old boy and
wounded other children as they played. In the name of justice
the skillful Samuel Leibowitz won an acquittal for Coll. But by
then gangland itself had decided on its own justice and a
$50,000 price was put on Coll's head. One of "Dutch" Schultz's

deputies collected it, for in this same year Coll was machine-gunned in a phone booth. "Big Frenchy" had been freed, and died fairly full of years in the manner of many business executives—in the phrase of Dan Healy "the Big Frog had a bum ticker."

Healy's Cotton Club productions were quite elaborate for a night club; there were miniature sets, dramatic lighting, and spectacular costumes—or lack of them. In keeping with the name the décor was rustic; there was a small stage against the wall opposite the entrance. Tables were arranged in tiers around the large dance floor. The stage served the needs of the show, with the action spilling onto the dance floor as required. The club's capacity was about five hundred, and it was often crowded enough to make getting through the ropes impossible, unless you happened to be somebody. It was probably the first night club that went in for sets and elaborate lighting; helping with these aspects of the shows engaged Ted Koehler as much as writing lyrics.

Working with so solid, though quite unorthodox, a craftsman as Koehler proved congenial to Harold Arlen. It was good training, too. Then, as now, Arlen was impatient with the mechanics of composing and was always eager to get on to the next song. Koehler, on the other hand, liked to hear the tune over and over again even before he began the lyric. And once he began he requested more and more playings.

"He would never let you know what he thought of a melody," Arlen has said. "Quiet, philosophic—nothing about Ted smacked of show business or Tin Pan Alley. All that was certain was that he would go about his work methodically. Once a song was finished, he'd go on to the next, and that was that."

Though the Arlen-Koehler method varied, the usual pattern was this: Arlen sat at the piano while Koehler stretched comfortably on the sofa. Composer would play the work in progress, then again—no reaction from his collaborator—and again. "I may have played a song—literally—a thousand times," Arlen recalls with a chuckle. During the course of a work session Koehler would appear to doze, whereupon the suffering Arlen, resenting the Koehler comfort a little, would shout above his own playing, "Ted!" Koehler would snap up, tapping his feet in tempo and whistling the melody to prove that he was working too. Sometimes, tired of the repetition, Arlen would not shout and take a break, while the lyricist, in his own words, would lie there "saving his cells."

Arlen learned early never to try to see Koehler's work before it was complete. It was the lyricist's belief that if a composer saw an uncompleted lyric, and felt compelled to criticize it, it might spoil the lyric's chances of ever becoming acceptable. When Arlen tried to see what lines were evolving from his marathon playing, Koehler would hide it from him. No one would see it until it was complete and, in the lyricist's estimation, ready to go out on its own. Then he would place it on the piano for Arlen to see.

The completed lyric was always right, finely fashioned, and earthy. Koehler has an easy ear for the vernacular, that simple poetry of the man in the street. Koehler's skill lay in choosing the fitting point the lyric should make in a given melody, then setting it with words that were both poetic and simple, and chiseled into place with the skilled hand of a major craftsman. Thus did Ted Koehler achieve, in many of the songs he and Arlen wrote for the Cotton Club, a kind of folk poetry unique in the history of American popular music, a quality that has helped to make so many of the songs popular classics that have lived for decades after their original composition. Koehler's approach, for all the evident skill, was always matter-of-fact. There was no pose of the poet in his make-up, for his feeling is that song lyrics must come naturally and will not work if contrived. "When they stop dropping out of the skies," he will declare, "I'm a dead pigeon!"

For the twenty-first edition of the Cotton Club series, the first of the *Cotton Club Parades,* Arlen and Koehler had as their hit song (for each of the shows they did they managed to have at least one) "I've Got the World on a String," sung by Aida Ward. And since Calloway's "Minnie the Moocher," though alive as a Cotton Club personality, had run her course as a song, Arlen and Koehler tossed off "Minnie the Moocher's Wedding Day" as a specialty number for Calloway. On hand, too, was Leitha Hill to sing the very blue blues songs—such as "My Military Man," "Pool Room Poppa," and "High Flyin' Man," none of which bears Arlen's name because he felt that such highly specialized material belonged in the club. These were genre songs, actually, amazingly reproduced by two white men, the kind of song that could be obtained only on the so-called "race records," specially manufactured for the Negro market and that later became collector's items to the jazz collector. Bessie Smith and Ethel Waters recorded these often shockingly outspoken songs. None of the Arlen-Koehler songs was ever recorded or published—or even copyrighted, for that matter.

Other purely local culture traits were preserved in song by Arlen and Koehler: the "breakfast dance," for example. This was, literally, what the term implied, a dance that was held in the morning, usually after a full night out. There was, also, the "rent party," a fund-raising device whereby the month's major financial problem was solved. Friends were invited to one's apartment, where music and refreshments were furnished. A collection would be taken up in the course of the evening, out of which the entertainment and refreshments would be paid for and the remainder would be applied to the rent. Arlen and Koehler based their "Raisin' the Rent," from the *Cotton Club Parade* of 1932, on this practice. Another, less attractive aspect was set down in "The Wail of the Reefer Man," a Cab Calloway specialty.

The following year, 1933, proved to be a special one. Early in the year Arlen and Koehler had all but tossed off a song at a party. Arlen had been thinking of Cab Calloway when he wrote it, had even opened it with what he calls "a front shout." Going from this three-note phrase, Arlen worked up the song, played it a few times. In about half an hour both he and Koehler had completed their respective ends of the collaboration. Relieved to have one more out of the way, they left to get a sandwich. Thus, simply and without fanfare, was created "Stormy Weather."

As it turned out, Calloway was not to appear in that edition of the *Parade;* Duke Ellington had been signed instead. As the song turned out, lyrically it was not tailored for a male singer anyway.

Ethel Waters, the song writers believed, would be the perfect interpreter of their song. Miss Waters had only recently returned to New York from Chicago and Cicero, then Al Capone territory. Her career was at ebb at the moment and she listened with interest to Arlen and Koehler when they called upon her to talk about her appearing at the Cotton Club. Dan Healy had once devoted to the great singer an "Ethel Waters Night," which had made a favorable impression on her; besides, *her* friends, at least, were allowed in the Cotton Club. But Miss Waters agreed to appear in the twenty-second edition of the *Cotton Club Parade,* mainly because of the impact on her of "Stormy Weather."

The spring edition was scheduled to begin early in April 1933. Long before it opened Harold Arlen recorded "Stormy Weather" with the Leo Reisman orchestra. Reisman, a former Bostonian, led what Jerome Kern called "The string quartet of dance bands." The conductor, a graduate of Harvard and the Boston Conservatory of Music, had left the Baltimore Symphony Orchestra to form his own band. Kern had been instrumental in bringing him to New York, where he played the most exclusive hotels, predominantly the Waldorf-Astoria. Reisman not only featured fine musicianship in his arrangements, he also evidenced an unusual good taste in the songs he played, most of which were the better show tunes of the period. The kind of straightforward yet imaginative arrangements the Reisman band played in the early Thirties were a good deal like those that were heard several years later in the Astaire-Rogers films.

Reisman had first met Harold Arlen in 1929, when he conducted the popular *Ponds' Hour* broadcast on station WEAF and on which he had invited Arlen to sing. From their first meeting Reisman was convinced that Arlen was "a master craftsman by training or instinct; he was also a master performer and projected with complete conviction." Their recording of "Stormy Weather" was done by RCA Victor in February 1933 (on the reverse was the Reisman band's version of the Irving Berlin song "Maybe It's Because I Love You Too Much", the vocal by Fred Astaire).

When released the recording became an instantaneous bestseller; in fact for a while it helped to revive the all-but-expiring phonograph-record industry. By opening night at the Cotton Club the record had stirred up a great interest in the song, and consequently the show. The ropes were up that night as New York's elite, from the world of society, show business, and gangdom, crowded into the Cotton Club to hear Ethel Waters sing "Stormy Weather."

To give an idea of how the now legendary Cotton Club shows were devised, the program for the 1933 *Cotton Club Parade* went like this: Duke Ellington led the orchestra in the overture, after which the show's first act began. There were eighteen scenes in it ranging from skits through dance specialties, comedy, and songs. The first scene was titled "Harlem Hospital" a typical vaudeville skit with a local twist, complete with a Head Nurse (Sally Goodings), Dr. Jones (Dusty Fletcher), Doctor's Assistant (Cora La Redd) and Mr. Cotton Club (George Dewey Washington). This skit, with its blackout ending, got the show off to a good sensual start.

George Dewey Washington, who also appeared simultaneously in the Broadway production *Strike Me Pink*, starring Jimmy Durante, in the second scene sang the Arlen-Koehler song "Calico Days." The next song was used in the skit titled "The Harlem Spirit" and sung in the sixth scene by Henry "Rubber Legs" Williams—the song, "Happy as the Day Is Long." In the ninth scene Sally Goodings appeared to do the show's wicked song, "I'm Lookin' for Another Handy Man." Not until the eleventh scene did the star, Miss Waters, appear.

The scene was titled "Cabin in the Cotton Club." Healy

had staged it simply against a log-cabin backdrop; Miss
Waters stood under a lamppost, a midnight-blue spot on her,
as she sang "Stormy Weather." After her chorus the scene
imperceptively faded into the next as she was joined by
George Dewey Washington, singing responses to Miss Waters'
choruses; the Talbert choir joined them. By using special
lights Healy was able to fade the girls practically unseen
onto the dance floor. The transition from song to dance was
done smoothly and effectively. The number stopped the show.
On opening night, Healy remembers, there were at least a
dozen encores.

Six more scenes made up the first act, among them a dance
act by the Nicholas Brothers, a return of George Dewey Washington, and Miss Waters before an entire company finale.

The second act opened with a skit in which Miss Waters
appeared; the rest of the fourteen scenes were devoted mainly
to specialties of the individual members of the company.
There were two songs in the second half of the show (and
five in the first). It was a long program but marvelous talent
and the Healy "pace, pace, pace" kept it moving.

The "Stormy Weather" impact not only meant good business
for the Cotton Club, it was another hit for Arlen and Koehler
—and practically launched a new career for Ethel Waters. The
day after he had seen the show Irving Berlin called Healy offer-
ing to buy out Miss Waters' contract (a nonexistent document)
explaining that he hoped to have her appear in his *As Thousands Cheer*, about to go into rehearsal. Miss Waters left the
Cotton Club to go into the Berlin show and made another historic appearance singing Berlin's "Heat Wave" and the bitter
"Suppertime."

The year 1933 was pivotal in the history of the Cotton
Club also. Ratification of the Twenty-first Amendment officially brought prohibition to a close on December 5. The
depression, which seemed to be nonexistent inside the Cotton
Club, was at its nadir by 1933. And further, Owney Madden
was not around again.

Although not as regularly in attendence as "Big Frenchy,"

Madden, Harold Arlen remembers, was around now and then. They had met socially at Madden's penthouse apartment in Chelsea, not too far from the Phoenix Cereal Beverage Company. Frances Williams, the singer who like Arlen was living at the Croyden Hotel, took Arlen and Roger Edens to a party at Madden's. Another time Madden offered to drive the composer to his hotel from the Cotton Club—it was Arlen's first, and only, ride in a bulletproof Dusenburg. It may have been the same vehicle that transported Owney Madden up to Sing Sing, which he voluntarily re-entered in July 1932 because of some parole violation technicality. When released a year later Madden retired from the business world, which had changed greatly in the short time he was away, and sought the kinder, quieter, climates of Hot Springs, Arkansas.

Even Arlen and Koehler skipped a year at the Cotton Club, the twenty-third edition, to enable them to spend a few weeks in Hollywood on *Let's Fall in Love,* their first film assignment. Some of the songs in that non-Arlen-Koehler edition were contributed by, among others, Jerry (once Julius) Arlen and Jimmy Van Heusen. The younger Arlen supplied the music to Van Heusen's lyrics for "There's a House in Harlem for Sale."

In the Cotton Club chorus was a sixteen-year-old beauty, "hiding from the truant officer," named Lena Horne. When Arlen and Koehler returned from Hollywood, they did their last Cotton Club show together; it was Arlen's last—Koehler stayed on for a few more editions. For the 1934 *Parade* they did "Ill Wind," sung by Adelaide Hall; the song, it was hoped, would prove to be a meteorological sequel to "Stormy Weather." It wasn't, but "Ill Wind" is one of their best. Another song was done by the now promoted Lena Horne singing "As Long as I Live" in duet with the smooth young dancer Avon Long. Miss Horne was proving to be quite a draw because of her singing, dancing, and ineffable beauty. The management signed her to a "lifetime" contract, and when she wanted to break away from the Cotton Club representatives of the management visited her Brooklyn home to discuss

the matter, during which "discussion" Miss Horne's step-
father was terribly beaten. To escape, Miss Horne and her
family left town and remained out of sight until it seemed
safe for her to reactivate her singing career with the band of
Noble Sissle, touring away from New York.

By this time, 1935–36, the novelty and excitement of the
Cotton Club had evaporated. The exotic Harlem setting no
longer attracted the celebrities, who in turn brought in the
big butter-and-egg men. The depression kept the celebrities
at home, and there were few butter-and-egg men around.
Herman Stark tried to keep the club going, even to the point
of making it more accessible by moving it downtown to
Broadway at Forty-eighth Street. It wasn't the same. The
idea had run its course and times had changed. Though
liquor was again legally available, the country itself had
become more sober; the spree that had reached a crescendo in
1929 merely whimpered out by 1935. A victim of cyclic history, the Cotton Club finally closed its doors on February
15, 1936.

The Cotton Club holds an important place in the history
of American popular music, not only because of the extraordinary talents it employed, and the bands that first made
a name there, but also because of the songs written for
its shows. If a Cotton Club opening was as gala an event as
any Broadway première, its songs were on the level of songs
written for 'Broadway productions, unique for a night-club
floor show. Some three decades later many of the songs have
become a part of the fabric of American traditional music; in
Europe, in fact, they are thought to be folk songs in a direct
line of descent from the songs of Stephen Foster.

The Arlen-Koehler Cotton Club songs are hardly in the
romanticized vein of Foster's songs, and they are more authentically Negro or, rather, more purely American, and less
European than Foster's, in form and harmony. Products of
a harder time, and written for a different purpose, the Arlen-
Koehler Cotton Club songs are redolent of another time
and place. If Gershwin's songs are representative of the Twen-

ties (a point that could well be argued) Arlen's songs carry in them the haunting melancholy of a sadder, perhaps even wiser time. Some may attribute the characteristic qualities of both Gershwin and Arlen to the time in which they composed specific songs, but this kind of thinking subtracts the most important element: the personal touch.

Though the Cotton Club songs, particularly "Stormy Weather" and "Ill Wind," were to afflict Arlen with typing as a composer of blues, there is none among the songs that could properly be labeled a blues. There are rhythm numbers, novelties, ballads, but no blues. Neither "Stormy Weather" nor "Ill Wind" is a blues in the authentic, folk sense. They are mood pieces, and in this sense may be called blues, but not in form. It was George Gershwin who pointed out to Irving Berlin the singularly constructed "Stormy Weather." The analytical Gershwin noted that in the entire first statement of the melody there was no repetition of any musical phrase, from the opening "Don't know why" front shout through "Keeps rainin' all the time." This was an almost shocking departure from popular music practice, and one, incidentally, of which Arlen was not particularly aware until Gershwin mentioned it.

When Carl Van Vechten played the Leo Reisman recording for Gershwin for the first time, the latter became enthusiastic, calling Arlen "the most original of composers. You can never trace his melodies to the Lost Chord or Go Down Moses!"

"Ill Wind," too, is unusual in structure; instead of the conventional thirty-two bars it runs to forty (the traditional blues is built on twelve-bar phrases). On the other hand, "Between the Devil and the Deep Blue Sea," is the regulation thirty-two bars. What concerned Arlen at the time he was writing the songs was not the form but the function. He was composing for special talents for a special place. Just as the melody of "Stormy Weather" was influenced by Cab Calloway's singing style, so were some of the other songs tailored especially for a personality: "Between the Devil" for Bill Robinson, for example. Arlen's personal bent tended toward the harmonies and rhythms of the blues and jazz, enabled him to compose melodies—and for which Koehler did remarkably apt lyrics— that sounded completely at home in the Cotton Club. That so many have continued to live this day to be sung by other personalities is a tribute to their timelessness. Curiously, the only song written deliberately in the blues style, "I Gotta Right to Sing the Blues," was not written for the Cotton Club at all, but during the same period for an *Earl Carroll Vanities*.

Ethel Waters, it has been said, once called Harold Arlen "the Negro-ist white man" she had ever known. Arlen's easy, open, and friendly warmth and humor made it easy for him to meet anyone, despite his innate shyness. He could be at ease practically anywhere, whether in Owney Madden's penthouse or, decades later, in Gloria Vanderbilt's home on Gracie Square. The Cotton Club served Arlen doubly in that he was furnished with an exciting outlet for his songs and he did meet every type of person.

"Those were happy, carefree, naïve days," producer-songwriter Roger Edens has remembered as through a glass-tinted roseate. "Harold had—has—a mercurial capacity for happiness and it has a contagious quality. Some of the happiest times for me were at the Cotton Club. At that time they were rehearsing a new Cotton Club revue, and Harold and Ted Koehler had written the score. It was great excitement for me to go with Harold to the rehearsals. I shall never forget the sight and sound of Harold with the cast. Singing with them, dancing with them, laughing and kidding with them. He was really one of them. He had absorbed so much from them—their idiom, their tonalities, their phrasings, their rhythms—he was able to establish a warming rapport with them. The Negroes in New York at that time were possibly not as sensitive about themselves as they are today. But, even so, they had a fierce insularity and dignity within themselves that resented the so-called 'professional Southernism' that was rampant in New York in those days. I was always amazed that they completely accepted Harold and his super-minstrel-show antics. They loved it—and adored him."

CHAPTER 4

It's Only a Paper Moon

Not all of Harold Arlen's energies were channeled into Harlem in the early Thirties; nor did he spend his nights at the Cotton Club eating Frivolity Sandwiches. Though he was reconciled to his new career as a composer, Arlen's original dream of a career as an entertainer was long in fading; in fact he never gave up singing.

Late in 1931 he appeared at the Palace, vaudeville's last stronghold, accompanying Lyda Roberti, who sang and served as a stooge for comedian Lou Holtz (both had appeared in Arlen's musical *You Said It* earlier in the year). The bill was so popular it broke the long-run record at the Palace. Some months later, in February 1932, the same trio appeared at the formidable rival of the Palace, Warner's Hollywood, with pretty much the same routine now called *Lou Holtz' Vaudeville Revue*. On the same program were Clark and McCullough, the Boswell Sisters, and Vincent Lopez.

Arlen opened the second half of the show, playing and singing several of his songs popular up to then; he then accompanied Miss Roberti, who had become identified with the Arlen-Yellen song "Sweet and Hot," her theme song. Though this particular phase of Arlen's show business activity took a great deal of time, he greatly enjoyed it, and it did prolong his official leave-taking from the stage, his first love.

He managed to get composing done between rehearsals; during the first appearance at the Palace, while he and Ted Koehler were doing songs for the Cotton Club's *Rhythmania*, Koehler would come around to the Palace, where he and Arlen would work on the stage during rehearsals. Thus in

October 1931 Arlen and Koehler had written "Between the Devil and the Deep Blue Sea" at a piano on the stage of the Palace Theater.

Early in the summer of 1932 Ethel Merman was signed to appear at the Palace; her accompanist was Roger Edens, who later became a successful song writer and film producer. His association with Miss Merman began with her first appearance on Broadway in the Gershwins' *Girl Crazy*, two years before. As originally planned Miss Merman was to deliver the "Sam and Delilah" number with a pianist accompanying her onstage. On opening night her vocal coach and regular accompanist, Al Siegel, became too ill to go on. Roger Edens was playing in the pit band of *Girl Crazy*—the Red Nichols orchestra—and was drafted to replace the ailing Siegel. Edens reluctantly gave into threats and coaxings, consenting to appear on the stage of the Alvin, provided that the spotlight was kept off him during the singing of "Sam and Delilah." *Girl Crazy* launched not only the brilliant career of Ethel Merman but also her friendship and association with Roger Edens, that has continued ever since.

Having completed a long run in the 1931 *George White Scandals,* in which she introduced "Life Is Just a Bowl of Cherries," Miss Merman was billed into the Palace just prior to the beginning of rehearsals of another show, *Take a Chance,* for which she was signed to appear later in November 1932.

"Once Merman had signed for the Palace," Edens remembers, "we had the problem of finding someone to play the first piano with me. She liked to make a change in the act and it was necessary for the pianos to do a solo spot to fill in.

"Harold was the ideal choice. He had a couple of very popular songs to his credit; he was attractive to look at; he could play the piano better than I; and he could sing like an angel.

"It was a hit show—with all the excitement of a hit show. It was also a happy show with a great camaraderie backstage. Harold was very popular with the other performers. His bubbling good spirits and spontaneous antics were irresistible."

The duo-pianists were also irresistible targets for the gags of the veteran vaudevillians Lou Holtz and William Gaxton, also on the bill. Because the pianists played on-stage they were expected to wear make-up, and Holtz and Gaxton were only too happy to offer advice to the neophytes. Arlen and Edens, under their tutelage, innocently went out and "bought enough make-up to last for years. Harold and I were enchanted with all the pots of rouge and jars of cream. We proceeded to put all of it on. We were excited and elated. And a little narcissism crept into it, for we both were admiring ourselves in the mirror.

"You can imagine our deflation when the stage manager (or maybe Ethel) told us that, because the two pianos were so far backstage, not enough light hit them to make any make-up necessary, and all we needed was a little powder."

The backstage high jinks reached a new high one day when the pianists invented a gag that almost detonated the entire act. Edens describes Ethel Merman as making "a stylish entrance to open her act. She always had a cape or jacket that matched her gown and would sing the first song wearing this cape. During the applause she would take the cape off and place it on top of Harold's piano. Before one matinee performance Harold and I decided to liven up the proceedings by leaving a little memento for Ethel when she left her cape on the piano.

"Ethel finished the opening song, came over to the piano, and was struggling to get the cape off when she saw the note" that Edens and Arlen had left on the latter's piano. It stated simply that a portion of her anatomy was, in a phrase, "hanging out."

"She read it; gasped; read it again. Then exploded into a gale of laughter. And if you've ever heard the Merm laugh you'll know what I mean. She laughed so she forgot all about the cape and did the next number still wearing it. When she made her exit for the change we could still hear her screaming with laughter."

So successful a coup encouraged sequels; each day some new and equally ribald message was left for the explosive Miss Merman. If not an unprintable note, some mute message might be left, such as the day when the *divertissement* took a lockerroom turn and there on Arlen's piano lay an athletic supporter, in which had been touchingly placed a single red rose.

For each performance the backstage crew gathered in the wings to observe Miss Merman's reaction to the day's new two-part invention when the ritual of placing the cape on the piano was due. They were never disappointed, for the singer never failed to whoop it up. At one performance, however, Arlen and Edens had arrived too late to prepare a new Cyprian device and barely had time to rush on-stage for Miss Merman's entrance. On finishing her first song and expectantly moving toward Arlen's piano, Miss Merman was disappointed not to find anything waiting for her. This upset her and she had to be assured that she had done nothing that might have offended the pianists. For the next show the ritual was reinstated and all was cozy again.

Miss Merman, no mean wit herself—though she could never bring herself to the Rabelaisian proportions of her accompanists —began her own running gag, though it was to be turned against her. While she made a costume change, Arlen and Edens took over with a two-piano medley of Arlen's most popular songs: "Get Happy," "Hittin' the Bottle," "You Said It," "I Love a Parade," all in quite complex two-piano arrangements. Arlen also sang "Between the Devil and the Deep Blue Sea" and "Kickin' the Gong Around" to very good applause.

This piano spot afforded Miss Merman with an opening for her own little joke. Though she took a special pride in the two fine talents working with her, she also needled them a little by announcing their spot with increasing extravagance as the days went by: ". . . will play for you a medley of Mr. Arlen's great, wonderful, *immortal*, song hits!" and so on.

"This rankled in Harold's modest soul for a week or two,"

Edens continues in his reminiscence. "And we decided we would have to put Madam in her place. Once we decided on the method it became an obsession with us; we would go over to Harms, the music publishers, to work it out.

"That afternoon Ethel made her usual lavish introduction of us and left to change her costume. Harold and I lit into the bombastic *maestoso* introduction that usually led into 'You Said It.' But, instead, we went into 'Ol' Man River.' I heard Merman shout off-stage. She forgot about making her change and came running out to stand in the wings, dumfounded at first, but then playing along with us. At the finish of 'Ol' Man River' she yelled out, loud enough for the whole theater to hear, 'And then he wrote . . .' and we smoothly sequed into 'Tea for Two.' Our 'hits' were 'The Man I Love,' 'Hallelujah,' 'My Heart Stood Still.'

"It was great fun—at least for us backstage. The audience must have been confused. Certainly the men in the pit were, as they, waiting for their cue to play 'Hittin' the Bottle,' which was the finish of our medley, never got the cue. We finished with 'I Got Rhythm.'"

It has been suggested, with little possibility of actual confirmation, that vaudeville never recovered from the effects upon it by the trio of Merman, Edens, and Arlen. Actually, as far as the Palace was concerned, the downward trend had begun as early as 1929 with the beginning, in March, of the "three-a-days." And not long after "all-talking" pictures came in, the draw of that novelty began affecting receipts at the Palace. Radio, too, was a serious competitor. In retaliation the Palace refused to book radio acts, but eventually gave in when the popularity of big radio names proved to draw at the box office. Film personalities brought them in too, and that brought about another revolutionary change in the Palace policy, the eventual change-over of the Palace from a vaudeville house to a movie house.

The bill on which Miss Merman appeared with her two wayward pianists—and of course Holtz and Gaxton—was one of the last historic long runs. When Miss Merman left for the *Take a Chance* rehearsals, she was replaced by the "Songbird of the South," Kate Smith.

Harold Arlen was to have one final vaudeville experience about a year later. Robert Wachsman, an active young thinker, newly arrived from Chicago and holding down an advertising job at forty dollars a week, had become a great admirer of the song "It's Only a Paper Moon." At a party given by composer Dana Suesse he was introduced to one of the song's composers, E. Y. Harburg, who with Billy Rose had written the lyric. On meeting Harburg, Wachsman inquired if Harburg had worked on the lyric or the melody (which was what Wachsman admired most about the song). Harburg informed him: the lyrics, to which Wachsman expressed an ill-concealed disappointment and apparent little interest. Eventually, at another party, he was to meet the composer of "Paper Moon," who in 1932 Wachsman found to be soft-spoken, gentle, "very slender—he had an almost ascetic look. And when he sang it was as if he were praying or in a spell." Arlen usually sang with his eyes closed and with a great deal of feeling. Roger Edens has stated that "I've always thought he could sing his own songs better than any other man or woman." Arlen often visited Edens and his wife, at the time living in a little house at Nyack, "on the hills above the Hudson River. Harold spent many weekends with us there. I have some faded snapshots of him learning to ski down the slope to the railroad station. We like to think that, on one of these weekends, Harold wrote 'Stormy Weather.' Of course this is not true. Not really. He had already found the melody and, I believe, Ted had a first rough lyric. And, on this weekend, he sang it for us many times—each time with an added note, or a different phrase, or possible change in the lyric. I do think that he possibly found the 'repeat phrases' as he was playing it. Undoubtedly he polished and perfected it to his satisfaction, for it went into rehearsal at the club several days later. Whatever, it became a legend for us. And I must say, as a legend, it could always command a good audience. I suppose it is really a subtle evidence of Harold's stature."

"Stormy Weather" gave Wachsman the idea for what proved to be Arlen's last excursion into the "Barnum and Bailey world" of show business as a performer. One day Wachsman called on Arlen at the Croyden. "He impressed me," Arlen remembers. "He came in wearing a derby and carrying a brief case. He had, and has, a great mind for facts plus imagination and ambition. Somebody had to prod me; Bob did."

With "Stormy Weather" selling on records and sheet music, being sung by Ethel Waters at the Cotton Club, it occurred to Wachsman, after having heard the composer sing the song, that an act could be built around just that. He also thought that a Negro choir as a backing made for a good touch also. He successfully talked Arlen into the idea, then approached the management of the Radio City Music Hall. He brought in Harold Arlen to audition for "Roxy" (S. L. Rothafel) himself and the musical director of Radio City, Leon Leonidoff. When he convinced them of the showmanship in the idea of having the composer sing his own song, it only remained for Arlen to sell himself as a vocalist. The two astute showmen liked what they heard and were willing to sign Arlen to a ten- to twelve-week contract. (Secretly they had planned to use the song in their stage show, for, although they had not yet cleared the use of the song with the Cotton Club, Roxy had already arranged for the purchase of a wind machine.) While Wachsman and Arlen waited during the auditions, Gertrude Niesen came in to audition also, and, coincidentally, sang "Stormy Weather."

The Roxy wanted Arlen and "Stormy Weather." It only remained for Wachsman to talk with Herman Stark at the Cotton Club, for the song was still current in that year's *Parade*. Stark reacted as would be expected, feeling that using the song in vaudeville would "hurt the show." Wachsman argued otherwise, but Stark was firm, though conceding—under pressure—that "the other fellow" must make the final decision. "The other fellow" was Big Frenchy DeMange.

That night Wachsman and Arlen arrived at the Cotton Club at midnight; they waited for DeMange until seven in the morning, when he finally appeared for his usual breakfast. Talking fast and persuasively, Wachsman outlined his idea of having the composer of "Stormy Weather" sing his song in vaudeville, which in turn would encourage customers, possibly even from an untapped source, to seek out the Cotton Club. Big Frenchy appeared not to attend to Wachsman's words at all, but when the speech was finished and Wachsman appended a rather desperate "What do you think?" to it, De- Mange's reply was a direct and simple: "I t'ink it's de nuts— where's my ham an' eggs?"

Permission was granted.

The "Stormy Weather" act was built around Harold Arlen and his songs. Juano Hernandez, of the Cotton Club, coached the choir, one member of which was Katharine Handy, daughter of the celebrated "Father of the Blues," W. C. Handy. Wachsman arranged for a tour of the Loew's circuit after the Radio City stand. On May 19, 1933, Harold Arlen opened at Radio City Music Hall. Interestingly, the Cotton Club group, having recognized the merit of Wachsman's idea, arranged for an act, also titled "Stormy Weather," that opened at the Capitol Theater a week after Arlen and company had played Radio City. The Capitol featured Duke Ellington and orchestra, Ivy Anderson, Buck and Bubbles. Abel Green, re- porting the latter event in *Variety*, found it "done in a mediocre manner," particularly if compared with the previous week's production, when "the Radio City Music Hall, with Arlen engaged for a pianolog specialty, put it on—'n' how!"

After New York the "Stormy Weather" troupe made a round of the Loew's theaters in Baltimore, Washington, D.C., where the composer's parents met him and were able to hear their son do one of the country's most popular songs. After Washing- ton the company returned to New York to appear in Jamaica (Queens) and the Bronx.

The fertile Robert Wachsman came up with another idea —this time for a radio series for which Ira Gershwin and E. Y. Harburg were to do the script and collaborate on special songs with Arlen. Arlen was also to serve as conductor and vocalist. Worked into the scheme were Frances Langford, Arlene Francis, Arthur Schutt at the piano; Russ Morgan was to supply special arrangements. "We had an exciting audition," Wachsman recalls, "but we didn't sell the show."

Another not strictly creative activity engaged the composer during the same period of the early Thirties. From 1931 through 1934 he did quite a lot of recording. Radio had practically ended all interest in phonograph records, but a little was still being done.

All of the recordings Arlen made with Leo Reisman, Red Nichols, Arthur Schutt, and Eddy Duchin were renditions of his own songs. The only recording he made of a non-Arlen tune was made in 1932, "Pardon Me, Pretty Baby" (by Vincent Rose, Jack Meskill, and Raymond Klages). Released on the obscure Harmony label, the disc had an accompaniment supplied by Joe Venuti's orchestra comprised of several fine jazz musicians, among them Miff Mole, Frank Signorelli, and Eddie Lang. Harold Arlen supplied the hot vocalizing.

Thus was Arlen able to keep his voice in trim, preserve authentic interpretations of his own songs, and add slightly to his income. He was barely aware of the depression at all. Only once since he had struck off on his own was he forced to ask his father for financial help. When a surgical operation was required, he needed money to pay for it; he first approached the Cotton Club heads, hoping for an advance, but was turned down. Cantor Arluck then, as always, was happy to lend a helping hand. Before long the younger Arlen would be taking new steps in music that would take him away from the Cotton Club completely, not to mention his career onstage.

CHAPTER 5

What Can You Say in a Love Song?

Lyricist Jack Yellen was in the morning's shower; from the other room his newly acquired radio was blasting (in 1930 everyone who could afford a radio had one, even if only to hear "Amos 'n' Andy," from 7:00 to 7:15 every evening). "I heard a tune with a very distinctive rhythm but had missed the announcement of the title. When I got to the office I sang it for one person after another, asking, 'What's the name of this tune?' Finally I found someone who could identify it—'Get Happy.' My secretary went out and got a copy and there it was: 'by Harold Arlen and Ted Koehler.' Obviously Harold Arlen was the former Hyman Arluck of Buffalo."

Yellen not only recalled the time he had been asked to talk Harold Arlen out of a musical career, he remembered too, a decade back when the synagogue presented a minstrel show in the community house. Arlen, about fifteen at the time, had been given a Yellen song to do in blackface. With composer Abe Olman at the piano in the auditorium, Yellen singing the melody to "Land o' Lullaby" in the wings, Arlen supplied, in a high clear voice, the obbligato from the stage.

Yellen had heard "Get Happy" by chance; a further coincidence was about to precipitate Arlen into another musical phase, for Yellen was planning to produce a show with comedian Lou Holtz. When the two producers met, Holtz had a composer in mind also, even opened the conversation with, "I've got a great composer for you."

"I've got the composer," Yellen stated with some emphasis.

"Who?" asked Holtz.

"Harold Arlen."

"Who the hell is Harold Arlen?" was Holtz's reaction.

Yellen filled the comedian in on Arlen's small but impressive catalogue; "Get Happy" was very current, and "Hittin' the Bottle" was doing well also in the summer of 1930.

Arlen and Yellen happened to meet in Lindy's one day. Yellen greeted Arlen with "Chyiam, you're going to write the score of a book show." Arlen could not work up much enthusiasm for that idea. Up to that moment he had contributed individual songs to revues, but a complete score for a musical was another matter. He even failed to keep an appointment with Yellen in his office at Ager, Yellen and Bornstein.

"I went looking for him again, found him at Lindy's, took him to the office, and made him sign contracts before he left the office." The show Arlen had signed to do was *You Said It*, in Yellen's estimation, "probably the worst show ever to run on Broadway. The book was frightful, the dances were terrible, the score was not good—but there was enough in that score to show the promise of Harold Arlen. The lyrics were bad, not nearly as good as the music. But it became one of the biggest laugh hits on Broadway."

The summer of 1930 was spent by Arlen collaborating with Yellen on the songs for *You Said It* and with Ted Koehler on the Cotton Club songs. Yellen was a hard-working, hard-driving, man; he was called "Napoleon" by his colleagues, so commanding was he in his statements. The younger Arlen was quite in awe of Yellen, still considers him "one of the great lyric writers." But working with so dynamic a man, after the low-pressure Koehler, set up problems for Arlen. Yellen pushed him at times. "Harold would write a tune, then stand in the corner and pray for the next one!"

The pushing and the tugging went on and eventually the score was complete. The show went to Philadelphia for the tryout. Yellen, who had done the book with Sid Silvers, considered it so bad that he found himself apologizing to Lee Shubert, who had put up some of the backing. According to Yellen all was going badly until "we got to this number. I'd never seen anything like it. We couldn't stop the applause, and we had never figured on an encore. That girl saved the show." Shubert's comment was, "This'll clean up in New York."

The number was "Sweet and Hot" and that girl was Lyda Roberti. Yellen had seen her first in Hollywood. "She was a natural blonde with a terrific sense of humor and remarkable sense of rhythm." When Yellen caught her act in Buffalo, some months later, Miss Roberti was not at all interested in going to New York. "I want no show," she had told him, "I want no New York, on Broadway is actors selling apples." By working through the William Morris Agency, then handling Miss Roberti, Yellen finally managed to sign her for *You Said It.* The show was already in rehearsal, but Yellen wrote her into the script. When given a copy of the script Miss Roberti giggled. "It can't be that funny," Yellen commented sardonically. The commedienne then informed him that she couldn't read English. With the help of another member of the cast, Benny Baker, Miss Roberti learned over the weekend, not only her part, but everyone else's.

"Sweet and Hot" was recognized as a pretty good number, and Holtz objected to its being given to a completely unknown girl to sing. But Yellen, naturally, had his own way.

What had captured the opening-night audience in Philadelphia was Miss Roberti's peculiar pronunciation of the "h" sound in the word "hot" (it always came out "*chot*"), a concession to her Polish accent. New York's opening-night audience, as Shubert had predicted, received her in the same manner. "We didn't need a press agent after that," Yellen remembers. "She was a personality—like a diamond, not beautiful but pretty, she radiated charm. She got more free publicity than we could have possibly bought. We had a good run in New York, but when the show went on the road, it went to pieces. The depression didn't help."

Although Jack Yellen had been responsible for Arlen's first book show, he makes no claim to having "discovered" Harold Arlen; in fact he has said that "*You Said It* was, I think, a lesson in what *not* to do. I could see he was destined for better things than I could give him." When Yellen formed his own publishing company, he again talked Arlen into collaborating on a few songs they hoped would be taken up by Kate Smith but that were songs both now look upon as pretty inferior. Still, *You Said It* had been a success, so were the title song and Miss Roberti's "Sweet and Hot," and that felt good.

As his fortunes improved so did Arlen's accommodations at the Croydon. From the rather dismal, dimly lit, first-floor he moved upward to the tenth, until he was able to take over the more spacious penthouse.

More room was required, for one rainy Saturday night his brother Julius (Jerry) arrived from Syracuse with a wet saxophone under his arm. He was indebted to a member of the high-school's football team for his change in name. "From now on," the quarterback announced, "this kid will be called Jerry. I don't want anybody named Julius on my team." Jerry Arlen had already adopted his brother's professional last name, even while playing in the orchestra pit in the Loew's Theater in Syracuse. In 1931 he tired of the limited band opportunities of Syracuse and decided to come to New York. After getting comfortable in his brother's apartment Jerry Arlen became a member of the Paul Whiteman band, and sang as a member of the second Rhythm Boys. The first had consisted of Bing Crosby, Al Rinker, and Harry Barris; the newly formed Rhythm Boys were Jerry Arlen, Jack Goodman, and a Southerner calling himself John H. Mercer.

But Jerry Arlen's major ambition was conducting, which he got a chance to do at Billy Rose's Music Hall. Benny Goodman and his orchestra supplied the swing and Jerry took over the conducting during the show itself. There was a dog act appearing at the Music Hall out of which came, if not much else, a litter. One of the mongrel puppies quite easily won the younger Arlen's sympathies to the point that he took the dog home. Now Harold Arlen not only had a boarder, but a dog of questionable ancestry. He took one look at the puppy and made a simple statement: "Out!"

But "Shmutts," as the new arrival was soon named, moved in also, the composer having easily succumbed to its pleading brown eyes. He soon took over full ownership in fact. Shmutts was pampered considerably, accompanied the composer on his walks in Central Park, and was allowed to raise his voice to the music on the phonograph; his favorites were Stravinsky's *Rite of Spring* and Ravel's *La Valse*.

Also living at the Croydon was a young surgeon Dr. Miguel Elias. He and Arlen became close friends and consequently spent a great deal of time together. As part of his penance for having chosen the medical profession, Dr. Elias was required to be on call for emergency charity cases. One evening, late, Arlen happened to be with the doctor when a call came in, and both went out on the call. Arlen watched, fascinated, while the doctor performed an emergency operation.

"Harold, I've always felt," the doctor observes today, "was a frustrated physician. His basic goodness, his humanity, came out clearly in his sincere interest in medicine. He would come along with me at times on my round of afternoon calls. He borrowed my medical books and read them carefully. And, no matter what time of night or early morning a call came in, he was ready to come along. In the hospital he would put on a surgeon's smock—I would introduce him as 'Dr. Arlen'—and observe while I performed the surgery.

"One patient, I remember, needed postoperative treatment and a full-time private nurse. Of course, the patient could not afford this kind of care. Harold paid for it."

Dr. Elias discovered that the pain Arlen had been suffering during the last weeks of his "Stormy Weather" tour was caused, not by an appendix, as could easily be assumed from the similarity of symptoms, but by the Meckel's diverticulum —in effect an undissolved umbilicus. Arlen had been bothered with it for four months before he decided, on Dr. Elias's suggestion, to have an X-ray made. On the print the doctor discovered the diverticulum, so rare a medical feat that it was eventually written up in a medical journal. The history did not interest Arlen as much as the curing of his stomachache, and the completion of his tour.

Earl Carroll called Arlen and Koehler for songs to go into his forthcoming *Vanities*, the tenth edition, due to open in September 1932. The dialogue was to be devised by Jack McGowan, author of among other works, the Gershwins' *Girl Crazy* (with Guy Bolton) and *Hold Everything*, by DeSylva, Brown, and Henderson. The settings and costumes were to be done by Vincente Minnelli, working on his first show. The dances were to be staged by Cotton Club veteran Gluck Sandor. Milton Berle, Helen Broderick, and Will Fyffe headed the large cast.

Also in the cast was a celebrated Powers model, Anya Taranda, just barely in her mid-teens. The strikingly beautiful blond model had little else to do in the *Vanities* but stand around in approved Earl Carroll fashion. Which was enough. Arlen was naturally taken with her, though much too shy to do anything about it. When he worked up enough nerve to invite her to his apartment for the first time, he managed that by inviting another girl to attend the same dinner. Once, however, the spark had been struck, Arlen and Anya were rarely apart or, if their respective careers intervened, they kept in touch by telephone.

Carroll didn't approve of his top echelon fraternizing with the help, but in Jack McGowan, Arlen found a friend and ally whose Irish streak of defiance kept Carroll in check. Like all producers Carroll longingly looked into the future with continual references to the past. He summoned Arlen, Koehler, and McGowan to him one day to remind them that the previous *Vanities* had produced a hit song in "Goodnight, Sweetheart." He then, in effect, suggested that the song writers come up with another like it. This order particularly rankled McGowan, who told Carroll, once the more or less confused Arlen and Koehler had left, that he felt it to be an unfair request. He further argued that Arlen and Koehler were distinguished song writers who had developed a distinctive

style and whose talents were beyond any such demands as
Carroll had just made.

Carroll's manner worked on the McGowan imagination like
a catalyst; after some hours of brooding a brilliant idea came
out of the inner reaches of his Irish soul. He called Arlen
and Koehler (already asleep in Brooklyn), insisting that they
all meet somewhere. "I've got an idea for a goddam Sweetheart song; come on over!" The by now quite dazed song
writers listened to McGowan's idea, which kindled, too, the
Irish in their respective souls. They set to work immediately,
the night air ringing out with their guffaws as they wrestled
with a new song in the process of borning.

The next day, bleary-eyed, they practically stormed into the
theater; Carroll's face lit up when he learned that his faithful
employees had so speedily complied with his wise orders. The
beam quickly extinguished when McGowan raised his voice
to sing "Wake Up, Sweetheart, I Want to Say Goodnight
Again."

Needless to say, this song is one of the rarities of our
popular music; it was never published, nor was it heard in the
tenth edition of the Earl Carroll *Vanities*. Arlen and Koehler
had not let Carroll down, however. They did turn out a song,
introduced by Lillian Shade, that amounted to something,
"I Gotta Right to Sing the Blues." But for some reason neither
Arlen nor Koehler was asked to do any more songs for any
of Carroll's shows after the 1932 edition. Carroll never paid the
song writers for their songs, "not even a tie for Christmas,"
Arlen said.

About a month after the *Vanities* opened, another revue,
Americana, opened at the Shubert Theater. Most of the songs
was the work of Jay Gorney and E. Y. Harburg. One of
their songs from that show became the classic lament of the
depression, "Brother, Can You Spare a Dime?" For *Americana*
Arlen did one song, "Satan's Li'l Lamb," interesting musically
as well as for extramusical reasons: it was the first Arlen song
for which the lyric was done by two writers with whom he was
to become an important collaborator, E. Y. Harburg and John

H. Mercer. In addition "Satan's Li'l Lamb" was treated to a
rather arty staging. After it had been sung by Francetta
Malloy and the Musketeers, it was danced by the Doris
Humphrey Dancers, a trio made up of Miss Humphrey,
José Limón and Charles Weidman.

Soon Arlen was to collaborate with Harburg again. "Satan's
Li'l Lamb" for Arlen required little more than writing out
the melody and sending it to the producer's office. He actually
did not collaborate with Harburg and Mercer in the fullest
sense. The next Harburg collaboration involved a co-lyricist
also, producer Billy Rose. The three men worked up a song
titled "If You Believe in Me," for a play Rose was producing,
The Great Magoo, by Ben Hecht and Gene Fowler. The play
had a sleazy show-business background, the song was a
leitmotiv-like commentary upon the setting. *The Great Magoo*
remained at the Selwyn for all of eleven performances, but the
composers managed to salvage their song, which was interpolated into the film version of *Take a Chance,* newly titled "It's
Only a Paper Moon."

What with steady assignments, royalties coming in from
several successful songs, Arlen settled down to the life of a
successful composer. He was studying harmony with Simon
Bucharoff. He dressed well, if conservatively; he began to
sport a bachelor button in his lapel (referring to it as a
"blue-ie"). And for a time he even carried a cane, in which
practice he was joined by his friend Bob Wachsman in their
Arlenian walks along Fifth Avenue of a brisk afternoon. Both
men soon abandoned the canes, but Arlen then took up a craggy
brier, which went with him and Shmutts in their walks
around the reservoir in the park.

The bookcases in his apartment soon filled up. Reading the
New York papers opened new vistas to Arlen, the beloved
books of his father. His tastes ran to philosophical works
and for a time he carried a well-read, annotated copy of
the *Meditations* by Marcus Aurelius. He favored aphoristic
books such as this, or the essays of Montaigne, or the poems
of Rilke, which could be read almost anywhere and even

on the run. Wachsman described Arlen's reading habits:
". . . he was a dipper. He might even be reading eight books
at a time, most likely non-fiction."

Early in 1933, not long after the exciting reception of
"Stormy Weather," there came evidence of interest in Arlen
from Hollywood. He happened to be in the William Morris
Agency office when the word came in on the teletype machine
that the film in mind would be titled *Let's Fall in Love.*
Arlen glanced at the film's title and, a little sickish with excitement, left the office and found refuge in the men's room.
There he jotted down the first few bars of the title song, "Let's
Fall in Love," and returned to the meeting. By October 1,
according to their agreement, Arlen and Koehler were to report at the Columbia studios for a month's stay.

"In those days traffic was light on the Chief," Koehler
remembers, "and we had the whole observation car to ourselves, in fact, had the 'A' stateroom in the car, and no one
came into the car except the conductor and the porter. Harold
remarked that if only we had one of those little fold-up
organs we could do some work. Just then the waiter from
the diner came in hitting the chimes and calling 'Last call
for lunch.' Harold took the chimes and started kidding the
waiter by playing on it." The composer could play some of the
opening notes of "Let's Fall in Love" on the limited compass
of the chimes, so that by the time he and Koehler arrived in
Hollywood they had practically completed the song.

On arriving in Hollywood they had only to do four addi-
tional songs. Arlen was somewhat in awe of Herbert Fields,
who had done the screen play of *Let's Fall in Love,* but
"Koehler wasn't; nothing fazed him." They found life in Beverly
Hills less invigorating than it had been on Lenox Avenue and
Broadway; besides, Koehler's family had remained behind in
Brooklyn, and Arlen's cross-country phone calls to Anya Tar-
anda mounted up. Once their five weeks were up, Arlen and
Koehler hurried back to New York.

The Hollywood pattern was set early: of the five songs
written for *Let's Fall in Love* only three remained in the

final film, and, at that, one was heard only as background music. To the song writers, accustomed to turning out material under pressure and often on the spot, and to attending rehearsals, even to making changes during the planning of a show, the California Method was incomprehensible. The songs were played and sung for the producer; if he did not object (and generally he was qualified to pass judgment by the mere magnitude of his musical ignorance) the songs were accepted. The song writers were then expected to go away. What happened then was decided by the studio's musical director, the arranger, the vocal arranger, the director, the star, the producer—possibly even the star's brother's uncle: everyone, that is, but the composer. Still, Arlen and Koehler were fortunate in their very first musical film. *Let's Fall in Love* will, however, be remembered chiefly because of that fact; cinematically and dramatically it made no great impress. Richard Watts, Jr., film critic for the New York *Tribune,* found "a pleasantly unpretentious quality about the new picture . . . Although it belongs to the familiar school of the film musical show, *Let's Fall in Love* is fortunately lacking in elaborate chorus numbers and it employs only two songs during its plot manipulations. It happens, however, that both of them are agreeable melodies and one of them, the air that gives the title to the photoplay, is particularly good."

While Arlen and Koehler were tasting the heady air of California for the first time, and not finding it especially agreeable, another Cotton Club show went into production, the edition without Arlen-Koehler songs, mentioned earlier. When the next *Parade* was rehearsing, in the spring of 1934, Yip Harburg came to Arlen with an offer to do the music for a full-scale revue to be produced by the Shuberts. Harburg's "Brother, Can You Spare a Dime?", having become absorbed into the American idiom, enjoyed a popularity the Shuberts fully appreciated. The Shuberts were planning to produce a John Murray Anderson show and wanted Harburg to do the lyrics; he was given carte blanche in the choice of his collaborator. Or collaborators, as it turned out, for Harburg, exhausted from the work he had done with Vernon Duke on the 1934 *Ziegfeld Follies,* asked Ira Gershwin to collaborate with him on the lyrics. Gershwin was free at that moment, his brother being then involved with DuBose Heyward on *Porgy and Bess,* and had not yet arrived at the point that would require the lyricist's help.

Arlen's position wasn't so clear-cut. Anxious to collaborate with such fine men and to do a Shubert revue, Arlen found himself deeply troubled about how he might tell Ted Koehler, with whom he had such a warm and productive relationship. Anya was then in California working on the film *Murder at the Vanities,* so Arlen turned to his close friend Bob Wachsman. They discussed the dilemma and decided that all Arlen could do was merely tell Koehler.

They met one evening at a Cotton Club rehearsal; Wachsman asked, "Did you tell Ted yet?"

"No."

"Well, what are you going to do?"

"I wrote him a letter," mournfully answered Arlen.

"What did he say?"

"I don't know, I just gave it to him."

Once the rehearsal was finished Koehler read the note so reluctantly prepared; his reaction was typical: "You'd be a fool if you didn't do it," he commented.

"Does that make you feel any better?" Wachsman asked Arlen.

"Not much," was the reply.

"Harold got loaded that night," Wachsman recalls. "Then he talked only about Ted—what a fine person he was, what an excellent lyric writer. He even praised the Cotton Club sets that Ted had worked on, how much detail went into them; and other good things about Ted—of which there are many." Although they were to collaborate again, the 1934 Cotton Club score was their last joint work of any size for some years to come.

Harold Arlen's former roommate, Ray Bolger, had been approached by John Murray Anderson to star in the proposed revue, but Bolger decided against that. He took the Shuberts and their right-hand man, Harry Kaufman, to see the comedian Bert Lahr, suggesting that rather than have the revue carried by a single star, at least two would make the job less formidable. Once Bolger and Lahr were set, other fine talents were signed: Luella Gear, Frances Williams, Dixie Dunbar, Brian Donlevy. Anya Taranda, having returned from her film chores, was also signed. David Freedman was engaged to write the sketches and John Murray Anderson would stage the Winter Garden production. Bolger was particularly happy to learn that his old friend was to write the music; it had become a habit for Bolger and his wife, when the dancer was asked to appear in a musical and the question of the composer came up, to answer automatically: Harold Arlen.

The bulk of the work on the revue was done at the Ira Gershwin apartment on East Seventy-second Street, where he and his wife, Leonore, made their home, directly across the street from the building in which George Gershwin lived.

Arlen's co-collaborators could not have been temperamentally more opposite. Ira Gershwin was benign, Harburg dynamic; Gershwin peace-loving; Harburg militant. Both, however, shared aesthetic principles: the satiric point of view in the matter of love songs, the polish of perfection, and a certain elusiveness. Gershwin liked putting work off, while Harburg had a habit of arriving at the Gershwin apartment a little late, say three or four hours.

Gershwin remembers Harold Arlen from those relatively early days of his professional life as "a gay young man, but with an almost supernatural belief in 'inspiration.' He never would approach the simplest musical requirement or idea without first calling upon 'the fellow up there'—jabbing his finger at the ceiling."

As he had been so unexpectedly and suddenly launched as a full-fledged "hit song" composer, Arlen's imagination would naturally have romantically embraced the concept of inspiration. Contributing, too, were his religious training as a boy and his current rather mystical and philosophical reading.

The immediate success of "Get Happy," as well as several of the later songs, some the result of "inspiration," others—most, in fact—resulting from hard work, impressed Arlen with the efficacy of capturing the stray melodic wisp that somehow always came in the middle of the night. He habitually carried small pads of music paper with him, even kept one at his bedside, to capture such melodic ideas, or, as he called them, "jots."

These were literally melodic germs, out of which seeds grew the final melody. When he began noting down his jots, Arlen did this as a precaution, for he had no idea that another "Get Happy" might come to him, or, if it did, might slip away. Very few composers are without their notebooks containing melodic ideas for future use. As a young composer Arlen took the precaution of carrying his notebook wherever he went. After a few years' practice and a great deal of success Arlen abandoned his jot book. He knew that when the time came for "that unsought-for phrase" it was a matter of sitting at the piano and looking for it. He has never, on the other hand, abandoned the system of using jots, a form of shorthand, running to perhaps five or six notes. From this fragment Arlen can construct a complete melody when it is required. With this system the entire score of a show, running to possibly twenty numbers, can be put down on a single manuscript page. Like his father, Arlen works on the principle of taking a theme and developing it. This method of working, subtracting momentarily his musical personality, accounts for the uniqueness of Arlen's melodies.

The fact that he considered the Shubert revue "a big showcase for me" explains also Arlen's seriousness of purpose that so impressed Ira Gershwin.

In his delightful book, *Lyrics on Several Occasions,* Ira Gershwin deftly and charmingly furnishes insight into how songs are made, song titles arrived at, and even how a show title is born. Somehow omitted from his own book, the story of how the Arlen-Gershwin-Harburg Shubert revue got its name is best told in Ira Gershwin's own words:

Show Title. One day Harburg, Arlen, and I were having lunch at director John Murray Anderson's apartment on Park Avenue. One of the matters under discussion was a title for the revue. There were many suggestions, but none sounded inevitable. When we were leaving, I happened to notice a book on the table in the apartment's foyer. It was the then non-fiction best-seller, Walter Boughton Pitkin's *Life Begins at Forty.* I turned to the others and said, "How about *Life Begins at Eight-Forty?*"

Later, producer Lee Shubert wasn't sure of it (even after he had tried it out on a Boston ticket agency which he controlled and had admitted it was liked there). So, one night after rehearsal at the Winter Garden he called a meeting on stage for a further title-discussion. There were a dozen of us under the arc light, including some Shubert staff men I didn't know. Several alternate titles were suggested, among them one of mine: this one, *Calling All Stars,* I had paraphrased from the police radio signal, "Calling all cars." But the earlier title stood the gaff and remained. I was amused a year or so later to learn that Lew Brown had bought a title from someone (I am pointing no finger) for his new revue to be called, *Calling All Stars.*

Ray Bolger is still able to sing the score of *Life Begins at 8:40,* even those songs he himself did not sing. "It was a completely perfect score for a show," he will tell you. "It was the freshest score that had been on Broadway in a year. Harold's music was completely different from anyone else's. Take the opening, 'Spring Fever,' why the push-beats we do today, and call modern, he did then in that song. He would make the afterbeat a part of the melody; it was a new kind of music. Maybe because he had been an arranger, Harold could write the song complete, with all the wonderful musical ideas written in—so that no arranger was really required.

"Harold has always tried to avoid the cliché; he would hate to write a 'pop' tune; I think he would do everything *not* to write one! He has a tremendous creative urge, yet he cringes from the egoistic, and all the obvious things. Melody is the staff of music—and there is where Harold also shines. But his songs, in 1934, seemed in advance of their time and took time before they were properly appreciated."

The *Life Begins* score was Arlen's most substantial up to that
time, a veritable showcase, indeed. The Arlen invention, wit,
and versatility are delightfully in evidence—and not a blue
note in the entire score. Work on the show was a pleasure, not
only because of the excellence of the company, Bolger, Lahr,
Arlen's neighbors from the Croydon, Frances Williams and
Adrienne Matzenauer, Luella Gear, not to mention Anya, but
also because the spirits of the company were good, for it was
soon evident that the show would be a hit.

John Murray Anderson, for example, rarely called anyone by
his proper name. Instead he devised private nicknames: Ira
Gershwin was called "The Rock of Gibralter," Yip Harburg,
"Zipper," Arlen, "Ol' Man River," and Anya answered to
"Schmanda Fair." One of the boys in the chorus, who shall
otherwise remain nameless, was called "Consommé Eyes."

Before the Boston opening Isaac Goldberg, the first biographer of George Gershwin and an unusually well-informed
student of the popular arts, interviewed Harold Arlen and
found that the composer, no doubt to the Bostonian's surprise,
did not "give an impression of Tin Pan Alley loudness. In one
respect, as even a casual meeting may suggest, the man and
his music are one: well-bred, soft, quietly confident, ingratiating. I believe, indeed, that 'ingratiating' is the key-word. About
Arlen or his music there seems to be nothing raucous. You
feel it in his voice, as he sings his pieces; you get it even
from his touch on the piano.

"He is a well-set youth . . . fair, blue-eyed (unless my eyes
are none too certain), easy of motion and manner. The picture of the Tin Pan Alley composer as a somewhat civilized
thug who chisels out tunes on a piano with one finger, or
whistles them at an arranger, became anachronistic some time
ago. Arlen is decidedly of the new generation. He is a fine
pianist and not at all a bad singer. When he lets his voice out
—for he is apt to begin his songs in a soft, even introspective,
legato that may be an influence of his cantor-father—he makes
an excellent propagandist for his wares. These songs, often
as not, have a true melodic feeling for wide yet smooth skips,

and I suspect that the marked quality of what I call ingratiation comes from the frequent employment of these half-glissando leaps. As he sits at the piano, playing and singing, his face tilted upward and his eyes half-closed, you seem to detect a relationship between his manner and his matter.

"He plays, by the way, as unostentatiously as he sings—as unconsciously as most people write, in privacy, a letter. His music, too, has this—shall we call it epistolary?—character. Arlen (and this is one of the reasons why I am inclined to herald him as one of the new hopes for our better popular music) has a rare combination of tenderness and humor. In other words, he has both the necessary sensuousness and the wise-crackiness of the Broadway wit, I speak of his sensuousness in a purely esthetic way, regarding it as a purely generative source. For I have heard him object to words in a song that seemed to go off-color, and his objection was based, not upon puritanical fussiness, but exclusively upon canons of good taste and what the particular song happened to call for. Arlen is no esthete of the parlors, nor is he a goody-goody; but he has intense artistic perceptions, even for the genre in which he is working at present."

Goldberg concludes with an observation on good song writers in general, ". . . intent first of all upon avoiding clichés. Sometimes this results in a melodic line that is tortuous, self-conscious, abortive. The impulse, however, is a valid one, and finds Arlen one of the most successful of the newer exponents. His aim is to achieve at once a singable, quotable tune that shall not be too easily predictable. It must have, besides the quality of self-sufficiency, the spice of surprise."

The Boston opening of *Life Begins*, on August 6, 1934, was made delightful by the storytelling of Ira Gershwin, in rare form after having downed a few beers. George Gershwin had come to Boston for the opening, healthily tanned after a five weeks' stay at Folly Island in South Carolina working on *Porgy and Bess*. He and his cousin the artist Henry Botkin brought back the report that in their searching for authentic Negro materials they had found "Stormy Weather" being sung along with spirituals, as if it too were a folk song.

Attending the Boston opening also was Charles Martin Loeffler, the composer—a friend of Leo Reisman's. Loeffler, unfortunately, was ailing the night *Life Begins at 8:40* opened and during the performance complained to Arlen that he was tired. Arlen's customary opening-night jitters led him to believe that Loeffler didn't like the show.

When it opened at the Winter Garden in New York on August 27, his opening-nightis had reached epic proportions. Arlen stood in the lobby with Dr. Elias watching the first-nighters stream in, among them Irving Berlin, Paul Whiteman, Oscar Levant, George Gershwin, Fanny Brice, Heywood Broun. Just as they were about to go into the theater Arlen said to Dr. Elias, "Wait a minute," and led him back to the street. They then walked along Broadway, returning only in time to watch the same glittering crowd leaving the Winter Garden. Conductor Walter Damrosch came up the aisle muttering, "Ah, such pulse, such rhythm!"

"I read the reviews word for word and thought I came off badly," Arlen admits. "I was literally sick to my stomach. My parents had come down from Syracuse; when my father saw my reaction he scolded me for it. I decided then and there never to be troubled by reviews. It's worked ever since."

Arlen may have not read the review of the astute Gilbert W. Gabriel in the morning's New York *American:* "There are good songs, good numbers, throughout. The spacious plan is chockful of happy Harold Arlen music . . . 'What Can You Say in a Love Song?' will probably linger longer on the nation's pursed lips . . . so will that neighborly coo, 'Let's Take A Walk Around The Block.' After a summer of poison ivy, *Life Begins at 8:40,* is all orchids and laurel. It seemed last night like the top-drawer of tunefullness, jollity and charm."

Percy Hammond began his comments with a question: "'What,' a soprano inquires at the Winter Garden, 'What Can You Say In A Love Song That Hasn't Been Said Before?' And what can a theater reporter print about a Shubert revue that hasn't been printed time and again? The answer seems to be that the new extravaganza in Fiftieth Street, while twin to all the members of its ancient lineage, shows symptoms of development and is brighter and richer than its predecessors and almost as unblushing."

The last is a reference to the "Quartet Erotica," the song that Goldberg had found Arlen resisting in Boston. It was sung by "Rabelais" (James MacColl), "De Maupassant" (Brian Donlevy), "Boccaccio" (Ray Bolger), and naturally, "Balzac" (Bert Lahr):

> When parents could contrive it,
> They read our books in private
> But now we're sold in Liggett's and the kids think we're a bore:
> Because it seems that latterly
> They're reading *Lady Chatterly*
> And the *Life and Loves of Evelyn Nesbit* they adore.
> Rabelais, De Maupassant, Boccaccio and Balzac—
> We've reached the bitter end
> We've staged the final fade-out;
> Those happy days are played out
> When a Lesbian was an Islander and not your wife's best friend.
> Rabelais, De Maupassant, Boccaccio, and Balzac—
> Babes in the wood are we,
> For even with the censors
> And Mr. Hays,
> The kids know all the ensers
> Nowadays.
> We'll go back to our rockers
> For we're just four *Alte Kockers*
> Rabelais, De Maupassant, Boccaccio, and Balzac!

Ira Gershwin and Yip Harburg were in fine form. Aside from such references to timeless topics, they also treated some subjects close to home, as they did in one of the two complete sketches they contributed to the show, "Beautifying the City (Life Begins at City Hall)," spoofing, among others such contemporaries as Mayor LaGuardia and Eleanor Roosevelt.

> I'm Dictator Fiorello,
> I'm a many sided fellow—
> When you look at me you almost see Napoleon,

I love music, I'm artistic,
I'm a stateman pugilistic,
As a brain I'd even take Professor Moley on.

       ✿   ✿   ✿

Tammany Hall is growing graver
For I never curry favor
And I never, never, never favor Curry.

On September 10 Mrs. Roosevelt attended a performance of
Life Begins at 8:40 and was reported to have been greatly
amused at Luella Gear's impersonation of her as she sang:

At seven o'clock this morning at Poughkeepsie,
I spoke at the opening of a bridle path;
Had breakfast in Savannah, then flew to Indiana,
To dedicate a woman's Turkish bath.
I christened a ferris wheel in Chattanooga,
And then I unveiled a Western Barbecue.
A Warner Brother's Palace—I opened next in Dallas,
And here I am to launch a gondola for you.

Musically "Beautifying the City" was interesting not only for
the new material it contained but also because Arlen wove into
it references to some of the other songs—"Fun to be Fooled,"
"Let's Take a Walk around the Block," "What Can You Say
in a Love Song?" and "You're a Builder Upper." Only these,
plus "Shoein' the Mare," satirizing the current Latin dance
craze, were published. Another interesting though unpublished
song is "The Elks and the Masons" for which Arlen used as his
jot the NBC radio chimes signature. Bert Lahr did wonderfully
with a song that devastated the typical popular love song, the
remarkably inarticulate "Things."

Life Begins at 8:40 had a long run in New York before
beginning a tour in Pittsburgh in March 1935 that visited
Washington, D.C., and traveled as far west as Chicago. With
work completed on the show and the excitement of the openings past the song writers found other work to do; Ira Gershwin
began his collaboration with his brother and DuBose Heyward
on *Porgy and Bess.* Yip Harburg and Harold Arlen had offers
from the West to consider.

It was during one of the working afternoons when all three

Samuel and Celia Arluck,
with their son Hyman, in
Buffalo around 1912.

Moses Arluck, father of Samuel and
grandfather of Harold Arlen.

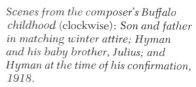

Scenes from the composer's Buffalo childhood (clockwise): Son and father in matching winter attire; Hyman and his baby brother, Julius; and Hyman at the time of his confirmation, 1918.

The Buffalodians: Defying the law of gravity (above) and onstage during
the band tour. Members of the Buffalodians, in the usual order:
Dick George, Jack McLoughlin, Jules Piller, Harold Tapson,
William Wullen, Charles Pennica, Harold Raub, Ivan Beaty, Leland
Kromparth, Norman Booth, Harold Arluck.

Transferring a "jot" from the small pad at the left, to a piano copy. "Shmutts" observes.

Harold and Jerry Arlen in the penthouse of the Croydon Hotel. The painting behind them is the work of Henry Botkin, titled "Ten Miles From Charleston," and was painted by Botkin while he and George Gershwin stayed at Folly Island. The latter was working on Porgy and Bess. Arlen, as did Gershwin, admired the work of Botkin.

At the Palace. Seated in the front row are Johnny Green, Lew Pollack, Harold Arlen, Lyda Roberti, Lou Holtz, Ethel Merman, and William Gaxton. Roger Edens is standing directly behind Johnny Green.

Anya Taranda,
painting by Abram Poole.

Lena Horne

Dan Healy

Ethel Waters

Cab Calloway

COTTON CLUB PERSONALITIES

Duke Ellington

Hollywood, 1933: Ted Koehler, Ruth Etting, and Harold Arlen. Miss Etting, a discovery of Koehler's, introduced the first Arlen-Koehler hit, "Get Happy."

Harold Arlen and Anya Taranda at the Goldwyn studios during the filming of Strike Me Pink.

Ted Koehler and Harold Arlen in an early-morning conference with producer Felix Young. They are discussing the songs written by Koehler and Arlen for Let's Fall in Love, *their first film.*

On the Strike Me Pink *set. Director Norman Taurog engages the attention of the film's star, Eddie Cantor, lyricist Lew Brown, and Harold Arlen.*

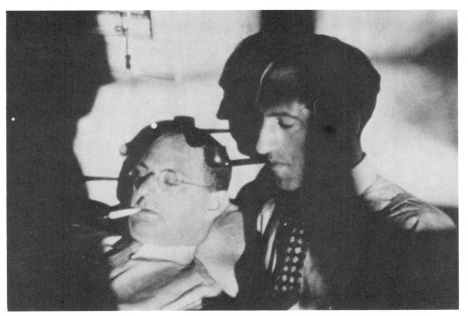

Ira and George Gershwin photographed by Harold Arlen. This is a still from a 16 mm. film.

George Gershwin, though playing hard to get, is sitting on Anya's lap. The photography is by Harold Arlen, the locale is the Gershwin patio, near the swimming pool.

Anya and Harold Arlen
at home in Beverly Hills.

The composer with
"Stormy" and "Pan."

At a rehearsel for a radio boadcast of songs from The Wizard of Oz.
Standing are Bert Lahr, Ray Bolger, MGM executive L. K. Sidney,
E. Y. Harburg, Meredith Willson, and publisher Harry Link.
Judy Garland and the composer are at the piano.

A still from The Wizard of Oz. The good Witch Glinda (Billie Burke) sets
Dorothy (Miss Garland) off on the Yellow Brick Road. The
Munchkins observe. Metro-Goldwyn-Mayer photograph.

George Gershwin and Harold Arlen on the Gershwin tennis court in Beverly Hills.

Irving Berlin, Anya and Harold Arlen at Ciro's, Hollywood.

W. C. Handy, Shelton Brooks, Harold Arlen, and Irving Berlin at the ASCAP meeting in San Francisco, September, 1940.

At a Decca Records recording session: Bing Crosby, Jack Kapp, and the composer. Crosby recorded songs from Bloomer Girl.

Scene from Bloomer Girl, *1944.*

With André Kostelanetz at the Blues Opera Suite *recording session.*

At the California Country Club with Harry Warren and Burton Lane; the latter is keeping his eye on the ball.

Pearl Bailey and Diahann Carroll rehearsing House of Flowers.

House of Flowers *production discussion. Oliver Messel explains a model*
of one of the sets he has designed to (standing, l. to r.) *director*
Peter Brook, Harold Arlen, author and co-lyricist Truman Capote,
producer Arnold Saint Subber, and musical director Jerry Arlen.

Portrait, 1954,
by Clifford Coffin

were engaged with the problems of *Life Begins* that they took time out to visit George Gershwin, across Seventy-second Street. With Gershwin was his good friend William Daly. Arlen played a new song idea he had just struck upon. Daly, skilled musician though he was, admitted that he did not get the melody. Gershwin, brimming over with his own melodies from *Porgy and Bess,* barely noticed it. The song, later to be titled "Last Night When We Were Young," still incomplete and without a lyric, was of an unusual structure. Its melody, hauntingly melancholy, though without a trace of the blues, seemed poignantly seeking for resolution and, as it did, took unexpected turns—its form did not rest conventionally upon the ear. Arlen set it aside for future work, though its initial hearing had hardly seemed encouraging.

He did receive pleasant recognition from another quarter, however, when asked by Dr. Frank Black, conductor of the *General Motors Symphony Hour,* to compose an orchestral piece especially for him and a radio première. Arlen went to work and produced a piece about twice the length of a popular song. As he played it through Bob Wachsman timed it: 5′ 59½″—Arlen then decided to call it *Six Minute Ballet;* Wachsman suggested instead, *Mood in Six Minutes,* its final title.

Robert Russell Bennett provided the orchestration. It was an exciting experience for Arlen. Hearing his work, orchestrated by a man of Bennett's stature, and conducted by Dr. Black, was an exhilarating experience. Wachsman never forgot the picture of the elated composer "practically flying along Madison Avenue after having attended a rehearsal, so happy was he with the results."

He was once asked if he enjoyed his work as a composer even though the full values of his work often went unappreciated. Arlen replied, "That happens to be the most interesting question of all. Fate stepped in. It all happened so suddenly. I was given a contract with a certain amount of money each week, whereby I could do whatever I pleased. That was terribly inviting. And as soon as the first song was written

I knew then and there that everything I had touched before this—traveling, arranging, singing for auditions—wasn't quite suited to my temperament.

"What happened next doesn't always happen to most writers. Practically everything I wrote in those years was accepted by the publishers. I was one of the fortunate. Now and then it gets troublesome—there's much heartache—but I'd be an unappreciative fool if I weren't deeply thankful. In my lowest moments I am grateful for whatever gift I have and the audience I have found."

Unlike the incomplete untitled song, *Mood in Six Minutes* was never heard from again (except for a brief theme) following its initial broadcast late in December 1935. Shortly after, Arlen again boarded the Chief for California. His popular musical success had attracted the Hollywood aestheticians in high positions in the burgeoning art of the cinema, a voice heard throughout the land.

CHAPTER 6

We're Off to See the Wizard

"Hollywood," it has been sagely observed by the sometime philosopher and all-time lyricist Yip Harburg, "is a place where you're here-o today, goniff tomorrow."

In 1933 Harburg had collaborated with Jay Gorney on the songs for the film *Moonlight and Pretzels,* songs that proved successful enough for Universal to sign him on as a writer-producer. He spent most of 1934 developing a script around the idea suggested by "April in Paris," a song he had written with Vernon Duke. The depression finally struck Hollywood around this time and in the upheaval, reorganization, and retrenchment at Universal, former here-o Harburg was out.

He had rented Lawrence Tibbett's home, a spacious, handsome, typically Californian house in Beverly Hills. It was a large place, so when Harold Arlen came out in 1935 there was room for him also. Arlen had been signed by Samuel Goldwyn to do the songs for the Eddie Cantor vehicle *Strike Me Pink.* All that remained of the Broadway original was Lew Brown, who had collaborated on the book and lyrics. Brown was in revolt at the time; he had decided to split from the honored DeSylva, Brown, and Henderson combination that had produced some of the greatest songs of the Twenties: "Black Bottom," "Birth of the Blues," "The Best Things in Life Are Free," "Varsity Drag," "You're the Cream in My Coffee," "Button Up Your Overcoat," and dozens of others. Brown felt that DeSylva was receiving too much of the credit for the work he and Henderson were doing and decided to strike out on his own. A. L. Berman, who had become Arlen's attorney and good friend from their first meeting during the negotiations on *You Said*

It, was also representing Brown. He suggested then that Arlen and Brown collaborate on *Strike Me Pink.*

Arlen had met Brown in New York and while he greatly respected the veteran song writer, knew that he would have to collaborate with Brown much differently from the way he had with Koehler, Yellen, or Harburg and Gershwin. It was Brown's habit, when he presented his lyric to the composer, to sing it at him, complete with Brown's own melody. If he wanted to compose the melodies for any Arlen-Brown songs, Arlen knew he would have to devise a method whereby he would not have to be in the forceful presence of Lew Brown. Arlen's solution was simple: he merely asked Brown to phone him at the Tibbett house and read the lyrics. Arlen jotted the words down, and then set them to music. Without an audience Brown did not tend to vocalize, and thus was Arlen able to compose the music without unsolicited suggestion.

The four songs that remained in the final print of *Strike Me Pink* were split between stars Eddie Cantor and Ethel Merman. The film took on all aspects of a family reunion: Anya Taranda appeared in it; Arlen's visits to the Goldwyn lot had more to do with her presence there than with his interest in the progress of the film. Also, he was able to warm over the Palace memories with Ethel Merman and with Roger Edens, who had come along to attend to Miss Merman's arrangements and was responsible for the fine treatment of one of the film's better songs, "First You Have Me High (Then You Have Me Low)."

Once work on *Strike Me Pink* was completed, Arlen was able to take up his partnership with Yip Harburg; in September 1935 the Hollywood *Reporter* announced that they had been signed to a year's contract by Warner Brothers. Before beginning on their first score they decided to complete the song Arlen had begun in New York. Possibly because of the influence of their surroundings, or because of the melody's very character, they wrote the song with their landlord, Lawrence Tibbett, in mind.

Harburg most skillfully and poetically reflects the melody's bittersweetness in his outstanding lyric for "Last Night When

We Were Young." Like so many songs combining unusual high qualities in music and lyric, "Last Night When We Were Young" has a curious history of scant success. Tibbett naturally recognized its quality and wanted the song for his film *Metropolitan,* but the song was dropped from the final print. The baritone, however, took the song into his repertoire, and even recorded it for RCA Victor—interestingly around the same time he recorded songs from *Porgy and Bess* in October 1935. On the other side of the Arlen-Harburg disc was a song that had remained in *Metropolitan,* "On the Road to Mandalay."

"Last Night When We Were Young" is too special a song to have been taken over quickly by popular singers; the Tibbett recording and the concert performances were satisfying to Arlen and Harburg, and for the former it has always served an additional function as the logical answer to the inane, inevitable, interview question: "What is your favorite song?" Over the years, since 1935, it has grown in popularity among vocalists also. The Tibbett recording introduced it to Judy Garland, who has become one of the song's champions and best interpreters. "I happened to find it in a pile of old records in a record shop," Miss Garland recalls, "and because it had Harold Arlen's name on it I bought the record. I was about sixteen years old when I first heard it. It was my favorite song then and I was always trying to work it into a picture. When I finally did get it in *The Good Old Summertime* I was so pleased, but then as luck would have it, it was cut out. Frank Sinatra heard my recording of it and did it in a picture called *Take Me Out to the Ball Game* and it was cut out of that too. However, I recorded it for Capitol. I also did it on a television show and I think that lyrically and melodically it is one of the great love songs of all time."

With art out of the way Arlen and Harburg began work on the first of a series of three musicals for Warner Brothers, none of which was destined to make film history. The first starred Al Jolson, whose own star in 1935 was hardly in ascendance. Arlen remembers Jolson during the early discussions, remaining self-effacingly in the background. Actual shooting on the film, *The Singing Kid,* began around the first of the year (1936), shortly after which the studio opened up its campaign to push the songs, with particular emphasis on "I Love to Sing-a," a satirical treatment of a mammy singer. Running three times longer than the average song, "I Love to Sing-a" in its original form was presented in an elaborate street scene number; another attractive song was "You're the Cure for What Ails Me."

Even before shooting was complete on *The Singing Kid,* Arlen and Harburg began, in March, to work on their next assignment, *Stage Struck,* a Dick Powell-Joan Blondell vehicle that rode in the old rut of the backstage story about the musical saved by the girl in the chorus when the star cannot go on on opening night. Into the timeworn and uninspiring mold Arlen and Harburg poured the excellent "In Your Own Quiet Way" and the even better "Fancy Meeting You," which was staged in a museum in deference to Harburg's erudite references to evolution in the lyric. But the film did not, like the one before, please. Howard Barnes, in his review of *Stage Struck* in the *Tribune,* observed that "its pleasant score and chorus numbers make a palpably false front for a tedious show. Except for the . . . catchy Harburg-Arlen tunes, it is a dull and muddled screen musical." Frank S. Nugent concurred and innocently made a false prediction: "There are a few redeeming features . . . two pleasant songs by Harburg and Arlen . . . which you will be hearing, unless you already have, on the airways."

None of the songs composed for the Warner Brothers films was destined to be played on the air. Just at the time the pictures were released an intramural quarrel developed in ASCAP, with the result that Music Publishers Holding Corporation, licensee of all Warner Brothers songs, withdrew from ASCAP. Music Publishers Holding Corporation, because of its stellar roster of composers (the Gershwins, Kern, Porter, Rodgers and Hart, Herbert, and others), accounted for some 20 per cent of ASCAP's total catalogue, demanded a larger slice of ASCAP's melon. When this was not forthcoming, MPH withdrew its songs.

When this occurred, it so happened that the radio networks and ASCAP were at peace, so that naturally all of MPH songs, and consequently all Warner Brothers songs, were banned from the air. When Al Jolson wanted to do "I Love to Sing-a" on the air in 1936, one executive expressed radio's stand by stating that "it will cost Warner Brothers $50,000 to get even one of its songs played on NBC." The battle went on for many months until Music Publishers Holding Corporation went back to ASCAP, but not before a lot of damage had been done to its composers and several affiliated publishers. To Arlen and Harburg it had cut off an avenue of performance for their songs.

A second Dick Powell-Joan Blondell musical followed *Stage Struck*, this time another in a popular series, *Gold Diggers of 1937*. Arlen and Harburg did four songs for it, of which only two were used; other songs were contributed by Harry Warren and Al Dubin. *Gold Diggers* fulfilled the song writers' contract with the studio; the year had given them valuable insights into the ways and means of working in Hollywood.

Beginning in 1933, Hollywood launched its second cycle of film musicals since the advent of sound, which had come with Jolson's *The Jazz Singer* in 1927. The first film musicals were static attempts at reproducing the Broadway prototypes, or were mass studio efforts into which everyone on the lot was thrown in one gigantic filmed variety show. Among the early historic film musicals was *The Broadway Melody*, with songs by Nacio Herb Brown and Arthur Freed, the first musical to receive the Academy Award (1929). This kind of recognition, plus the film's fiscal popularity, encouraged the making of musicals. However, by 1931–32, the movie-going public had tired of the stream of all-star musicals, the behind-the-scenes stories (it never failed—there was always someone standing around shouting, "All right, kids, everybody on stage!"), causing a musical box-office slump. This came at the time when the Gershwins had finally been wooed to the Coast to do their undistinguished *Delicious*, and Rodgers and Hart to do their now forgotten *Hot Heiress*. As early as 1929, Ernst Lubitsch had shown what could be done when wit, taste, and intelligence were applied to the making of a musical film—as he had in *The Love Parade*—provided that the director knew how to use the camera. Rouben Mamoulian followed in the same inventive path with his *Love Me Tonight* in 1932, a film that starred, as did the Lubitsch production, Maurice Chevalier and Jeanette MacDonald, but with songs by Rodgers and Hart.

The tongue-in-cheek, mildly suggestive (decades later it would be termed "adult") Continental handling of a musical was further enhanced by a more skillful weaving of the songs into the story under the hands of Lubitsch and Mamoulian. While the conventional musical exploited to an almost stultifying degree the possibilities of the vast sound stages for spectacular "production numbers," the Lubitsch-Mamoulian musicals favored a simpler handling of the songs and substituted subtle humor and taste for mere spectacle. The Arlen-Koehler *Let's Fall in Love*, while no filmic milestone, was a turn in the newer direction. What could be done with song and plot integration was effectively shown by Harburg and Arlen in their "I Love to Sing-a" number, as originally conceived for *The Singing Kid*, and "Fancy Meeting You," for *Stage Struck*. The songs naturally grew out of the action, were related to plot and characterization, were simply presented, in addition to being good songs. However, they were not noticed in undistinguished films. Rodgers and Hart attempted an even more radical departure in their film *Hallelujah, I'm a Bum* (1933), but that too went unrecognized, as did the recitative-like rhyming dialogue. It was obvious, despite these failures, that film musicals were developing into something approaching art.

Flying Down to Rio began the film musical renaissance in 1933. For it Vincent Youmans wrote four excellent songs (lyrics by Gus Kahn and Edward Eliscu), and the film served to introduce a newly formed dancing team comprised of two fugitives from Broadway, Ginger Rogers and Fred Astaire. That same year other important film musicals were released, among them *Forty Second Street* (songs by Harry Warren and

Al Dubin), *Gold Diggers of 1933* (Warren and Dubin again), *College Humor* (songs by Sam Coslow and Arthur Johnston), and *Footlight Parade* (songs by Irving Kahal and Sammy Fain and the ubiquitous Warren and Dubin). Whatever their doubtful value as screen entertainment, these musicals produced memorable songs.

Rogers and Astaire followed *Flying Down to Rio* (Youmans' last score) with *The Gay Divorcee*, a film remake of Astaire's stage success *The Gay Divorce*. The adaptation was par for the Coast: one song by Cole Porter ("Night and Day") remained from the original, and new songs were added by resident composers: the real hit of the film turned out to be "The Continental," by Herb Magidson and Con Conrad. The pattern for the Astaire-Rogers films was established: the settings were glitteringly non-depression, the people in them were charmingly scatterbrained and quite youthfully irresponsible (no one ever seemed to have a job, or even bothered to work), and each film was scored with marvelous songs; one further characteristic: there was always at least one big dance sequence in every picture.

With the depression forcing stringent economies upon Broadway, Hollywood became the composer's haven. Such home-based talents as Nacio Herb Brown, Arthur Freed, Arthur Johnston, Mort Dixon, Allie Wrubel, Irving Kahal, Sammy Fain, the transplanted Harry Warren, Leo Robin, and Ralph Rainger dominated the film musical scene in the Thirties. Many had left Broadway and Tin Pan Alley; with the purchase of the publishing houses by the film industry the music industry was now also based in California.

When he came to California in 1935, Harold Arlen thus did not find himself among strangers. Harry Warren was an old friend; Ted Koehler was writing lyrics for the very popular Shirley Temple films; Irving Berlin was turning his attention to the songs for such Astaire-Rogers musicals as *Top Hat* and *Follow the Fleet*; Jerome Kern had come out also and had done *Swingtime* for the soaringly popular dance team.

Cole Porter was contracted to M-G-M to do scores for Eleanor
Powell. The Gershwins came to California in 1936.

The result was one of the richest periods in American popular music. If the Twenties produced some of the finest Broadway scores, the Thirties equaled that output with its film songs.
The major difference was that more people were able to see
the movies. Even though the depression had devastated most
forms of entertainment, the inexpensive motion picture flour-
ished by supplying the demand for light amusements and
escape from the harsh realities of the economy.

For Arlen economic realities took on a typical Hollywood
form with the weekly arrival of his check—via motorcycle.
This dramatic promptness, which enabled him to hear his
earnings arriving from blocks away, had its drawback. He was
soon to learn that when he was to inquire about the fate of
one of his songs, the stock answer was, "You get your check,
don't you?" The entire neighborhood knew Arlen had got
his check; no arguing with that.

Harry Warren has supplied the best example of the attitude
toward the composer in films: a composer was summoned up
to a producer's office. The great man sat behind a great desk,
suggested to the composer that some of his songs might easily
be improved by a little change here and there. The composer,
a bit shaken, for he knew that the producer was profoundly
ignorant on the subject of music, rather delicately asked him
how it came to be that a man with the producer's musical
tastes could tell a composer what to do. Even without recourse
to a musical dictionary the producer came up with a straightforward answer: "You're *standing* there and I'm *sitting* here—
that's why!"

Not all production, however, was handled by the unen-
lightened, particularly when a producer also happened to be
a composer, as was the case with Arthur Freed, Roger Edens,
and later Arthur Schwartz. Or the wise producer who did not
know music left that department to his musical director.

The greatest obstacle, particularly to the composer accustomed to work in Broadway shows, was the expectation that

once you had turned in your songs you could forget about them; some were never heard again. A Broadway musical called for auditions, rehearsals, and changes right up until opening night. The studio method was impersonal and objective. You were, after all, paid for a certain product and were asked for no more. Others might be called in to cut it to fit, change it, color it up a little, or it was simply discarded. The climate was fine, the pay was good, but song writers found themselves often homesick for the living theater.

While they were still under contract to Warner Brothers, Arlen and Harburg received a request from Bert Lahr for a song he hoped to use in a revue, *The Show Is On*. The team produced the famous "Song of the Woodman" for Lahr, recorded it, and mailed it to him. Vincente Minnelli, who was directing the revue, talked the Gershwins into contributing a song to *The Show Is On* also, the waltz-spoof "By Strauss." Harburg was called to New York to help doctor the show a bit; it opened on Christmas Day, 1936, to become a hit.

Not long after, Arlen came to New York to see *The Show Is On;* he even filmed Bert Lahr's "Woodman" number. With him at the performance was Anya Taranda. One evening, as he left her at her door, Arlen gave her a note; it read:

> Dearest Anya—
>   We're getting married tomorrow—
>   'bout time don't you think?
> All my love,
>   H.

Almost five years of hard thinking resulted in that charming note. He had not made up his mind on the spur of the moment, as might be interpreted from the almost spontaneous and casual note. Some months before he had been visiting his parents in Syracuse. He decided to accompany Cantor Arluck on one of his daily walks to the broker's. His father quite unexpectedly mentioned Anya. Obviously the question of the difference in religions concerned him, and he had sensed a deepening in their relationship. "Are you sure you know what you're doing?" he asked his son. "Yes," Arlen had answered, "don't worry, Pop."

After the marriage, which was gracefully accepted by all parents concerned, the subject was never brought up again by Cantor Arluck. Anya was warmly welcomed into the family, as was Arlen into the Taranda family and religion was not a factor in its relationships.

Having read the note that Arlen had given her, Anya had only to round out the surprise by actually showing up the next morning after so unusual a proposal. They were married at eleven in the morning on January 8, 1937, in Harrison, N.Y., with the heavy-lidded Jerry Arlen and A. L. Berman sleepily serving as witnesses.

Back in California the Arlens took a house on Lookout Mountain Road in Laurel Canyon. It was a beautiful house of a rather spectacular design; the living room was on the top floor and the bedrooms below that. But, barely having settled in their new home, the Arlens found themselves involved with a new Broadway musical.

Yip Harburg had greatly enjoyed his brief return to Broadway; besides there were events, particularly on an international scale, that were stirring him up. The United States gunboat *Panay* had been sunk by the Japanese near Nanking in China; in Germany, Hitler canceled out the Treaty of Versailles; the Spanish Civil War was dramatized by the siege of Madrid and the aid given by Italian dictator Mussolini to Franco. It was evident to Harburg that warlike events were brewing, that there was not much right with the world at all: "Hooray for what?" became a troubled question for him.

E. (for Edgar) Y. (for-who knows?) Harburg was born on April 8, 1898, in New York's Lower East Side—"under the El," according to an early autobiographical account. His early life "was a desperate struggle against poverty and squalor." He began writing essays and verse for the school paper while still in P.S. 64. He also evidenced a talent for oratory and acting for which he was awarded prizes in amateur competitions; eventually he became known in his neighborhood as "the best Goddamned little actor on the East Side." To help himself through high school, he sold newspapers and lit street lamps for the Edison Company. At Townsend Harris Hall, a school for gifted students, he wrote for the *Academic Herald* and contributed a column to a neighborhood paper, the *Tompkins Square News*. Attending Townsend Harris Hall at the same time was Ira Gershwin, a neighborhood friend. When they went on to City College, both future lyricists contributed prose and verse to college publications and to even more professional outlets such as the famous "Conning Tower" columns of Franklin P. Adams. Harburg and Gershwin were also associated with the entertainments presented at the local neighborhood center, the Christadora Settlement House.

On finishing college young Harburg took a job representing a business in South America; two weeks after his arrival there the business collapsed. The resourceful Harburg barnstormed South America for three years until, by now in Uruguay, he had earned and saved enough money not only to return to the United States, but also to start his own business.

The Consolidated Electrical Appliance Company set up offices at 916 Broadway and managed to be doing nicely until October 1929 set in and Prop. E. Y. Harburg found himself bankrupt and owing some $250,000.

Looking around for something to do, and some means to pay off his debts, Harburg decided to turn his gift for light verse to profitable use. He formed a song-writing partnership with Jay Gorney, a former lawyer from Detroit. Gorney had noticed some sprightly rhymes published in F.P.A.'s "Conning Tower" signed "Yip," and they had impressed him: they bore a decided technical rightness, at the same time making their points, often satirically.

The name "Yip" was a holdover from Harburg's East Side days; it had evolved from "Yitsel" into "Yipsel" (the "Squirrel"), which, shortened to Yip, has remained Harburg's preferred name ever since. His collaborators frequently refer to him as "Yipper." It somehow suggests his terrier quality when he knows there is a point to be made.

With Gorney, Harburg turned out his first songs—for Earl Carroll's *Sketch Book* of 1929—such titles as "Legs, Legs, Legs," "Like Me Less, Love Me More," and "Kinda Cute." That same year they contributed a song, "What I Wouldn't Do for That Man," to a Paramount film, *Glorifying the American Girl,* when that studio was still shooting films on Long Island. In 1930 Harburg collaborated with the talented Vernon Duke and with Ira Gershwin on "I'm Only Human After All," and with Jay Gorney on the Earl Carroll *Vanities,* which first brought him together professionally with Harold Arlen.

"Brother, Can You Spare a Dime?" (music by Gorney) was a great hit in 1932, and made many a dime for the song writers. That same year Harburg turned out the lovely "April in Paris" with Vernon Duke for *Walk a Little Faster;* they collaborated again on the *Ziegfeld Follies of 1934* for which they came up with such songs as "Suddenly," "What Is There to Say?," and "I Like the Likes of You," which is one of Ira Gershwin's favorite lyrics by any lyricist. Harburg, like Gershwin, is one of the very few men of the well-chosen word. Like Gershwin, also, Harburg is constantly concerned, not only with the idea of the song, but also with its proper grammatical wording ("April in Paris," for example, contains the line: "Whom shall I run to?").

"Yipper," Harold Arlen has said, "is a Gilbert-and-Sullivan lover. This means a torrent of lyrics. I had to adapt myself to his kind of thinking, and find a way to please myself at the same time. Working with him didn't limit me—that is, I didn't have to set lyrics, we really collaborated. It was a change of pace, for Yip has always been brilliant at lampooning."

When the idea came to Harburg in the summer of 1937 to lampoon the international situation in a musical, it seemed an admirable one. It also seemed to the Shuberts to be a possible source of profit, for they were willing to back it; they placed the business management of the show in the hands of Harry Kaufman, who had worked out so well on *Life Begins at 8:40.* Howard Lindsay and Russel Crouse were then given the job of developing Harburg's idea into a musical for Ed Wynn.

The comedian was to portray an inventor who accidentally stumbles upon a poison gas (he is actually hoping to invent an insecticide) that proves potent against humans. Naturally all the "peace-loving" nations of the world are interested in the gas as a weapon in the next war all are planning.

This rather grim subject actually served as a springboard for the zany routines of Ed Wynn, who had spent six years as radio's "Fire Chief" and was returning to Broadway to appear in the Arlen-Harburg-Lindsay-Crouse, Shubert-sponsored *Hooray for What?*

One of the pleasanter aspects of California living they were leaving was the outdoor living and socializing in the musical colony; the afternoons at the Gershwins', the card-playing evenings at the Kerns', the tennis matches with Dorothy Fields and Moss Hart, the afternoons at the track. "We used to go out quite often with the Berlins." Arlen recalls with a warm chuckle, "when we'd go to a Chinese restaurant, he'd walk right through to the kitchen and supervise whatever dish he decided we'd have—and he always ate with chopsticks."

Before they left for New York, where they were to begin work on Ed Wynn's yacht, Arlen and Harburg stopped at the Gershwins' to say good-by. They were shocked to see George Gershwin terribly ill, his face an ashen pallor. Debilitated, he could barely speak, but he managed to say, when he heard that the Arlens and Harburg were going to New York, in a weak voice, "All my friends are leaving me."

Because Gershwin's illness was thought to be a physical manifestation of an emotional reaction to his frustrating experiences in the film capital, it was decided then and there that perhaps if he were to get away from the continual traffic of the Gershwin home he would feel better and could rest. Harburg offered the use of his home, while they were in New York, as a retreat away from the Gershwin social center. Gershwin moved in on July 4; Arlen and Harburg left for New York. On July 11, 1937, while spending a restful Sunday in the country, they were stunned and deeply saddened to hear that Gershwin had died after an unsuccessful attempt to remove a tumor in his brain. Both men had lost a dear friend; one that Harburg had known since boyhood in the Lower East Side.

Arlen was particularly affected by his death, not only because Gershwin had often gone out of his way to champion Arlen's work, but because they had become, since their meeting some half-dozen years before, very close friends. They frequently met in that fluid life in Beverly Hills at parties, around a pool, in the tennis court, and they would talk about their work or personal problems. The last year of his life Gershwin seemed bent upon getting married.

When he visited the Arlens, usually unannounced, Gershwin immediately made for the piano, where he would play his latest song. To Arlen this rather symbolized Gershwin's true dedication, and once made Gershwin a little touchy on advising him not to marry.

Arlen affectionately remembers an incident that occurred at the Clover Club, where the composers and lyricists gathered to gamble. On one evening Arlen offered to drive Ira Gershwin home. On the way the lyricist confessed that he had lost five hundred dollars. "But don't tell George," he cautioned. The following night Arlen was driving George home from the same place—and heard the same confession (even the amount was the same). And the same request: "But don't tell Ira."

Not long after Gershwin's death work on *Hooray for What?* was held up because of the headaches Arlen had; Gershwin had complained of headaches too. Arlen was accused of sympathetic hypochrondria, even by his doctor. But the headaches persisted, becoming severe enough for Arlen to stop work completely to have something done about it. A thorough examination uncovered a cyst in the maxillary antrum pressing upon the fifth nerve; it was this that caused Arlen's headaches, not Gershwin's tragic death. A removal of the cyst stopped the headaches and work was resumed on the new show.

The aims of *Hooray for What?* were high, but by the time the show opened in New York on December 1, 1937, the artistic sights were considerably lowered. Vincente Minnelli had been chosen to stage and direct; even Agnes de Mille was called upon to devise some significant ballets; they found themselves consistently hampered.

Miss de Mille had done a little work in the Broadway vein previous to *Hooray for What?* In London she had choreographed a Cole Porter musical, *Nymph Errant*, and later, in 1932 back in New York, the Arthur Schwartz-Howard Dietz *Flying Colors*. On neither show had Miss de Mille's experiences been other than exasperating, frustrating, her work distorted, mangled, and rejected. Some further misfortunes in Hollywood (detailed in her book *Dance to the Piper*), however, did not dampen Miss de Mille's hopes in show business. *Hooray for What?* would offer her postgraduate courses in her now considerable education.

Miss de Mille's bête noire proved to be the Shubert's Harry Kaufman, whose forte was hardly art. As the Shubert's overseer, hatchet man, and holder of purse strings, Kaufman wielded a mighty hand. An initial disturbance came as early as the dance auditions, when Kaufman insisted on hiring dancers who could hardly have been expected to do any justice to the de Mille art. The girls looked good, but couldn't dance, and—as intimated by Miss de Mille in her book—were extremely willing to be more than friendly with the backers.

Harburg's original idea of attacking the world's tendency toward war, unlike the tendency itself, was shifted off target by the book that now concentrated on the star; the point of the anti-war thesis became blunted, if not lost altogether. Vincente Minnelli's costumes did not prove to be revealing enough for the flesh-loving management. And so did the compromising begin.

Besides Ed Wynn, also signed to appear were Kay Thompson, a very popular radio personality, Hannah Williams (then Mrs. Jack Dempsey), and, as juvenile lead, Roy Roberts. Miss Thompson brought a group of singers with her from her radio show.

Ralph Blane, a young hopeful singer from a city with the unlikely name of Broken Arrow, Oklahoma, desperately wanted

to be in a Harold Arlen musical. When the call came for
auditions, he was there in line, music under his arm, along with
the other hopefuls. He had barely managed to sing two bars
of his song before being crushed with the stock, "Thank you—
we'll call you." Blane then placed himself on the dancer's
line and made an even less appreciated impression.

In desperation Blane called an agent friend for advice. He
learned that because the singers were under Kay Thompson's
direction she made the decisions on the singers, and had in
fact almost all she needed anyway with her own Kay Thompson Singers. Blane, however, instructed his agent to call Miss
Thompson on the hour, every hour, until he was permitted to
audition for her. This went on all day until the distracted
Miss Thompson invited the singer to come to her apartment—
where he was greeted with earned hostility. While he was
singing, members of Miss Thompson's group began arriving,
among them a young ex-concert pianist from Birmingham,
Alabama, Hugh Martin. As for Blane's audition Miss Thompson was noncommittal.

When time for the evening's rehearsal at the theater came,
Blane merely attached himself to the group and went along.
Having listened at Miss Thompson's apartment while she rehearsed, he had learned one of her vocal arrangements. Once
at the Shubert, the group filed on-stage, the girls in front,
the men behind. Blane was especially behind, for he was making himself practically invisible in back of one of the girls.

Harry Kaufman recognized a by now quite familiar face. He
stopped the rehearsal even as Blane attempted to make himself
smaller, and asked, irony in his voice, "Didn't I throw you out
of here twice today?" Blane attempted to say that he was a
member of the chorus, though technically he wasn't, even suggesting that Miss Thompson had hired him.

With a cold fury Kay Thompson came to Blane's swift
defense, at the same time showing her contempt for Kaufman.
The incident so amused Arlen, Minnelli, and Harburg that
they outvoted Kaufman and the indefatigable Ralph Blane
became a member of the Kay Thompson Singers.

Arlen was not without his problems, for even Lee Shubert offered advice on how the melodies should be written. Robert Emmett Dolan, the show's musical director, found the composer "unusually patient and understanding. Some of the orchestrations were a radical departure from the standard practice." Often devised so that the vocalists carried the melodic line, the orchestral accompaniment might not be much more than a glorified oom-pa. Unless the singers were present, Arlen rarely had the opportunity to hear his melodies.

For *Hooray for What?* Arlen composed the *Hero Ballet*, his first extended writing since *Mood in Six Minutes*. The theme of the ballet had to do with the pointlessness of war, the "hero," and was danced by Paul Haakon. The music is predominantly percussive and modern (Arlen's description: "very Stravinsky") and unorthodox for a show. Unfortunately for de Mille's art and dancers, Minnelli went all the way with *his* art: the stage was cluttered with simulated barbed wire, the girls wore gas masks, and other war paraphernalia, including guns with bayonets, were pressed into use. Miss de Mille now dismisses the *Hero Ballet* as "terrible," but by the time *Hooray for What?* opened, it was all that remained of her work.

Boston was the scene of the massacre. The show began its two-week tryout there on October 30. The morning after Agnes de Mille, who by now was finding it difficult to be certain whether she was hired to be a choreographer or a part-time madam, was told that she was through. Even before the company had left for Boston she had become a part-time choreographer for a Broadway dance director had already been called in to "fix" the dances. Kay Thompson was fired in Boston, so was Roy Roberts, so was Hannah Williams. This last almost precipitated an incident, for it brought Jack Dempsey to the stage of the Colonial Theater, blood in his eye, ready —and more than able—to avenge his wife's cavalier treatment. In the face of this even Harry Kaufman had nothing to say, but Mrs. Dempsey never returned.

After Miss de Mille had returned to New York, nursing her

latest Broadway-inflicted wounds, she received a phone call
from Kay Thompson, still in Boston but on the way out,
though not aware of it yet. It was 2:30 in the morning, but
Miss Thompson had news she felt could not wait. "I have
good news for you," she declared. "Harry Kaufman has just
fallen off the stage and has broken his back!"

"You're just telling me this to make me feel good," was
Miss de Mille's bitter reply.

Kaufman, indeed, had taken a header into the pit, landed
in the bass drum, and was injured seriously enough to require
hospitalization. Though he had not broken his back, he was in
great pain with a back injury; the sympathetic though unsen-
timental management reluctantly gave him the time off to
recover. Their sympathy did not cover the cost of the broken
instruments—which Kaufman had to replace.

Up to that time Kaufman had been after Arlen and Harburg to write what he called "a jingle," a very simple, easy-to-
take song—just the thing for a Shubert show. The writers had
not come up with anything. When they visited Kaufman in
the hospital, he philosophized from his bed of pain: "I've
decided, boys, from now on the important thing, the most
important thing in life is your health; nothing else matters
—WHERE'S THE JINGLE?"

The news of the Boston wrangle reached New York; it
seemed that each train from the north carried a newly fired
ex-member of the cast of *Hooray for What?* It devolved upon
Russel Crouse to bring some of the usual gossip to rest, for
the talk of "out-of-town trouble" can doom a show before it
opens. For the New York *Times,* Crouse wrote an amusing
though hardly veracious "So You Heard a Rumor," in which
he skillfully explained away the exits of Kay Thompson (replaced by Vivian Vance), Roy Roberts (replaced by Jack
Whiting), and Hannah Williams (replaced by June Clyde).

But the show did open at the Winter Garden; Harburg's
original idea conceived in 1937, while he contemplated the
world's terrifying state, was softened by the winter—though
the world's condition worsened. The production wrangling had

taught him, as it had Agnes de Mille, Kay Thompson, Hannah Williams, and others, something about man's contentious affinities.

In all the chaos it was natural that some of the work of Arlen and Harburg was put on that overworked train from Boston. A non-jingly song, "Buds Won't Bud," originally sung by Hannah Williams, was thrown out; so was "Napoleon's a Pastry," an idea to be salvaged some years later for another musical, though the song itself was abandoned.

With Kay Thompson's exit (she did receive program credits: "The Singing Ensemble coached by Miss Kay Thompson"), the remaining arrangements fell to Ralph Blane and Hugh Martin. For one, "In the Shade of the New Apple Tree," they formed a quartet of Martin, Blane, Harold Cook, and John Smedberg. The four formed the nucleus of the group that would later be known as "The Martins," and Martin and Blane formed a musical partnership that would result, some years after *Hooray for What?* in their own scores for such outstanding productions as *Best Foot Forward* and *Meet Me in St. Louis.*

Hooray for What? received a warm critical reception in New York; all were obviously happy with the return of Ed Wynn to the Broadway scene. Reaction to the book was, in a word, mixed, although John Mason Brown noted that it was "extremely satiric . . . it laughs at munitions manufacturers, the League of Nations, and the absurdities of war." The spirit of the show might be conveyed in Wynn's comment, in character as "Chuckles" the inventor, who says to members of the League: "Don't you know that if you fellows miss a couple more payments [on war debts] America will own the last war outright!"

The songs that received special mention were the ballad "I've Gone Romantic on You," the bluesy "Moanin' in the Mornin'," the waltz "Life's a Dance," and the irreverent "Down with Love." The stirringly patriotic "God's Country" went unnoticed but was later interpolated into the film *Babes in Arms* in 1939, when the war that *Hooray for What?* predicted had become a reality. Sidney Whipple, in the *Telegram*, pointed out that the *Hero Ballet*, "a bayonet dance . . . was an outstanding and understandable ballet."

With the show finally, and successfully, launched, Harburg and the Arlens returned to the comparative peace of Beverly Hills. The fact that *Hooray for What?* was a hit had a decided salutary effect. Metro-Goldwyn-Mayer was looking around for the right composer for a special project; for a time they were considering Jerome Kern.

Although Mervyn LeRoy was the producer of the proposed film, all major musical decisions were made by the capable associate producer, Arthur Freed. He had been an Arlen enthusiast for years, had liked the songs written for *Let's Fall in Love* and had a fondness for "In the Shade of the New Apple Tree," from *Hooray for What?* He felt that that one song evidenced all the sparkle and lightness he hoped could be put into the score of the new film. Freed used the song as an arguing point when he brought up the names of Arlen and Harburg as possible composers for the new production. Harburg, Freed felt, had a wonderful feeling for fantasy that, coupled with Arlen's musical fancy, might produce the right songs for the contemplated filming of the childhood classic *The Wizard of Oz*. Freed made his point, and in July 1938 the Hollywood *Reporter* published the announcement that Harold Arlen and E. Y. Harburg had been chosen to do the songs for what M-G-M planned to be their most ambitious musical production up to that time.

When Arlen visited his friend "Mr." Kern, the older man studied him with a new regard as he inquired, his voice pitched almost in a tone of incredulity, "You got the job?" Dorothy Fields, who worked a good deal with Kern in Hollywood, found Kern "had a great respect for Harold, and considered him enormously talented."

Arlen's respect, in turn, for Kern was epical—a couple of years went by before he dropped the "Mr." and called Kern "Jerry," as did all others close to him. His regard, however, did not deter his sense of humor; he would frequently tease Kern by opening the windows before he played Kern songs on the piano. To set the proper scene for a Kern song, for the atmosphere of "tinkling chandeliers," Arlen felt that the breeze must set the curtains in motion, with the candelabras lighted, the lighting subdued. Or, if Kern were involved in a card game, Arlen might take an uncompleted Kern song in manuscript on the piano and complete it. Kern enjoyed this kind of inside joking, but only if he happened to like you. If not, he could be absolutely withering.

Once Arlen and Harburg were assigned to *The Wizard of Oz*, they set to work immediately, for shooting was scheduled to begin in September; there remained but two months to turn out what was expected to be a unique and extended film score. Veteran though he was, Arlen now admits that this assignment "really troubled" him. The initial ballyhoo promised big things, and M-G-M was pouring everything into it. The studio had had one disappointment: unable to get Shirley Temple to portray "Dorothy," they settled for Judy Garland.

Harburg, who did some work in the script, however, made a show of confidence. "We think we've found a way to eliminate stop-plot numbers from the screen," he announced. The technique they had used in their earlier films, though it went unnoticed, was put to good use in *The Wizard of Oz*. Its score must be one of the very first successfully integrated film scores, for all the songs, all musical bridges, all the choral numbers are related to the story and the characters.

One day, having completed one of the songs, Arlen and Harburg went to the studio to play it for approval or rejection. Harburg was so filled with ideas that he offered some of them to the producer, "in such involved language," Arlen remembers, "that I had trouble following him; it was a pretty complex speech delivered with a great passion. We never did get to demonstrate the song.

"When we left the office I jumped Yipper. 'What were you up to, what were you trying to tell them? We didn't even get to play the song.'"

Harburg, still dazed by the force of his own elocution, looked blankly at Arlen and asked, "What did I say?"

"We had finished the lemon-drop songs," Arlen continues, referring to the lighter creations, "We're Off to See the Wizard," "The Merry Old Land of Oz," "Ding-Dong! The Witch Is Dead," and it was felt that a ballad was needed to balance them. "I felt we needed something with sweep, a melody with a broad, long, line. Time was getting short, I was getting anxious. My feeling was that picture songs need to be lush, and picture songs are hard to write."

The song came to Arlen literally out of the blue. He and Anya had decided to drive to a movie at Grauman's Chinese Theater—that is, Anya drove, the composer was too nervous with anxiety about the ballad he hoped to find. They had reached the spot where the original Schwab's drugstore was located, on Sunset Boulevard, when the "broad, long-lined, melody" came to Arlen; he jotted it down in the car. "It was as if the Lord said, 'Well, here it is, now stop worrying about it!'"

The next day he wrote the middle—the bridge—and the song was ready for Harburg to hear. The lyricist did not react to it with the joy Arlen had hoped for; instead he said, "That's for Nelson Eddy, not a little girl in Kansas." Harburg felt that the direct simplicity and lightness of the other songs might clash with the rather grand proportions of the new one. Arlen defended his hard-won tune. The writers played the song over for Ira Gershwin, who had come to offer an opinion. On hearing it Gershwin found it good, which was enough for Harburg; he titled it "Over the Rainbow" and composed a fine lyric for it.

But that was not the only resistance to the song. Judy Garland and Roger Edens, then also at M-G-M, were immediately delighted, but other ears were not. Miss Garland has written, "When I first met Harold I was just 14 years old and the first song of the score for *The Wizard of Oz* they played for me was 'Over The Rainbow.' I was terribly impressed by Mr. Arlen's great genius and very much in awe of him.

"As I recall, it seems that Harold always treated me as an equal and not as a child. We have been great friends through the years." As for her work on *The Wizard of Oz*, Miss Garland "enjoyed it tremendously although it was a long schedule and very hard work; it was in the comparatively early days of technicolor and the lights were terribly hot. We were shooting for about six months but I loved the music and I loved the director, Victor Fleming, and of course, I loved the story.

"I wasn't aware until the first preview of *The Wizard of Oz*, that they were thinking of cutting 'Over The Rainbow' out of the picture. I couldn't understand it because it was such a beautiful song. However, in those days I had very little to say about anything.

"[As for] my feeling toward 'Over The Rainbow' now, it has become a part of my life. It is so symbolic of everybody's dream and wish that I am sure that's why people sometimes get tears in their eyes when they hear it. I have sung it dozens of times and it's still the song that is closest to my heart. It is very gratifying to have a song that is more or less known as my song, or my theme song, and to have had it written by the fantastic Harold Arlen."

"Over the Rainbow" was deleted from the print of *The Wizard of Oz* three times; after each deletion Arthur Freed would storm into the front office and argue it back into the film. Further opposition came from the publisher, who objected to the difficult-to-sing octave leap in the melody on the word "some-where," and to the simple middle, ". . . why it's like a child's piano exercise." But Freed and Arlen stood up to the powers and the song remained, ironically to receive the Academy Award as the best film song of the year.

Arlen's reaction to the treatment of his song by the powers was one of simply washing his hands. After the third preview of *The Wizard of Oz* "I came home to Annie and said, 'No more previews. From now on I'm just going to write the best I can, turn 'em in and forget 'em.'" And he always held fast to that vow, just as he did to the vow he had made to his father about theater reviews.

Shooting was not completed until May 1939, at a cost of some three millions of dollars; when Judy Garland was absent with a cold for five days, the delay cost the studio $150,000. The production was tastefully lavish. The scenes in Kansas were shot in sepia tint; the Oz scenes in color, to heighten the effect of fantasy. Special effects created a remarkably realistic Midwestern tornado, the Oz settings provided ample opportunity for the virtuoso use of color, there was plentiful trick camera work, and even the sound track was speeded up in spots to give the Munchkins their highly pitched voices.

Make-up, too, was masterful, especially as applied to Dorothy's companions on the road to Oz, the Cowardly Lion (Bert Lahr), the Tin Woodman (Jack Haley), and the Scarecrow (Ray Bolger). Frank Morgan appeared in the role of the Wizard, a part that was to have gone to W. C. Fields, who held out for more money than M-G-M was prepared to pay him—long enough to have lost the part completely. Morgan did a fine job as the kindly, befuddled, Wizard, and proved to be extraordinarily versatile in many disguises; he was most effective in the scene written for him by Harburg in which he awards Dorothy's companions a heart, a brain, and nerve.

The scoring by Herbert Stothart skillfully captured the essence of the songs, for this he too received an "Oscar." Judy Garland was given a special award for her "distinguished services" to the screen.

That *The Wizard of Oz*, originally designed as a children's film, has been capable of standing up for two decades without dating is a tribute to all concerned. It is regularly revived by the movie houses and has become a holiday perennial on television (for which its authors receive only the glory).

An additional irony in connection with *The Wizard of Oz:* after it Arlen and Harburg were not given any assignments that were equal to their now obvious abilities. The *Wizard* was followed by *At the Circus,* a Marx Brothers film that hardly required a musical score. "Two Blind Loves," sung by Kenny Baker and Florence Rice, was musically interesting —the theme was based on the nursery rhyme "Three Blind Mice." Harburg shines in a "lyric-fun" (Arlen's term) song, "Lydia, The Tattooed Lady," written for Groucho Marx. The song was written specifically for Marx as a comedy number and not as one to be danced to. When Arlen played it for one of the producers, he turned around from the keyboard and "to my amazement he was dancing around the Metro office." The producer, with typical Boeotian musical comprehension, had mistaken the comedy song for a romantic number. When he noticed that Arlen was watching, the producer commented, "Very dancy."

Anya was involved at the time in furnishing their new home, for in the fall of 1938 they had moved into a beautiful white house in Coldwater Canyon on Lindacrest Drive. Fanny Brice's hobby was interior decorating and she was delighted to help with the new home. She and Anya visited antique shops to find unusual pieces.

Arlen, on the other hand, was tiring of unmusical producers; he was tired of their suggestions and criticisms beginning, "I don't know anything about songs, but . . ." He was tiring of being expected to leave his work at their door. He was, in short, ripe for another Broadway show.

Of the post-*Wizard of Oz* musicals he and Harburg did for M-G-M, among them the Abbott and Costello comedy *Rio Rita*, and a Marlene Dietrich vehicle, *Kismet*, and a Negro musical, *Cabin in the Sky*, only the last proved truly worth while.

Of the three songs written for *Rio Rita* only one, "Long Before You Came Along," remained, and one of their best, "Poor Whippoorwill," was deleted.

Cabin in the Sky was an adaptation of the 1941 musical, which had a score by Vernon Duke, John La Touche, and Ted Fetter. The studio bought the rights to the show, then assigned Arthur Freed to it as producer, and Vincente Minnelli as director—it was his first full directorial assignment. Ethel

Waters was drafted from the original Broadway cast; the Dooley Wilson role fell to Eddie (Rochester) Anderson; and the part of the temptress done on Broadway by Katherine Dunham was given to Lena Horne. Of the original Duke songs only three were retained for the movie: "Taking a Chance on Love," the title song, and "Honey in the Honeycomb." Arlen and Harburg supplied five additional songs, of which three remained, "Li'l Black Sheep," "Happiness Is a Thing Called Joe," and the show stopper, "Life's Full of Consequence," sung by "Rochester" and Miss Horne.

The *Cabin in the Sky* songs "came fairly easy" to Arlen, and he liked the work, but has never approved of having "Happiness Is a Thing Called Joe" interpolated into the Duke score when the show is done in summer stock. At the time the film was being made Vernon Duke was not available for working on it; he was then in the U. S. Coast Guard. *Cabin in the Sky* proved to be a good film, and "Happiness Is a Thing Called Joe" an enduring song.

Nat Goldstone, Arlen's agent at the time, approached him in 1944 with an idea for a musical that touched on, among other things, women's rights, slavery, the Civil War, the underground railroad. The play by Dan and Lilith James was built around some episodes in the life of Dolly Bloomer, champion of women's suffrage and inventor of the garment named for her. Arlen, eager to get out of what many called the "Hollywood sausage grinder" for a while, tried to interest Yip Harburg in the idea. Arlen felt that the book contained many elements that could make for a most colorful musical. After six months of begging off, and a nudge from his wife, Harburg was enlisted as lyricist and the play was reshaped into a musical's book by Fred Saidy and Sig Herzig under the title of *Bloomer Girl*.

Most of the work was done in Beverly Hills, some easy, some difficult: one song, called then "The Railroad Song," later titled "I Got a Song," existed in no less than twelve variants before the final one emerged.

Goldstone brought out producer John C. Wilson to hear

some of the completed songs. Impressed and armed with several homemade recordings, Wilson returned to New York to raise the required production money.

Early in July 1944, Arlen and Harburg had completed enough of the score to be able to leave for the New York rehearsals. The night before they left they sang their songs at a party to a very appreciative audience; they shared the program with Abe Burrows, who sang one of his oblique love songs; Walter Huston did "September Song."

Before reporting in at New York the Arlens stopped off at Syracuse to stay with his parents on University Avenue for four days. In New York they were plunged into the usual activity of a show in preparation.

The day before, Goldstone and Wilson had announced that Agnes de Mille would do the *Bloomer Girl* dances. By 1944 she had received the recognition she had not had when she did *Hooray for What?* Her work on Rodgers' and Hammerstein's *Oklahoma!* and Kurt Weill's and Ogden Nash's *One Touch of Venus* had made hers a name to reckon with in the theater; taking her themes and patterns from her understanding of American forms, Miss de Mille almost singlehandedly created a native dance form combining both popular and folk elements with classic ballet. She had also learned to stand up and fight after years of being pushed around in "show biz."

Bloomer Girl's cast was relatively unknown, though at least two had come to the fore because of their work in *Oklahoma!* Celeste Holm was cast as Evelina and Joan McCracken as Daisy. David Brooks was signed as the male lead.

Arlen and Harburg were still writing while all other activities went on; one of the last numbers was "Sunday in Cicero Falls," the satiric opening of the second act—it was written, by chance, on a hot July Sunday in the Dorset Hotel. Arlen conceived "Sunday in Cicero Falls" in three-part form, which afforded Miss de Mille a fine possibility for choreography, and Harburg could make highly revealing commentary on the pious citizens of Cicero Falls.

Arlen's *Bloomer Girl* score is one of his richest and most varied. The period setting called for less brittle songs than the conventional Broadway production. Into such a background Arlen was able to put a lovely waltz ("The Rakish Young Man with the Whiskers") or a lullaby ("Satin Gown and Silver Shoe"); the hero, a Southerner, sang ballads inflected with below the Mason-Dixon line flavors, such as the distinquished "Evelina" and "Right as the Rain." A slave sang a hymn to human dignity in "The Eagle and Me" and the blues-tinctured "Man for Sale." Both songs, Harburg feels, express the major thesis of the musical: "the indivisibility of human freedom." The plot and subplots of *Bloomer Girl* centered on the theme of freedom—for the slave, for women—and all came together in a unity that bound the score into a remarkable whole.

Harburg's lyrics reflected the mood of a unified America in wartime. In the third scene of Act 2 there is an interpretation of *Uncle Tom's Cabin* in which the theme is beautifully stated as a single voice rises out of the chorus to sing to one of Arlen's richest melodies:

> But Lord, if the goin' is cruel
> Then let him die like man, not live like mule.

This recitative-like melodic strain, sung by a Negro woman about her baby, is, though brief, beautifully complete. It is hardly more than a jot, and might easily have been developed into a full-length aria, but remained just a small melodic fragment in "Eliza Crossing the Ice."

Joan McCracken, the falling-down girl of *Oklahoma!*, sang and danced. Her songs were the amusing "T'morra', T'morra'" and "I Never Was Born" and she also appeared in some of Miss de Mille's most inspired choreography. There were several dance sequences—a "Grandma Ballet," a style show, "Sunday in Cicero Falls," among others. The most ambitious, and no doubt most meaningful, ballet was Miss de Mille's treatment of war in the "Civil War Ballet," the one, naturally, that caused the most trouble.

Bloomer Girl entertainingly carried its message. That it was a "musical comedy" was never forgotten, and the messages were put across lightly. But the "Civil War Ballet" was felt to be too grim, too serious, too saddening, and consequently too jarring to the enterprise. Even Harburg found himself exclaiming, "Can't we get rid of this somber, dreadful ballet!"

Miss de Mille stubbornly fought for a work she felt expressed "women's emotions in war." It was at once a universal and a personal conception, for her husband, Walter Prude, was away in the Army. Her idea, however, was too innovational for a musical, and the years had dimmed the existence of the *Hero Ballet*. When the wrangling reached a high pitch, Miss de Mille seemed to give in: when any of the top production echelon was around she rehearsed her dancers in a watered-down, prettified version of her ballet. But she continued to work on her original idea on the sly; no one was aware of this but the dancers, Miss de Mille's faithful rehearsal pianist Trude Rittmann—and Harold Arlen. He could understand what the choreographer was attempting, even felt that so unorthodox a ballet would add to the value of *Bloomer Girl* and not detract from its comic aspects. "I hope to God it stops the show opening night," he told Miss de Mille, "and shuts their clamoring mouths."

But by opening night in Philadelphia it had been decreed that the entire ballet was out, whatever version. Miss de Mille had planned to go along with her adversaries until that opening night and stake her fate on the reception of the "Civil War Ballet" by an actual audience. The decision to eliminate the ballet from the spot completely spoiled her plans. With Arlen behind her she fought like a tigress—and won a reprieve.

The audience of typical Philadelphia first-nighters, a few local people, and many professionals from New York cheered the "Civil War Ballet." The mood of the show was not destroyed, but a bitter poignancy was added in the touchingly projected anguish of women waiting for their men to return from the wars—those who did return. Miss de Mille's sincerely heartfelt theme had reached out and touched everyone; it was not jarring, but timeless. Producer Wilson, who had reluctantly but firmly sided with the anti group, admitted that he had been wrong; even the dynamic Harburg told her, "Goddamit! I've begun to like the dreary thing."

Arlen was happy with the success of the ballet, for it vindicated him in his mild conspiracy against his colleagues and proved him right in his belief in de Mille's work. Miss de Mille has retained a fondness for the *Bloomer Girl* score over the years and considers it one of the finest she has ever heard, and Arlen one of the important talents in the theater. "He has much better taste," she has observed, "than anyone else around him. But he must learn to stand up for his rights." The choreographer feels that much of Arlen's work, especially its most sensitive and original aspects, is often spoiled by contamination of those around him, who cheapen it by sacrificing the meaningful to the commercial.

The Philadelphia run proved to be quite triumphant, though other incidents besides those inspired by the "Civil War Ballet" kept the preopening jitters at a high pitch. Though Arlen had worked hard and long teaching Richard Huey "I Got a Song," the singer found the song's rhythms difficult to learn. This meant hours at the keyboard for the composer and hours of singing the same lines over and over again for Huey. At one dress rehearsal the night before the opening Huey simply walked off the stage without finishing the song. Arlen then decided perhaps they should write a new song for the spot, but Harburg refused; they had worked hard on the song and it must remain. Remain it did—and, the story takes a typical show-biz turn, for on opening night—and every night thereafter—Huey stopped the show with his singing of "I Got a Song."

Some word had come to New York about *Bloomer Girl* and its too sad war ballet that came too late in the evening, and that there were high-level quarrels going on: all very doubtful. But the reception in Philadelphia, and the three weeks there devoted to polishing completely reversed the rumors, and when the show came to New York the word had got around: *Bloomer Girl* was a hit. Even before it opened Arlen had the thrill of seeing a line, a mob rather, stretching from the Shubert Theater on Shubert Alley all the way to Eighth Avenue.

By then the critical reception was predictable and the raves were almost in chorus. There was a tendency to overemploy the critical crutch of comparison, so that *Bloomer Girl* and *Oklahoma!* invariably turned up in the reviews linked, as if there were a deeper relationship besides the fact that they were both costume musicals dealing in Americana. In retrospect there are no other valid points in common.

Even the major dissenter, Burton Rascoe, found good things to say about the songs. Rascoe's criticism took an unusual turn when he began attacking *Bloomer Girl* because he had found "pro-Roosevelt propaganda" cunningly dispensed in the book (there was an anti-Lincoln reference in which he is called "that man in the White House"). An unexpected rebuttal to Rascoe came from the critic on the *Worker*, who found that "by taking the cudgels for woman's rights and abolitionism, the musical captures the spirit of 1861."

According to Rascoe, *Bloomer Girl* was "probably the least entertaining musical in town." (Current musicals were *Carmen Jones*, *Follow the Girls*, *Mexican Hayride*, *Oklahoma!*, *One Touch of Venus*, and *Song of Norway*.) Rascoe's wrath even reached the point where he began scolding Arlen and Harburg for not using their songs properly. But when the end of the year came he picked, as one of the season's high spots in the theater, the singing of "I Got a Song" by Richard Huey, Dooley Wilson, and Hubert Dilworth.

Other reviewers working for less militantly anti-FDR papers than that of Rascoe concentrated their views on the show itself. Ward Morehouse, in the *Sun*, found that "Harold Arlen's score is probably his best job for Broadway to date. E. Y. Harburg has written some excellent lyrics and has done the staging of the production. Agnes de Mille has contributed an exciting and imaginative civil war ballet and

Lemuel Ayers, with the scenery and lighting, and Miles White, with the costumes, have excelled themselves." The only reservation Morehouse had was in the book, which he felt was "ambling, and a little more humor wouldn't hurt."

Louis Kronenberger, writing in *PM*, opened on a very bright note: "Not to scurry about for exotic phrases, *Bloomer Girl* is an unusually good musical. It will be a roaring hit, and sets a standard that the season's other musicals may have trouble living up to." The last word came with *Variety's* "Bloomer Latest Broadway Smash $20,000 in 1st 4 Shows."

After the opening the Arlens returned to Syracuse to visit the composer's parents. In October, Andre Kostelanetz broadcast on his regular radio hour a medley of songs from *Bloomer Girl*. Arlen was piped into New York briefly from Syracuse, played a few measures of "When the Boys Come Home," commenting that this song was his and Harburg's expression of the hopes of many whose sons and husbands were away at war. "Music," he said, "doesn't argue, discuss, or quarrel, it just breathes the air of freedom." Kostelanetz then presented a stirring rendition of "When the Boys Come Home" and other songs from the show, among them a beautifully sung "Right as the Rain" by Eileen Farrell.

The success of *Bloomer Girl*, Arlen feels, might be attributed in part to its wartime opening, "when people were hungry for theater—not like today." But more recent successes might be attributed to the timeless quality of the songs, dances, and the book. Revivals at New York's City Center in 1947 and at the St. Louis Municipal Opera in 1949, as well as tours and regular musical tent performances, prove it to be an enduring work. *Bloomer Girl* was one of the first musicals attempted by television (in April 1956). Unfortunately, in adapting the large-scaled musical for home viewing, a lot of the original was lost; too much was squeezed into an hour-and-a-half "spectacular." The singing of Barbara Cook was lovely for the songs, and the de Mille "Civil War Ballet" was effective on the television screen, though cramped. *Bloomer Girl* is a musical that will be heard frequently for a long time to come.

With the completion of *Bloomer Girl* the Harold Arlen-Yip Harburg collaboration went into a hiatus. They returned to Hollywood, where each worked with other collaborators for twelve years. Three years after *Bloomer Girl,* Harburg enjoyed another Broadway success with the fantasy *Finian's Rainbow,* with music by Burton Lane. In Hollywood he collaborated on a Deanna Durbin film, *Can't Help Singing,* with Jerome Kern. Another fantasy written with Sammy Fain, titled *Flahooley* (1951), proved to be one of the rare Harburg failures. But, typically Harburg, the lyricist refused to accept the failure of the show and has spent time repolishing it, confident that its values will eventually be recognized as had been those of *Finian's Rainbow* and *Bloomer Girl.* The determined Harburg has never stopped fighting what he calls "the hostility toward the creator" in the theater and films.

CHAPTER 7

This Time the Dream's on Me

When Harold Arlen returned to California in the winter of 1944, it was to take up again a collaboration with Johnny Mercer, begun some years before. The film they did after his return was an inconsequential bit of nothing titled *Out of This World*, a satire on the Sinatra bobby-soxer craze. The twist lay in using Bing Crosby's voice on the sound track while leading man Eddie Bracken mouthed the words. If nothing else, at least two good songs came out of the project, "Out of This World" and "June Comes Around Every Year."

Though they would produce some very memorable and lasting songs, Arlen and Mercer were not given strong material to work on. Their first collaboration came close. Early in 1941 they were assigned to a script titled *Hot Nocturne*. It purported to be a reasonably serious attempt at a treatment of jazz musicians, their aims, their problems—the tug-of-war between the "pure" and the "commercial"—and seemed a promising vehicle, for the two men shared a common interest in jazz.

Johnny Mercer practically grew up with the sound of jazz and the blues in his ears. He was born in Savannah, Georgia, in 1909. His father, George A. Mercer, was descended from an honored Southern family that could trace its ancestry back to one Hugh Mercer, who had emigrated from Scotland in 1747.

The lyricist's father was a lawyer who had branched out into real estate. His second wife, Lillian, was the mother of John H. Mercer. By the age of six young Johnny indicated that he had the call. One day he followed the Irish Jasper Greens, the town band, to a picnic and spent the entire day listening, while his family spent the day looking. The disappearance caused his family to assign a full-time maid to keeping an eye on the boy. But one afternoon Mrs. Mercer met her; both were obviously on the way to the Mercer home. The mother inquired, "Where's Johnny, and why did you leave him?" "There was nothing else I could do," the maid answered, satisfied with a rather vague explanation. But Mrs. Mercer demanded more. The maid then told her, "Because he fired me."

With her son evidencing so strong a musical bent his mother could do little else but get him started on the study of music—though she waited until he was ten—beginning with the piano and following that with the trumpet. Young Mercer showed a remarkable lack of aptitude for both instruments. Still, he did like music making and even sang in the chapel choir of the Woodberry Forest School, near Orange, Virginia, where he sounded fine but did not matriculate too well.

When he was fifteen John H. Mercer turned out his first song, a jazzy little thing he called "Sister Susie, Strut Your Stuff." If his scholarship and formal musicianship were not all they might have been, Mercer demonstrated at an early age that he was gifted with a remarkable ear for rhythm and dialect. From his playmates in Savannah, Mercer had picked up, along with a soft Southern dialect, traces also of the Gullah dialects of Africa. Such speech differences made him acutely aware of the richness and expressivness of language.

During the summers, while he was still in school, Mercer worked for his father's firm as a messenger boy. It generally took well into the autumn for the firm to recover from the summer's help. "We'd give him things to deliver, letters, checks, deeds and things like that," remembers his half-brother Walter, still in the real estate business in Savannah, "and learn days later that he'd absent-mindedly stuffed them into his pocket. There they stayed."

This rather detached attitude toward life's encumbrances has seemed to be the dominant trait in Mercer's personality ever since. It is, however, a disarming disguise, or perhaps a shield, for not only has Mercer proved himself to be one of the few great lyricists over the years, but also one who can function remarkably under pressure. He has also enjoyed a successful career as an entertainer (his records have sold in the millions) and is a sharp businessman.

He has also an extraordinary conscience. In 1927 his father's business collapsed, and, rather than go bankrupt, Mercer senior turned his firm over to a bank for liquidation. He died before he could completely pay off his debts. Some years later the bank handling the Mercer liquidation received a check for $300,000, enough to clear up the debt. The check had been mailed from Chicago, the envelope bore no return address, and the check was not signed.

"That's Johnny," sighed the bank president, "the best-hearted boy in the world, but absent-minded." But Mercer's explanation was simple: "I made out the check and carried it around a few days unsigned—in case I lost it." When he remembered that he might have not signed the check, Mercer made out another for the same amount, instructing the bank to destroy the other—especially if he had happened to have absent-mindedly signed both of them.

When the family business failed, Mercer left school and on his mother's urging—for she hoped that he would become an actor—he joined a local little theater group. When the troupe traveled to New York to participate in a one-act-play competition—and won—Mercer, instead of returning with the rest of the company in triumph, remained in New York. He had talked one other member of the group to stay with him, but that friend had tired of not eating regularly and returned to Savannah. But Mercer hung on, living, after a fashion, in a Greenwich Village fourth-flight walk-up. "The place had no sink or washbasin, only a bathtub," his mother discovered when she visited him. "Johnny insisted on cooking a chicken dinner in my honor—he's always been a good cook —and I'll never forget him cleaning the chicken in the tub."

A story, no doubt apocryphal, for Mercer himself denies it, has him sporting a monocle in those Village days. Though merely clear glass, it was a distinctive trade mark for an aspiring actor who hoped to imprint himself upon the memories of producers. One day in a bar, so the legend goes, someone put a beer stein with too much force on the monocle and broke it. The innocent malfeasant, filled with that supreme sense of honor found in bars, insisted upon replacing the destroyed monocle—and did, over the protests of the former owner—with a square monocle. Mercer is supposed to have refused it with, "Anyone who wears a square monocle must be affected!"

Everett Miller, then assistant director for the *Garrick Gaieties,* a Theatre Guild production, needed a lyricist for a song he had written; he just happened not to need any actor at the moment, however. For him Mercer produced the lyric to "Out of Breath Scared to Death of You," introduced in that most successful of all the *Gaieties,* by Sterling Holloway. This 1930 edition also had songs in it by Vernon Duke and Ira Gershwin, by E. Y. Harburg and Duke, and by Harry Myers. Entrance into such stellar song writing company encouraged the burgeoning song writer to take a wife, Elizabeth Meehan, a dancer in the *Gaieties.* The Mercers took up residence in Brooklyn, and Mercer found a regular job in Wall Street "misplacing stocks and bonds."

When he heard that Paul Whiteman was looking for singers to replace the Rhythm Boys, Mercer applied and got the job, "not for my voice, I'm sure, but because I could write songs and material generally." While with the Whiteman band Mercer met Jerry Arlen. He had yet to meet Harold Arlen, for although they had "collaborated" on "Satan's Li'l Lamb," Mercer and Harburg had worked from a lead sheet the composer had furnished them. The lyric, Mercer remembers, was tailored to fit the unusual melody.

Mercer's Whiteman association brought him into contact with Hoagy Carmichael, whose "Snowball" Mercer relyriced as "Lazybones," in which form it became a hit and marked the real beginning of Mercer's song-writing career. After leaving Whiteman, Mercer joined the Benny Goodman band as a vocalist. With the help of Ziggy Elman, also in the band, he transformed a traditional Jewish melody into a popular song, "And the Angels Sing." The countrywide success of "Lazybones" and "And the Angels Sing" could only lead to Hollywood, where, besides Harold Arlen, Mercer collaborated with Harry Warren, Jimmy Van Heusen, Richard Whiting, Walter Donaldson, Jerome Kern, and Arthur Schwartz. Mercer has also written both music and lyrics for several songs. He may be the only song writer ever to have collaborated with a secretary of the U. S. Treasury; he collaborated on a song with William Hartman Woodin, who was Secretary of the Treasury, 1932–33.

When Johnny Mercer and Harold Arlen began their collaboration in 1940, Mercer, like Arlen, had several substantial film songs to his credit, among them "Hooray for Hollywood," "Ride, Tenderfoot, Ride," "Have You Got Any Castles, Baby?", and "Too Marvelous for Words" (all with Richard Whiting); with Harry Warren he did "The Girl Friend of the Whirling Dervish," "Jeepers Creepers," and "You Must Have Been a Beautiful Baby." Mercer's lyrics are characterized by an unerring ear for rhythmic nuances, a puckish sense of humor expressed in language with a colloquial flair. Though versatile and capable of turning out a ballad lyric with the best of them, Mercer's forte is a highly polished quasi-folk wit.

His casual, dreamlike working methods, often as not *in absentia*, were an abrupt change from Harburg's, so that Arlen had to adjust again to another approach to collaboration. There were times that he worked with both lyricists simultaneously.

Speaking of his work with Johnny Mercer, Arlen says, "Our working habits were strange. After we got a script and the spots for the songs were blocked out, we'd get together for an hour or so every day. While Johnny made himself comfortable on the couch, I'd play the tunes for him. He has a wonderfully retentive memory. After I would finish playing the songs, he'd just go away without a comment. I wouldn't hear from him for a couple of weeks, then he'd come around with the completed lyric."

Arlen is one of the few (possibly the only) composer Mercer has been able to work with so closely, for they held their meetings in Arlen's study. "Some guys bothered me," Mercer has said. "I couldn't write with them in the same room with me, but I could with Harold. He is probably our most original composer; he often uses very odd rhythms, which makes it difficult, and challenging, for the lyric writer."

While Arlen and Mercer collaborated on *Hot Nocturne,* Mercer worked also with Arthur Schwartz on another film, *Navy Blues.* Arlen, too, worked on other projects at the same time with old friend Ted Koehler. Besides doing a single song, "When the Sun Comes Out," they worked on the ambitious *Americanegro Suite,* for voices and piano, as well as songs for films.

The *Americanegro Suite* is in a sense an extension of the Cotton Club songs in that it is a collection of Negro songs, not for a night club, but for the concert stage. The work had its beginning in 1938 with an eight-bar musical strain to which Koehler set the words "There'll be no more work/ There'll be no more worry," matching the spiritual feeling of the jot. This grew into the song "Big Time Comin'." By September 1940 the suite had developed into a collection of six songs, "four spirituals, a dream, and a lullaby."

The Negro composer Hall Johnson studied the *Americanegro Suite* and said of it, "Of all the many songs written by white composers and employing what claims to be a Negroid idiom in both words and music, these six songs by Harold Arlen and Ted Koehler easily stand far out above the rest. Thoroughly modern in treatment, they are at the same time, full of simple sincerity which invariably characterizes genuine Negro folk-music and are by no means to be confused with the average 'Broadway Spirituals' which depend for their racial flavor upon sundry allusions to the 'Amen Corner,' 'judgement day,' 'Gabriel's horn,' and a frustrated devil— with a few random 'Hallelujahs' thrown in for good measure.

Here are singable tunes wedded to sensible texts, resulting in six songs which all lovers of real Negro music will enjoy."

Ira Gershwin found that the "incantations . . . have not only character and atmosphere but also the flavor of authenticity. They make an eminently worthwhile contribution to American folk music . . ." Irving Berlin agreed with Gershwin, feeling that the writers had "made an important contribution to the catalogue of American Negro songs." Deems Taylor found the songs "while not imitative, evoke the charm of the Negro spiritual, preserving the directness, humor, and underlying sincerity of the folk-song, enhanced by individual touches that give them a special quality all their own."

Deeply affected by the *Americanegro Suite,* the composer of "Ol' Man River," Jerome Kern, added to the professional accolades by suggesting that Arlen and Koehler were to "be congratulated particularly for successfully avoiding the sham of pseudo-Negro spirituals . . . they are almost without exception genuine musical creations, not experiments in imitation."

On hearing Arlen perform some of the songs on the Kern piano, Kern quietly left the room, to return with a curiously carved walking stick. It had once belonged to Offenbach (Alexander Woollcott had given it to Kern); Kern presented it to Arlen for reasons Arlen has never been able completely to fathom. It was a touching gesture, and Arlen gratefully accepted it from the man he was finally calling "Jerry." Kern had once admired an Arlen-Koehler song and insisted that it must be published by his own firm within the Chappell organization. The song was the graceful "Sing My Heart," which was interpolated into the Irene Dunne-Charles Boyer film, *Love Affair.*

The longest song (although "song" is hardly the right word; possibly "sermon" would be more apt) in *Americanegro Suite* is "Reverend Johnson's Dream," under which title the complete suite was recorded by Decca Records in 1940 with the composer supervising. "Reverend Johnson's Dream" is an apocalyptic view of the world in 1940. . . .

". . . de devil's down here posin' lak a natch'l man
An' spreadin' evil all over de lan'
He's got your chillun fightin' and raisin' san'

❋   ❋   ❋

You better come down here Lawd!

The lullaby "Little Ace o' Spades," on the other hand, is brief, thirty-seven bars in all. Arlen's lovely melodic line is based mainly on the interval of the third, with which he simply and ingeniously suggests a rocking motion. The melody is ornamented with typical Arlen grace notes (also typical, of course, of much Negro singing), and the harmonies of the blues. The song is a beautiful and sensitive creation.

Of the four spirituals in the *Americanegro Suite* three are remarkably authentic though conventional evocations of the form, and one, "Where Is Dis Road A-leadin' Me to?," a major contribution to American song, folk, pop, or otherwise. It is an impassioned, affecting outcry of a sinner who feels she has lost her way, calling upon her God to lead her back home. Koehler's lyric is a masterpiece of parlando poetry; so is Arlen's melody—and more. The accompaniment is pure, and most the time quite simple, much as in Bartók's settings of Hungarian folk songs. But as in these settings the hand of a master composer adds a further dimension of conscious art.

The meter is restless, shifting from 2/2 to 4/4 to 2/2 to 2/4 to 3/4. In the song's sixty-six bars the tempo changes no fewer than ten times, reflecting with disturbing accuracy the troubled mind of the singer. The structure is completely asymmetric (as is speech), the form being determined by the emotions expressed in the lyric rather than by strict mathematical subdivision generally adhered to in song. There are twenty-two bars in the first part of the song, twenty-eight in the second, and sixteen in the third—this last being a return to the idea of the opening, though in variant form.

The melody itself, which Arlen indicated to be sung "Very Free," is melismatically emotional, rising from C to G flat and curving downward again, as the emotion is released, and resting on a sustained G—which, in the key of the song (C minor), is a "blue note." The long middle 2/4 section builds to a climax in a strongly rhythmic style. The lyric exclaims that the singer is traveling a road that isn't "righteous" (twice), then one that is not "easy" (twice), reaching its peak on the word "glory" when the accompanying chords turn dissonant, then resolve, for the emotion is spent, into a return to the resigned feeling of the opening theme.

Although the original Decca recording has long since disappeared into the limbo of commerce, soprano Eileen Farrell has made "Where Is Dis Road A-leadin' Me to?" a part of her repertoire, has sung it in recitals, and has recorded it. Miss Farrell, like many fine concert artists, has a high opinion of the song—and of Arlen "and his magnificent contribution to the music world." Her singing of the song is a moving musical experience, and she sings it gloriously, to the composer's taste, too, for her recording of it is one of his favorite records.

While he was collaborating with Koehler on the *Americanegro Suite*, Arlen was commissioned to write an instrumental work for Meredith Willson, who liked to introduce more or less "serious" compositions by popular song writers on his radio program. Willson, a composer himself of larger works, had approached, besides Arlen, composers Louis Alter, Peter De Rose, Vernon Duke, Duke Ellington, Morton Gould, Ferde Grofé, Sigmund Romberg, Dana Suesse, and Harry Warren with the same idea. Each was to choose his own form.

At the time the request from Willson came in, Anya Arlen had studied ballet with Michel Fokine and was regularly being asked to dance at parties they attended. So with his wife in mind Harold Arlen chose to do his piece in the form of a minuet. Titled *American Minuet*, the work of considerable grace and charm was broadcast on Willson's *Good News* program in December 1939. Like so many other examples of Arlen's many-sidedness, the *American Minuet* is not very well known. Though it added to his already-sizable professional reputation, it was not the kind of work that payed the rent.

So back to Warner Brothers and his work with Johnny Mercer on the impending *Hot Nocturne*. The producers had come up with a song spot that sounded interesting. The scene was a jail into which the hero and his friends have been tossed. In a nearby cell a Negro sings out his blues in just the style the jailed musicians hope someday to play. Because the singer who would present the song was William Gillespie, a discovery of Arlen's friend Bob Wachsman, now also settled in California, Arlen was anxious to come up with something worthy of the fine voice, something musically strong.

Locking himself into his study (a converted garage, away from the house, filled with his books, and housing his piano) Arlen analyzed recordings of authentic blues and experimented with original ideas, discarding them if he felt they were not just right. Arlen has a passion for what he calls "the authentic ring," for writing in his own style and yet in keeping with the song's idiomatic setting.

The traditional blues is built on twelve-bar phrases, has a definite scale structure, and a harmony characterized by the so called "blue note," all of which Arlen was aware (and had in fact employed for years instinctively). Because he wanted the jail blues to reflect the authentic folk blues he adapted the folk form's twelve-bar pattern. After two days at it Arlen emerged from his study confident that he had found the right melody; as was customary he played it first for Anya. He then played it for Mercer, who began inventing lyrical ideas, so many in fact that he had covered four pages with notations. In shuffling through them Arlen admired Mercer's work, suggested only one change—that a line appearing on the fourth page be placed at the beginning of the song. The line was "My mamma done tol' me . . ." and the song was, of course, "Blues in the Night." It proved impressive enough to give a new title to the film too; *Hot Nocturne* became *Blues in the Night*.

Like "Get Happy," "Stormy Weather," and "Over the Rain-

bow," "Blues in the Night" was an overnight hit, an unexpected developement that did a generally undistinguished
film a great deal of good. With the song's popularity preceding
the release of the film, an artificial interest was generated
that helped attendance. Jimmy Lunceford, whose band appeared in *Blues in the Night,* scooped the record market, in
1940 just coming back into its own, with a double-sided
instrumental version of the title song. Devoting both sides to
a single song was an innovation, but the record became an
instantaneous best-seller. For reasons known only to Lunceford
he had resisted recording the song for a while. Once he had,
he had nothing to regret, however.

If not a glittering story, *Blues in the Night* did have an
outstanding cast. Richard Whorf portrayed the jazz pianist-
composer who was torn between the True Jazz and "Commercial" music; in human symbols the good girl (Priscilla Lane)
and the bad girl (Betty Field). Elia Kazan, now a brilliant
director, appeared as an ardent jazz fan tolerated by
the jazz musicians. He even joined in on one of the songs,
"Hang Onto Your Lids, Kids." Priscilla Lane sang an Arlen
melody of unusual contour, "This Time the Dream's on Me."
For the commerical band, the antithesis of the dedicated
jazz band, the novelty "Says Who, Says You, Says I!" was
devised supposedly as an illustration of the silly type of song
such a band would feature. On its own it is a delightful
song and for a time was quite popular.

Unfortunately *Blues in the Night* did not turn out to be
the documentary-like study of jazz music and musicians that
Arlen, Mercer, and no doubt others connected with it had
hoped. After the early reels it lost its power: its most compel-
ling scene was the singing of "Blues in the Night" and remains
an exciting experience in television reruns. The story disinte-
grated into the usual gangster-musician, good *vs.* evil, melo-
dramatic-cliché conclusion. For all its weakness as a film
Blues in the Night did begin a series of other jazz-oriented,
pseudo-historical films: *Birth of the Blues* (with Bing Crosby
and Mary Martin), *Syncopation* (with Jackie Cooper and

Bonita Granville), and *Stormy Weather* (with Lena Horne, Ethel Waters, Fats Waller, and others). But, like the prototype, they failed to achieve their high aims.

Jerome Kern greatly admired "Blues in the Night." He strongly felt that it should have won the Academy Award, but it so happened that Kern, not Arlen, received it instead. "The Last Time I Saw Paris" was written by Oscar Hammerstein in commemoration of the fall of Paris to the Germans in 1940. He read the words to Kern, who composed a melody for it. The song was then interpolated into the film musical *Lady Be Good*, for obvious reasons of timeliness and its excellence as a song. When Kern heard that the song had received the Academy Award, winning over Arlen's "Blues in the Night," he immediately began working at getting the Academy's bylaws changed so that only songs specifically written for the screen were eligible for the Academy Award; this has been the rule since 1941.

On completing the Warners' assignment Arlen and Mercer moved to Paramount; they practically tossed off a title song for a film glorifying the Royal Canadian Air Force, *Captains of the Clouds*. "We sang the song for some Canadians," Mercer relates in a typical laconic manner. "They liked it."

The movie industry, by early 1942, was geared for war. Service films were ground out regularly, and musicals took another turn toward the all-star picture into which went, as in the early days, everyone on the lot. Films with such titles as *Johnny Doughboy*, *Private Buckaroo*, *True to the Army*, and *The Fleet's In* were released in 1942. The last had some good songs in it, music by Victor Schertzinger and lyrics by Johnny Mercer: "I Remember You" and "Arthur Murray Taught Me Dancing in a Hurry."

Paramount's biggest all-star musical was *Star Spangled Rhythm*, for which Arlen and Mercer had been signed to do the score. Such stars as Bing Crosby, Bob Hope, Victor Moore, Betty Hutton, Dick Powell, Mary Martin, Franchot Tone, Paulette Goddard, and dozens of others, many "as themselves," even Cecil B. De Mille, appeared in it. One of the massive

production numbers was to be staged around a dance by Vera
Zorina for which Arlen devised an unusual melody, "That Old
Black Magic."

"I played the melody for John. He went away." Then
Mercer returned with the lyric that Arlen feels is greatly
responsible for the success of the song. "The words sustain
your interest, make sense, contain memorable phrases, and tell
a story. Without the lyric the song would be just another long
song."

Their next job was a less impressive one for RKO. Its story
was simple, something about a Flying Tiger pilot on leave,
but fortunately for Arlen and Mercer the pilot was charmingly
portrayed by Fred Astaire. Though Astaire spent most the
film in civilian clothes, it was considered politic at the time
to have the hero a serviceman, even if not in uniform. The
Astaire film was *The Sky's the Limit,* a level the picture
itself reached only occasionally.

Fred Astaire remembers a curious though characteristic reception of two of the songs. "The funny thing about these
two songs was that while the picture was in operation neither
of them registered as an immediate hit, but several months
later 'My Shining Hour' became the number-one song of its
day and 'One for My Baby' has become a standard classic
popular song and one of the best pieces of material that
was written especially for me."

In an otherwise-unstimulating film the "One for My Baby"
sequence, staged and choreographed by Astaire, was one of
the year's film highlights. The song Arlen half jokingly refers
to as "another typical Arlen tapeworm." (A "tapeworm" in
trade jargon is any song exceeding the conventional thirty-
two-bar length.) He considers it "a wandering song. Johnny
took it and wrote it exactly the way it fell. Not only is it
long—forty-eight bars—but it also changes key. Johnny made
it work. I don't care what you give him, he'll find a way to
save it, to help you."

As with "That Old Black Magic," "One for My Baby" is
set with a narrative lyric. The story and interest are sustained

by Mercer throughout the long telling and, though Arlen self-effacingly (and sincerely) tends to ascribe the song's popularity to the lyricist, the melody is in fact musically inevitable, rhythmically insistent, and in that mood of metropolitan "melancholy beauty" that writer John O'Hara finds in all of Arlen's music.

One of the songs written for *The Sky's the Limit* was a production casualty. It is a document of the times, and a typical Mercer lyric deserving preservation. The title, "Hangin' On to You":

> No more stuff 'n' things
> Trouser cuff 'n' things
> No more aluminum
> Cause Uncle Sam's consumin' "um"
> No more tires t' own
> Goodyear—Firestone
> Sugar's a rarity
> They've even cut down parity
>
> Bituminous—that made our fireside luminous—is gone
> By the way—if anyone has chromium—show me "um"
>
> Take my silk away
> Grade "A" milk away
> But if I lose the whole shebang
> I'm hangin' on to you
>
> No more beef in sight
> No relief in sight
> It's most disquieting
> But you could use some dieting.
> Turn that metal in
> Throw that kettle in
> As for vanadium
> It's scarcer now than radium
>
> Priorities—according to authorities—are through
> So you see—we'll soon be living drastic'lly—plastic'lly
>
> Take my meals away
> Rubber heels away
> But if I lose the whole shebang
> I'm hangin' on to you.

The Arlens soon experienced some shortages of their own, that might easily have resulted in tragedy had they not done some hanging on to one another. As Arlen tells it: "We had been to Palm Springs over the weekend; we came back, went to bed. Everything was quiet. Then about one o'clock, half-asleep, half-awake, I saw what looked to me like the glare of the garden lights. I got up and was about to turn them out. Then I smelled smoke—could feel the heat from the floor. It was a fire. I awakened Annie and told her. As a rule, she wasn't one to awaken easily—only after two cups of coffee. But she got what I had told her, with her eyes wide open and her mind capable of taking it all in with amazing speed. I was about to go downstairs. She lunged at me and cried, 'Don't open the door!,' then pushed me toward the window, and said, 'Follow me.' We were both barefooted; as luck would have it our next-door neighbor had run over and was directly beneath the window, and broke Annie's fall when she dropped. I fell into a rosebush—without a scratch. The first thing we did was to run around the garden to get the dogs, 'Pan' and 'Storm,' out. Then I rushed into the house, Annie screamed 'Where are you going?' I managed to save George's painting of Kern. Then we went next door to phone the fire department, only a quarter of a mile away from us, but they couldn't come because we were in Los Angeles County, though our address was Beverly Hills. By the time the firemen came from over the canyon, the main part of the house, the living room and the little den, was gutted. In they went at it as if they needed some Freudian release, to chop up everything there was in order to put out the fire.

"We lost all our paintings in that part of the house, furniture, the piano, some books—fortunately most of them were in my big study, which wasn't touched.

"After this horror was over we decided to redo the house and went all the way and built a pool which Anya designed. There were two charming bath houses and a small bar. We learned that the fire had been caused by a short in the radio in the small den."

For their next pair of films Arlen and Mercer switched again, back this time to Paramount to do a score for Bing Crosby and Betty Hutton. Still wartime, *Here Come the Waves* was another service film with Crosby and Sonny Tufts as sailors and Betty Hutton cast as twins, both Waves, one a demure type and the other "a jive-happy chick," whom the sailors love but must properly identify and assort before the final reel.

For *Here Come the Waves* the song writers produced at least three excellent songs, the sensitive but neglected (now—it was popular for a while in 1945) "I Promise You," the kind of a song Arlen would refer to as "pure and simple," though once again he managed to keep it from falling into the conventional thirty-two-bar structure. It has a hauntingly beautiful melody, with a lyric to match. The same may be said for "Let's Take the Long Way Home."

Work on *Here Come the Waves* had reached the point where inventing just one more song seemed a major impossibility. Arlen was tired of it and showed it; Mercer, as always, was inscrutable. Lyricist-pixie though he may be while working, Mercer generally presents a rather dour poker face.

Deciding to freshen their views by taking a drive, the song writers continued discussing their work in terms of bleak discouragement, when Mercer suddenly asked, "How does that little thing go, I've heard you humming—the spiritual?" Arlen complied though it was difficult to be cheerful. Mercer brightened with, "You've got to accentuate the positive . . ." The phrase fitted the music, and Arlen sang it back to Mercer (Arlen frequently will take a conversational phrase and sing it back to you, as if even the most ordinary speech might inspire music).

By the time they had finished their drive, they had the song pretty much complete and, as Arlen now tells it, "It must have really pleased John; it was the first time I ever saw him smile."

He was pleased, too, with the royalty statements, for "Ac-

Cent-Tchu-Ate the Positive" was a difficult song to avoid during the early months of 1945. "That Old Black Magic" was interpolated into *Here Come the Waves,* as an amusing commentary on the then current Frank Sinatra craze.

The joke went over well enough to become the *raison d'être* of their next film, *Out of This World.* Howard Barnes, of the New York *Tribune,* found nothing of value in the film but the songs. "Otherwise," he observed with telling perception, "it might better have stayed where the title would suggest."

The film's reception did not concern Arlen and Mercer; they were already at work on their next project, a musical for Broadway. Edward Gross, the producer, had come across a book by Arna Bontemps and poet Countee Cullen based on the former's novel, *God Sends Sunday.* Now titled *St. Louis Woman,* the play, Gross felt, would be transformed into a most colorful musical. He was able to get Arthur Freed and Samuel Katz to back it, and it was hoped that Lena Horne, then appearing in M-G-M films, would be the star.

Gross took the idea to Arlen and Mercer and met with some resistance from the lyricist, who didn't care for the book, though he was eventually talked into it. "I wasn't really keen about it, but I'm always doing jobs I don't want to do."

Still, working with Harold Arlen on a full-scale Broadway show, with a book, whatever he thought of it, by such distinguished writers as Bontemps and Cullen, held promise— and a lot can happen during rehearsal. Lena Horne, however, withdrew, not wishing to appear as the flashy lady of easy virtue. But Lemuel Ayers was signed to direct, as well as to design the sets and costumes. *St. Louis Woman,* while not foolproof, was not without promise.

The late summer and autumn of 1945 were devoted to work on the new musical. One of its best songs came out of a single evening's work in October. Mercer had come over to the Arlens' and had remained in the study while Arlen went into the living room and "toyed around with an idea, then came down and played it for him."

Mercer liked the tune, even came up with a fitting opening line, "I'm gonna love you, like nobody's loved you," after which he paused for a moment. Into the brief silence Arlen jokingly injected, "Come hell or high water . . ." To which Mercer reacted with, "Of course, why didn't I think of that— 'Come rain or come shine.'" Before Mercer went home that night they had the song complete. Interestingly, "Come Rain or Come Shine," while it does not employ the usual introductory verse, just happens to fall into a thirty-two-bar form. But it does begin in one key and end in another.

The death of Countee Cullen before rehearsals began was the first stroke of bad luck to afflict *St. Louis Woman*. The usual "out-of-town" problems arose: there were replacements; choreographer Antony Tudor left and Hollywood dance director Charles Walters came in; rewrites, songs dropped, new ones written. Even so seasoned a director as Rouben Mamoulian—who was called during the out-of-town run (he had staged *Porgy and Bess, Oklahoma!* and *Carousel*)—even he could not pull the disparate book together. *St. Louis Woman* was a not very cohesive musical comedy that might have been an opera. The first act's high jinks were all but neutralized by the last scene of the second act, set in a funeral parlor. Though the third act provided the traditional happy conclusion, the pervasive gloom infected the entire evening; it was as if an unremitting duality of purpose prevented the musical from being all of a piece. Labeling *St. Louis Woman* a musical play was more accurate than describing it as a musical comedy, but the latter was expected and the audience was treated to both.

Although *St. Louis Woman* was excellently cast, there was not one "name" in it that might have carried the show long enough to overcome the handicap of the book and to further the chances of the show's values to be recognized. Pearl Bailey stopped the show with two songs, "Legalize My Name" and "A Woman's Prerogative"; the Nicholas Brothers—who had danced to Arlen music at the Cotton Club—proved to be fine dancers, but vocally they were not much more than pleasant (Harold Nicholas appeared in the leading male role of Little

Augie, the superstitious jockey). To June Hawkins, a graduate
of the University of Minnesota and a former teacher, fell
three of the score's outstanding songs, "I Had Myself a True
Love," "Sleep Peaceful, Mr. Used-to-Be," and the eventually
deleted, "I Wonder What Became of Me?" Leading lady Ruby
Hill was discovered by accident in the studio of vocal coach
Al Siegel by producer Gross, who arranged for her to travel
to California to audition for Arlen and Mercer, who found
her good. Yet despite the fine voices and superior talents
St. Louis Woman was not well received.

Ironically, *St. Louis Woman* has, with time, become hailed
as the Arlen-Mercer masterpiece. Several of its songs have
become enduringly popular, and many of its initially undis-
covered beauties have come to be greatly admired by musicians, composers, show people, as well as discerning collectors
of fine songs. Its original cast album released by Capitol Records, out of print, brings a stiff price in collectors' shops.
Divorced from its book, *St. Louis Woman* has outlived its
original receptions.

Even so sensitive a critic as Louis Kronenberger, writing in
PM, revealed a blind spot, typical of drama critics, when
he stated: "First-rate music might have yet turned the tide,
but Harold Arlen's songs and orchestral tags are second-rate
even for him. They are most of them romantic and atmospheric
enough, but they lack distinction, they lack melodic urgency,
they lack excitement and cohesive power that folk drama
demands. It is an agreeable score, but nothing more than
that."

Mr. Kronenberger does not define the "cohesive power that
folk drama demands," nor, for that matter, does he bother to
explain just why it demands it. Granted, he may have had
something definite in mind, but when he found the songs
lacking in melodic urgency he may not have been in the
theater when "Come Rain or Come Shine," "I Had Myself
a True Love," "I Wonder What Became of Me?" (it was
sung opening night), among others, were sung; perhaps, like

so many drama critics, he lacked the ability to recognize a distinctive melody when he heard one.

On the other hand, Rosamond Gilder of *Theatre Arts* offered an opinion that time has proved more accurate: ". . . though the Arna Bontemps' and Countee Cullen's book occasionally overweighs Harold Arlen's score and though some of Rouben Mamoulian's directorial gambits have become stereotyped, the show is full of gusto and vigor." Miss Gilder erred only in her prediction that *St. Louis Woman* "bids fair to remain for some time," for the show closed after a short run of 113 performances.

A drama critic is expected to judge all elements of a show, not merely its score; how he is able to do all this and still meet his journalistic deadline is a strange mystery, to say the least. That a drama critic might slight or misjudge one of the several elements while he is attempting to appraise the whole is understandable. But a drama critic rarely admits that he blithely attempts what even a trained musician finds difficult, if not impossible: judging music on a single hearing.

This means that some twenty songs may be flung at the critic in the course of the evening, a couple of songs perhaps twice, but mostly only once. Unless the songs have been widely played before the opening (which rarely happens), all will be completely new to the critic. He must be blessed with a unique musical sensitivity and intelligence to grasp all the material on a single hearing, let alone disassociate it from all the other proceedings. If a song happens to be particularly subtle, its effect must be completely lost on the critic contending with a typical first-night audience—not to mention a first-night cast, on edge. All he can actually bring away from the theater, if he would be honest enough to admit it, is a general impression: Did he like it or didn't he? The songs . . . ? Well, he did check a couple he liked, but did he recall any others? No (but then he didn't recall any of *Don Giovanni* either the first time he saw it). But the critic rushes off, in a flurry of importance, tosses off an opinion—and the work of several people—in a few moments' typing. Critics are, perhaps, useful, but their methods are dishonest when applied to musicals. The classic case of arrested appreciation is, of course, *Porgy and Bess*. A decade went by before its full importance came to be recognized, even by critics who came to reverse their original judgment of it.

How can any critic "get" "I Had Myself a True Love" from a single hearing? Does he recognize its sensitively beautiful melodic line, its harmonic richness, its unique structure, its poetic imagery, at once homely and lyrical, its effectiveness as a song? These are qualities that only study or, most usually, time will recognize.

Johnny Mercer's lyrics for *St. Louis Woman* are a rare achievement. Though he has written popular and brilliant lyrics before and after it, his work on this one show would be enough to assure him a niche alongside the few master lyricists. Some of his lines are disarmingly conversational and yet composed with a delicate craftsmanship, as, for example, from one of the Pearl Bailey songs:

> I don't know who it was wrote it,
> Or by whose pen it was signed.
> Someone once said and I quote it:
> "It's a woman's prerogative to change her mind."

> Or: Love words,
> Sweet talk
> You an' me talk—
> You say just a glimpse of my allure
> Is a glimpse of paradise, I can be sure
> Brother, if you wanna take the dollar tour
> Legalize my name
> Sparkin'
> Spoonin'
> Honeymoonin'
> That's the kind of talk I get from you
> And you often say you wish the whole world knew,
> Just a pair of witnesses and a judge'll do
> Legalize my name.

The range, from earthy humor to a searching lament on a wasted life, may be illustrated by Mercer's lines:

Lights are bright,
Pianos making music all the night—
And they pour champagne just like it was rain
It's a sight to see,
But I wonder what became of me?
Crowds go by,
That merry making laughter in their eye—
And the laughter's fine,
But I wonder what became of mine?
Life's sweet as honey
And yet it's funny,
I get a feeling that I can't analyze,
It's like,
Well, maybe,
Like when a baby
Sees a bubble burst before its eyes.
Oh, I've had my thrills,
They've lit my cigarettes with dollar bills,
But I can't be gay, for along the way—
Something went astray
And I can't explain,
It's the same champagne,
It's a sight to see
But I wonder what became of me?

Arlen's melody for this song is a haunting evocation of questioning sadness; the musical accompaniment employs a grace note piquantly to underscore the bitter, tremulous emotion of the singer. That the musical theater had reached, musically and lyrically at least, the level of art that spring of 1946 was not noted; by the winter *St. Louis Woman* departed the Broadway scene. It's songs, however, continue to live.

There was little else for Arlen and Mercer to do but return to California; Mercer boarded a train and was on his way. The Arlens decided to visit his parents and other relatives. They even paid Buffalo a visit. With his cousin, Mrs. Earl Crane, escorting them the Arlens visited the Pine Street *shul*, where Arlen's father had served as cantor before moving to Syracuse. As the group was about to enter the temple, Arlen recognized the *shamus* (sexton) he had known as a boy; the old man was seated on the steps taking the sun. Telling Mrs. Arlen and Mrs. Crane to go into the building, Arlen stopped to talk with the sexton.

"Hello," he began, speaking in Yiddish.

The old man studied Arlen for a moment, then asked, "You Cantor Arluck's son?"

Arlen nodded.

"And the girl—your wife?

Arlen assented again. The sexton, thinking, began taking snuff. "Hmmm," he said thoughtfully, then asked, "Got any children?"

"No," Arlen told him.

"Then," said the sexton with Old World finality, "what good are you?"

Chuckling, Arlen entered the old *shul* to continue their pleasant Buffalo visit. Anya Arlen found the large family warm, one in which she could feel completely at home and at ease. In Syracuse they had visited, besides the composer's parents, the Asher Marksons, his friend Mannie Manheim, and the Earl Cranes in musical evenings spent singing around the piano, before entraining for Beverly Hills.

Hollywood was, in 1946, in a postwar jitters; unemployment was widespread and cuts were expected to be taken by everyone. Arlen decided that, rather than lower his fee, he would take time out to rest. This decision kept him from working for two years in films.

Mercer had managed to begin work on a new musical before the panic set in. He was working with Harry Warren on the Judy Garland film, *The Harvey Girls*. They met in a little cottage on the M-G-M lot where they worked on the songs. One day Warren entered to find Mercer apparently preoccupied, starring into space, no doubt contemplating couplets. Warren greeted the lyricist with, "Hi, Johnny. How are Ginger and the kids?" Mercer didn't answer but continued to commune with his muse. Warren left, went to the studio commissary, had lunch, talked with friends for a while, then returned to the cottage, found Mercer still there. As he came in, Mercer looked up, brightened, and said, "They're fine thanks."

Arlen's favorite Mercer story has the lyricist taking a walk and meeting a friend who greets him with, "Hello, Johnny— where you going?"

"I don't know," replied the candid Mercer.

CHAPTER 8

It's a New World

Ira Gershwin, writing to an Army friend early in the war year 1943, brings him up to date on the news of Hollywood at the time. There are references to the OPA and the Lunch Time Follies (which furnished entertainment for workers in shipyards and aircraft factories), and to current films, as well as more personal news: "Played golf today with two boys whose work probably interests you—Harold Arlen and Harry Warren. The three of us may be fine song writers but we were certainly lousy golfers today. Golf is a great luxury these days of gas rationing but by pooling we manage to get in a game now and then."

Arlen was getting in more than a game now and then. During one of their games Gershwin rather wistfully mentioned to Warren, "Harold beat me for a hundred today."

"Why not," Warren asserted, "he goes over to Hillcrest every morning for a lesson!"

"Don't say that about Harold," Gershwin protested. "He's a nice fellow."

Gershwin had actually introduced Arlen to the game some years before. Ray Bolger and Gershwin golfed; Arlen went along for the walk. "I walked around with them with a club in my hand. I thought it was pretty ridiculous." But then he got the bug. The art and science of the game fascinated him. He joined Hillcrest Country Club and studied with its pros, George Fazio, Eric Monte, Olin Dutra, and Stanley Kertes. He worked out with other professionals also, among them Lloyd Mangrum, Jimmie Thompson, and Jimmy Demaret; he discussed golf with Ben Hogan and Byron Nelson. In the morning

Arlen could be found at Hillcrest for his lesson, then he would get a bucket of balls to practice his swing, after which he'd join Warren and Gershwin at the California Country Club for thirty-six holes; and he'd read himself to sleep with a book on golf. At the same time he had managed to work on the scores of *Blues in the Night, Rio Rita, Star Spangled Rhythm, Cabin in the Sky, The Sky's the Limit,* and others.

While her husband was completely immersed in his game and work, Anya Arlen—a golf widow—tended her garden and, as she recently observed, "took care of the white house." As Arlen dug up the turf at Hillcrest, Anya planted the flower beds, even laid the brick walk and painted it, in their beautiful back-yard garden. During the war the Arlens converted it into a victory garden.

Harry Warren recalls one of their games, during which the regular trio of Gershwin, Arlen, and he were joined by a stranger. Warren made the proper introductions: "Mr. Arlen, Mr. Gershwin—and I'm Mr. Warren." The stranger acknowledged the introductions but seemed most interested in Gershwin, whom he finally addressed, in an overture to conversation, with "What do you do, Mr. Goodman?"

Gershwin generally played with a cigar in his mouth, but it was Jerome Kern who contributed the most bizarre touch to the games. The song writers had formed a "Pitch 'n' Putt" society and it fell to Kern to whip up highly individual costumes and yet manage not be barred from the links. His specialty was impossible hats; Arlen's was freakish shoes. The golfing mania had afflicted Kern too, for after Arlen had picked him up in the car they would, on the way to the golf course, stop a milkman to buy a quart or two to go with the lunches they brought with them.

At Hillcrest they would join the group at the Roundtable, comprised of Groucho and Harpo Marx, Jack Benny, George Burns, George Jessel, and the Dannys, Kaye and Thomas. The Roundtable was more devoted to whooping it up than to playing golf. For six years Arlen was an almost daily golfer.

"The game consumed me," he has said. "I wasn't a fine golfer, but when I took my practice swing I looked like a pro."

One of his golfing companions was boxer Joe Louis, whom Arlen describes as "a man of very few words, but when he says something, it's really nailed down." One day Arlen noted that Louis appeared to be distracted. "What's the matter, Joe?" he inquired. The reply, complete, was simply: "Gal trouble." When they got together again a couple of days later Arlen noted that Louis was no longer troubled and mentioned it. "Joe, you look fine today." "No more gal trouble," was Louis's last word on the subject.

Another golfer was Lou Clayton, of the famed Clayton, Jackson, and Durante comedy trio. "I used to play with Lou Clayton quite often," Arlen will tell you as he recalls their classic encounter on the links. "He was as colorful off the golf course as he was on. I don't believe that anyone, to my memory, loved the game as much as he. Joe Louis, Lou Clayton, and I played many times and we'd play a 'five-dollar Nassau' (there's no need to try to explain that—most golfers will understand, if they care to read about a 'hackers' life), which meant if you lost all ways you would stand to lose only twenty dollars.

"One day Lou, who loved to bet, was about a six or seven handicap, while I at the time was a seventeen—which meant I usually got six strokes aside from him. But this day he had a strange notion that he'd like to play me even, which, to me, seemed ridiculous. But when he said, 'Beulah'—I was called that by all the boys because I couldn't hit the ball very far—'Beulah, I'll play you even, but I'll lay you five hundred to fifty,' I accepted, not because I thought I could win, but because the odds made it terribly exciting. (As every hacker knows, the ego in golf is unmatched by the ego in any other human pursuit.)

"I agreed and we teed off. Let me just add that when he was in front, Lou was a warm and wonderful companion, but this day I only saw him on the tees and the putting greens. He was one of the finest short-iron players and putters I've ever seen for a non-professional. But because I was shooting over my head, and for the first time in my golfing career shot an eighty-three, he was shanking and three-putting most of the way. Of course, you've guessed, I won. And may I add a footnote: he payed me off—in cash—as we went to the locker room. Of Clayton it was said he never banked his money, but carried it with him.

"There are very few golf enthusiasts like him around today and I, for one, miss him greatly not because of this strange match we had, but of the other many wonderful days we had together."

Harry Warren was not only Arlen's golf companion, but an old-time friend and neighbor. Consequently the Warrens and the Arlens spent much time together. One evening—it happened to be Oscar night—the composers decided not to gather with the waiting ones. Instead they chose to drive to Palm Springs to visit the E. H. Morrises. On the drive from Beverly Hills they kept the car radio tuned into the coverage of the dispensation of that year's Oscars. Arlen was surprised at Warren's lack of concern, despite the fact that one of his songs was up for an award, which, if he won it, would be his third. By the time they had arrived in Palm Springs his song, "On the Atchison, Topeka and Santa Fe" (lyrics by Johnny Mercer), had been chosen the best film song of the year. Still unruffled, Warren remained silent until the foursome had arrived at the Morris door, when he said to Arlen with mock dignity, "Walk two Oscars behind me."

E. H. "Buddy" Morris is one of the rare music publishers: not only does he understand business, he also knows something about music. He has known Arlen since the spring of 1929, when he handled the contract signing that made Arlen a full-fledged professional composer. By the time he was twenty-three Morris was head of the Warner Brothers division of Music Publishers Holding Corporation. After several years of working for others Morris decided in 1939 to form "Mercer and Morris" with Johnny Mercer. Unfortunately for Mercer, however, owning an independent publishing company not directly affiliated with a film studio practically assured him of no work with the studios. In 1941 Morris formed his own publishing company; he also began legal proceedings that helped end the virtual monopoly of the studio publishing combine.

Beginning with the songs for *The Sky's the Limit*, E. H. Morris & Company, Inc., began to publish Arlen's songs, though, of course, Feist published the M-G-M songs, Remicks the Warner Brothers songs. In April 1948 Arlen and Morris formed Harwin Music Corporation to publish Arlen's music. Ever since, beginning with the songs written for the film *Casbah*, Arlen's songs have been published by his own company.

While this may not make him a wealthy man, Arlen can be certain that his songs will be published as he conceives them, without editorial "fixing." He has some control of his work and a good idea of its popularity and, thus, value. He once learned, after two decades, that one publisher had neglected to report all foreign royalties on Arlen songs; this could no longer occur. Arlen has the benefit, not only of Morris's business sense, but also of his friendship.

"Belief in a writer is most important," Morris has said. "Anybody can walk in off the street and give you a hit. That doesn't make him a great song writer. Harold has always been a long-pull composer who expresses himself honestly—his songs last and are, ultimately, more valuable, even financially, than the off-the-street hit."

The youthful publisher longingly looks back to his earlier days in publishing when such composers as Gershwin, Rodgers, Schwartz wrote because they had to, because it was fun. "Today when a young composer shows up, he doesn't bring his music—he brings his lawyer."

The music business has changed a great deal since Harold Arlen broke into it, and Buddy Morris was a twenty-year-old executive. Today it is based, not on the sale of sheet music, but on the phonograph record. The term "publisher" hardly applies any more, for though songs continue to be published the publisher could hardly remain in business if he had to depend on the sale of sheet music. The publisher is, it might be remembered, primarily engaged in business and not the underwriting of art. He may give away more copies of a song than he sells. These "professional copies," printed on plain, undecorated black and white paper (as differentiated from the colorful commercial copies) are distributed to singers, band leaders, record company A&R (Artist & Repertory) men, and anyone who might be able to assist in getting performances of the song, from which record royalties and ASCAP performance credits might accrue. These are the major sources of a publisher's income today, not the average popular-song devotee who has a piano in his home.

The publisher remains in business, in the main, by virtue of his income from "mechanical rights" (phonograph records), "synchronization rights" (to motion pictures), and the income from radio and television, which lies in the province of the American Society of Composers, Authors and Publishers. By monitoring the networks and the smaller independent stations as well, ASCAP charges a fee based upon a sampling of the musical fare the network or station may use. ASCAP licenses well over a million individual works so that there is rarely a minute in the day when some ASCAP music is not being broadcast. The frequency of performance of a composer's work—which is, at the same time, a publisher's work—determines the amount that composer and publisher will receive when ASCAP's annual dividend is sent out. Because Harold Arlen has written many "standards" (songs that remain active for years) and is regularly performed and recorded, he is a valuable catalogue composer for any publisher—including himself.

Arlen's work is actually spread over the catalogues of various publishers, for one reason or another. Some of the early songs now belong to Music Publishers Holding Corporation, which bought out Piantadosi; MPH also controls these songs written for the Warner Brothers films. Mills Music published the Cotton Club songs because of a business agreement between Mills

and the Cotton Club. Mills was responsible for bringing Duke
Ellington and Cab Calloway into the Cotton Club.

Sometimes a "divided contract" makes for complications.
The songs for *A Star Is Born*, for example, are published by
Harwin. The lyrics are by Ira Gershwin, who has, ever since
he began writing around 1918, had all his work published by
Max Dreyfus of Chappell's. When two publishers are involved,
the songs are generally published by the composer's publisher,
"by arrangement." The divided contract arrangement is usually
a financial one.

The music publisher is not noted for his generosity, or
even to the furtherance of culture. Like any other businessman
he cannot remain in business unless his product sells. He deals
in intangibles and he watches his pennies. He cannot keep an
ear, even with the help of ASCAP, on every consumer of his
product.

It has even been breathed through the airless though tune-
filled halls of the Brill Building (the modern equivalent to
Tin Pan Alley) that publishers (not all, but some) even cheat
composers. (Perish the thought!) The publisher and the composer operate on different levels: the one creates, the other
markets. Though neither could exist without the other, each in
turn may feel that his own contribution to the operation is the
more important.

There are some song writers who are merely marketers themselves, but they hardly belong in the same category with Arlen—
or the Gershwins, Rodgers, Kern, Youmans, Berlin, and men
of their stature. The songs of the true creators are generally
more difficult to "sell" in the popular sense. Their work does
not produce (there are exceptions) the overnight smash hit,
selling millions of records and even several thousands in sheet
music. But like the folk song, the creators' songs have some
indefinable quality that endows them with a long life, even
after they have been given the hit treatment and practically
worn down by constant performance. These all-time hits, unlike the run-of-the-mill hit, remain a part of the nation's mu-

sical heritage. They weren't planned that way, however; they just happened.

What can a music publisher give to a song writer that makes their precarious and necessary relationship practical? One thing is experience. A man like Buddy Morris, or Max Dreyfus, or Irving Brown, or Dr. Albert Sirmay—each a man of rare good taste and musical intelligence—knows not only the business but also the art. He not only controls the presses that print the music, he also has "contacts" with the record companies, with singers, with band leaders. He has a tremendous and efficient machinery at his command that gives the composer an outlet for his work, and the protection it may require, too. The publisher may help encourage the composer when he is subjected to, in the words of Morris, "the morticians attending the Philadelphia opening." Above all the publisher must have money and an investor's gambling instinct—plus "belief in the writer." Arlen's association with Edwin H. Morris, based as it is on a long relationship, friendship, mutual respect, is gratifyingly closer to art than business.

The first film Arlen did after his layoff following *St. Louis Woman* was *Casbah*, a musical adaptation of the Pepe le Moko tale, which had been so successful as a Hedy LaMarr-Charles Boyer film *Algiers* in 1938. Ten years later Universal refilmed the venerable story as a musical with Tony Martin in the Boyer role and the late Marta Toren in the LaMarr part. The story was substantially the same; the major change lay in the addition of songs by Harold Arlen with lyrics by Leo Robin.

Robin, like most of the finest lyricists, is little known. Though he had his professional beginnings in New York in the mid-Twenties (his first song was used in the 1925 *Greenwich Village Follies*), it was not until he came to Hollywood in the latter Twenties that Robin began turning out an unending series of outstanding songs. His major Broadway show was *Hit the Deck*, written with Vincent Youmans in 1927. This was followed by his initial Hollywood work with Richard

Whiting, resulting in such songs as "Louise," "Beyond the Blue Horizon," "My Ideal," and "One Hour with You."

Around 1932 Robin began a fruitful collaboration with composer Ralph Rainger that continued until the latter's death in 1942. Together they produced several of the better film songs of the Thirties, many written specifically for Bing Crosby, among them "Please," "Love in Bloom," "June in January," "Blue Hawaii," and even one for Crosby's film nemesis, Bob Hope: "Thanks for the Memory." After Rainger's death Robin collaborated with Nacio Herb Brown, Harry Warren, Jerome Kern, and Arthur Schwartz. The Kern opus, *Centennial Summer* (1946) was the composer's last film score; Robin's lyrics for that film (others were by Oscar Hammerstein, Johnny Mercer, and E. Y. Harburg) were for the songs, "In Love in Vain" and "Up with the Lark."

Leo Robin is president of the mythical "Sweet Fellows' Society of Beverly Hills; Ira Gershwin is vice-president. The presidency is a tribute by his peers recognizing Robin's inability to say anything bad about anyone. The faculty both he and Gershwin have for defending the victim who happens to be on the Hollywood roaster puts them outside the pettiness of the rumor and gossip-laden subcivilization of the film world. That anyone can remain aloof from a society that draws its sustenance from character assassination and vicious gossip is a major accomplishment in itself. But it also keeps you out of that society, and consequently denies you the benefits of the notoriety membership brings.

Leo Robin's completely self-effacing personality and gentleness impressed Arlen. So did Robin's working habits. "We would always have healthy discussions about the songs," Arlen recalls. "Leo starts working about midnight, and like all the true greats is a great craftsman. He would give me a completed lyric with his usual 'Now, this is only a dummy,' but it always turned out to be the right one." (The dummy is a lyric in rough form not intended to be used in which the accents and rhymes are more important than the sense).

"I don't recall," Robin has said, "his asking me to make any changes in the lyrics I submitted to him. I was rather surprised when he offered no objection to the lyrics of 'Hooray for Love.' In my whole career I have never written a lyric quite like this and I don't know offhand of any lyrics by any other writer that are so repetitious. I have always had a sort of prejudice against monotony in a lyric and when I finished this particular one, I was shocked to notice that every line in the refrain ended with the words 'for love.' But it felt right! Evidently Harold reacted to it the same way because he made no comment about the repetition. He might not even have noticed it and this may be due to the fact that the rhymes come where the ear expects them to be.

"I had another experience while working with Harold that was unusual for me. Ordinarily, when a composer submits a tune to me, I take a lot of time—sometimes a month or more—before I hit upon a title that I like. But in the case of several songs for *Casbah* I hit upon a title within minutes after Harold played the melody for me! (And then I took a lot of time, as usual, to complete the lyric.)"

One of the songs Robin presented to Arlen, though protesting that it was just a dummy, was one of the finest in the score, "What's Good about Goodbye?" The "release" of this song effectively employs an octave leap from one word ("Your") to the next ("love"), a logical place for a climax. Within eight bars the melodic line settles down to a predominantly single-note rhythmic theme. Robin ingeniously matched his lyric climaxes to Arlen's in the melody.

"It was refreshing and challenging to work with a writer like Harold," Robin has said, speaking for all of Arlen's lyricists, "who is not bound by the conventional formulas of the music business. However, it is remarkable that while he avoids the commercial clichés, so many of his songs have been commercial in the sense that they have found favor with the people.

"Although I have never sat with him while he was 'digging' for a tune, as I have with other composers, I imagine that he must be a very conscientious craftsman to whom everything he writes is important. To mention 'Hooray for Love' again, this is an example of what I mean. This particular song was a sort of 'throwaway' spot in the picture because it was sung under a lot of dialogue and excitement in a party scene. Nevertheless, Harold's melody for this spot was so strong that this song is still popular, and, if I am not mistaken, it is the most performed song of all those in the picture.

"Another pertinent point is that, although the picture wasn't a success, the songs are still liked. Just recently Johnny Mercer mentioned to me that 'It Was Written in the Stars' is one of his favorite songs."

What Leo Robin remembers best about Harold Arlen is "his hearty laughter. I know of nobody who seems to enjoy a joke more than he does. In fact, he gives the impression of being a very lighthearted person, but some of his music, of course, belies this. Also, there is his peculiar way of demonstrating a song. With his wonderful sense of rhythm and phrasing, and his chanting style, he is as exciting a singer as many professional vocalists."

After completing the lyrics for *Casbah*, Robin joined Jule Styne in a Broadway venture, *Gentlemen Prefer Blondes*, further demonstrating his skill with words by evoking the spirit of the Twenties in several timeless songs.

Arlen remained in Hollywood. With Mercer he turned out a handful of songs for a miserable film tribute to girlie artist George Petty titled *The Petty Girl;* except for the sweeping "Fancy Free" the songs are hardly memorable; Mercer turned out some typically witty lines for the "Calypso Song." But the film itself was destined to early oblivion.

Producer Sol C. Siegel had asked Arlen to do a Betty Grable musical then being planned by Twentieth Century-Fox. No lyricist had yet been assigned when Arlen dropped in on his neighbor Harry Warren. Mentioning this to Warren prompted a suggestion. He had just completed *Summer Holiday* and had enjoyed working with lyricist Ralph Blane. "Ralph is very musical," Warren told Arlen, "and great to work with."

This was the same Ralph Blane who had had such a time

getting into the cast of *Hooray for What?* Blane, since 1938, had gone on to become a most polished supper-club vocalist, and a member of "The Martins" with Hugh Martin. Together, and independently, Martin and Blane wrote vocal arrangements for such shows as *Too Many Girls* (a Rodgers and Hart musical), *DuBarry Was a Lady* (Cole Porter), *Louisiana Purchase* (Irving Berlin), and another Rodgers and Hart show, *The Boys from Syracuse*. Finally, after a rich apprenticeship, Martin and Blane decided to go into business for themselves with *Best Foot Forward* in 1941. When the musical was transformed into a film later, the team moved to California to contribute an additional song to its score, and remained to do the beautifully nostalgic *Meet Me In St. Louis*. Martin and Blane contributed occasional songs to films, too, including the exciting "Love" introduced by Lena Horne in *Ziegfeld Follies*. The Second World War split up the team for a few years, after which their careers went along independent paths until they reunited to do *Athena* in 1954.

Ralph Blane, like his collaborator, holds Arlen in great respect; Blane's description of Arlen—"creator of forms"—is particularly apt. When Blane was asked to collaborate with a man he practically considered an idol, he jumped at the chance. Once the contracts were drawn up, Blane went over to the Arlens' for the first discussion of the film. It turned out to be *My Blue Heaven,* a typical Hollywood turn, for, though Arlen and Blane wrote a substantial score for it, the film's title came from an interpolated song by Walter Donaldson and Richard Whiting.

Having studied the script while on a trip to Honolulu with Anya, Arlen had evolved some definite ideas on song possibilities, even before Blane came to call. The first song he played for Blane was one of those typically unorthodox forms that Blane so admired, and which they tentatively titled "The Friendly Islands." Blane wrote the title across the top of the page of his nice new notebook and went home.

"For days I couldn't sleep a wink," he now laughingly admits. The awe in which he held Arlen literally stymied the success-

ful and completely professional Blane. He was terribly anxious
to make the lyrics just right, consequently he came up with
nothing. His wife reassured him, but that didn't help. Finally
Blane called his agent, Irving Lazar. "I want off this picture,"
he moaned. "All I have is a title and a blank page. I haven't
slept for three days!" And he dramatically concluded with
the announcement, "I am going to die!"

Shortly after that dire phone conversation Blane received a
call from Arlen. "It *is* a difficult song," he told Blane, "come
over and we'll work on it." Together they then worked on the
lyric to "The Friendly Islands," a satire on *South Pacific*—and
thus started Arlen's activity as a lyricist.

Over the years he had, in the give-and-take of collaboration,
suggested ideas for lyrics. But he had never before deliberately worked on the words. The work with Blane was so
engrossing that Arlen found as much pleasure in doing the
lyrics as he did in composing the music. Both Blane and Arlen
had a wonderful time working on the lyrics.

"Annie thought I was crazy," Arlen relates. "I was busy
every working hour. Of course, I was hell-bent on writing
lyrics then and I had a great time doing it. It wasn't labored
and we didn't have any trouble when we turned in the songs.
It was a whole new world."

Blane, too, once he had overcome his initial trepidations,
enjoyed himself—especially when he could, he now confesses,
get Arlen to play the piano, sing, and improvise. What had
begun as a seemingly impossible chore for Blane was turning
out to be a picnic. This is obvious in the songs, which are
among the sprightliest Arlen has ever written. They had their
fun with Rodgers and Hammerstein in "The Friendly Islands" and with Irving Berlin in "Hallowe'en." In the latter
song they pointed out, in the verse, that Berlin, in writing
about American holidays, had skipped Hallowe'en, and they
willingly filled in the gap. Blane now ruefully says that he
knows why the master song writer ignored it, "No one pays
any attention to it—or songs written about it."

In another song, "It's Deductible," Arlen and Blane produced a lyric that had pleased Ira Gershwin and that had some social points to make:

People are running from store to store, from Macy's to Sakses
Nobody wants to work anymore because of income taxes!

They gave an example of deductibility:

Producer gets an angel, producer gets a flop,
The angel doesn't worry, 'cause the flop comes off the top,
Crazy world, crazy times.

Another lyric-fun song is the relentlessly rhymed "Don't Rock the Boat, Dear." An excerpt from one chorus (there are several) preserves the flavor:

Don't rock the tug, dear,
Love is just a drug, dear,
All I need is a hug, dear,
We're not lost at sea.
Don't rock the scow, now,
Charm me off the bow, now,
Love me here and now, wow!
The way it ought to be.
Even tho' we're out in deep waters,
We must save the future for sons and daughters.
Don't rock the sloop, dear,
Don't be a nincompoop, dear
Lovers loop the loop, dear.
Just like the likes of you and me.

And so on through artful rhymings for boat, ship, yacht, launch, smack, junk, hulk, raft—a nautical education, in fact.

The results were happy enough to encourage a sequel to the collaboration. At first even the title of the second Arlen and Blane collaboration was taken from a song in their first, "The Friendly Islands," but by the time the film was released in the summer of 1953 the title had been changed to *Down among the Sheltering Palms.* Ironically, after the song of other song writers. It was an unlikely story; even the studio thought little enough of the film to sneak it into town, unheralded, unsung, and, as it turned out, unremembered. Blane and Arlen composed seven songs in a period from September through October 1950, only three of which remained in the completed film. In December they did an additional song, "The Opposite Sex," though that too was not used.

There is good satiric humor in "I'm a Ruler of a South Sea Island," and in "Inspection," both throwing barbs at the Army and military life in general. Even that kind of military nostalgia that afflicts the away-from-home GI is treated in "Twenty-seven Elm Street," singing the glories of that "favorite word, Home! F.H.A. home . . ."

> On Twenty-seven Elm Street,
> Near Sweet and Simple Square.

The problem of fraternization was tackled in *Down among the Sheltering Palms,* but was neither intelligently handled nor, naturally, solved. At least it was approached. The presence of the pre-TV Jack Paar in the film did not help it.

Arlen and Blane were ready to tackle another project when the opportunity came for Blane to do a musical, *Three Wishes for Jamie,* for which he did both words and music. This took so much of his time that he was forced to cancel film work for about a year.

Blane's unavailibility had its good side for Arlen, for in this period of rapid turnover in lyricists he next collaborated with another great one, the outstanding one of her sex, Dorothy Fields.

Miss Fields had preceded Arlen as a Cotton Club song writer in the late Twenties, after which she and her collaborator Jimmy McHugh switched to the Broadway stage to do the *Blackbirds of 1928,* out of which came their first great hit song, "I Can't Give You Anything but Love, Baby." Miss Fields and McHugh made the usual 1930 Hollywood trek, out of which came such songs as "The Cuban Love Song," "Lost in a Fog," "I'm in the Mood for Love," and "I Feel a Song Coming On."

Next Miss Fields joined Jerome Kern to work on his finest

film scores, among them *I Dream Too Much* and *Swingtime*. From the latter came the Academy Award-winning "The Way You Look Tonight." Returning to Broadway, Dorothy Fields collaborated with Arthur Schwartz on the songs for *Stars in Your Eyes* for Ethel Merman and Jimmy Durante.

Miss Fields comes from an honored show-business family. Her father was the great comedian Lew Fields; her brothers Herbert and Joseph were successful writers. With Herbert, Miss Fields collaborated on the books for a series of Cole Porter musicals, *Let's Face It, Something for the Boys,* and *Mexican Hayride*. She then returned to song writing when she collaborated with Sigmund Romberg on the romantic hit, *Up in Central Park* in 1945. She again joined Herbert Fields on writing the book for the Irving Berlin classic *Annie Get Your Gun,* and did both the book and lyrics for *Arms and the Girl* (music by Morton Gould) and the lyrics, to the music of Arthur Schwartz, for *A Tree Grows in Brooklyn*. She then returned to Hollywood to work on a film with Harold Arlen which was an attempt to capitalize on the renown Ezio Pinza had won with his appearance in *South Pacific*.

The film was *Mr. Imperium,* and proved to be one of the most forgettable to be released in 1951. It united the talents of Pinza with those of Lana Turner, who appeared as a singer of songs (her voice was actually dubbed in by Fran Warren). It did not go, as a motion picture. However, the Fields-Arlen songs were given vibrant renditions by Pinza.

Harold Arlen's "infinite variety" most impresses Dorothy Fields. "This man can write anything!" she declares. Disturbed over his typing as a composer of blues, Miss Fields will invoke one of the best songs written for *Mr. Imperium,* "Let Me Look at You" as an example of his versatility, "which must be shown!" A further example of versatility is the song "My Love an' My Mule," a light, amusing contrast to the more serious "Let Me Look at You." Another delight is "Andiamo," a kind of Italian folk song. Into its lyric Miss Fields works allusions to musical directions, "allegro," "vivace," and "presto." Unfortunately the movie's poor quality helped no one, and no song.

Arlen affectionately called Dorothy Fields "Red Arrow"; she, in turn reciprocated by calling him "Schnitta." Miss Field's pet name must be accepted on its face value, but Arlen's for her is a tribute to her speed in turning out lyrics. They worked in her suite at the Beverly Hills Hotel. "I'd get there about ten or eleven in the morning," Arlen has said. "Dorothy was always up early typing. We would discuss ideas—I'd play a tune and leave a lead sheet. We'd have lunch in the patio and then I'd leave. When I returned the next day, the song would be finished. It was wonderful fun, Dotty was easy to get along with—there was never any strain."

"Harold is the nicest and sweetest person I've ever known; this man is full of love," which Miss Fields hears reflected in "his pure lyric line and good taste."

About a year went by before Dorothy Fields and Arlen collaborated again. In the interim Arlen took time out for a trip to Europe with the Buddy Morrises and the Harry Warrens. The tour took in Italy and France. In Paris, Arlen became intrigued by the paintings of a young Spanish artist whose specialty was soulful waifs. Arlen decided to commission a portrait by the artist Montañes, who was extremely proud. He would not in fact paint Arlen until he learned that he was the composer of "Stormy Weather." On this trip, in 1952, Arlen traveled by air for the first time. "Harold was scared of planes," Morris relates. "He became a Lindbergh after that trip. We flew from London to Rome, with Harold taking pictures out the window all the way. We went to Naples, too, and Harold must have taken a photo of every statue in Pompeii."

At this time *Mr. Imperium* was mercifully forgotten, and Twentieth Century-Fox planned to remake *The Farmer Takes a Wife*, based on the novel by Walter D. Edmonds, as a film musical. The story, with its setting on the Erie Canal, its roistering bargemen in the 1850's, seemed a natural for the kind of songs Miss Fields and Arlen could write. The color and romance of history and folklore were irresistible to them.

Miss Field's brother Joseph collaborated on a screen play of some substance with Walter Bullock and Sally Benson. But the problems lay in the casting, or miscasting, rather. Betty Grable was to appear as a barge cook, an unconvincing assignment to begin with, but she could sing. Not as much could be said for leading man Dale Robertson, though he did manage to sound pleasant when he did. John Carroll could sing, so could Eddie Foy, Jr. *The Farmer Takes a Wife* was treated to a lavish production but just simply did not come off. What might have been an important effort turned out to be another in a series of undistinguished overproduced film musicals.

The opening, a beautifully filmed long shot of ships on the Erie Canal to the music of "On the Erie Canal," hinted at what might have been done had the entire film continued in the same spirit. But what finally emerged was merely expensively cheap and vulgar. The Fields-Arlen songs, actually of Broadway show-tune quality, were lost in all the glitter and glut.

For *The Farmer Takes a Wife* Arlen composed music fitting to the period and setting; Miss Fields's lyrics are sophisticated and folkish, as required—with Arlen's music matching them musically, in keeping with the kind of song sung in New York state along the Erie Canal in 1850. The songs were expressive of the earthy yet sunny people who lived and worked on the canal. Bosley Crowther found only the songs worth while; he wrote in the *Times:* ". . . someone had the notion that a winning folk musical could be made of the successful play and film by Frank B. Elser and Marc Connelly . . . and indeed, that notion was a good one and might have been brought to flower if the only thing necessary to this fulfillment was a nice Harold Arlen-Dorothy Fields score." Though the film provided "a thoroughly agreeable package of spirited and rollicking songs," in Crowther's estimation, the other ingredients that might have made a worth-while film were missing. And the songs, like the film, have not been heard from since.

Late in 1952 the final agreement required to make a musical of the 1937 screen classic *A Star Is Born* was signed when Ira Gershwin consented to do the lyrics. Since his brother's death in 1937 the lyricist had collaborated with composers

Kurt Weill (*Lady in the Dark*), Aaron Copland (*The North Star*), Jerome Kern (*Cover Girl*), Arthur Schwartz (*Park Avenue*), Harry Warren (*The Barkleys of Broadway*), and Burton Lane (*Give a Girl a Break*), on assorted shows and films. *A Star Is Born* was his first collaboration with Arlen since they had done *Life Begins at 8:40* in 1934.

Everything about *A Star Is Born* promised to make it an important film. The original screen play by Dorothy Parker, Alan Campbell, and Robert Carson was revised especially for Judy Garland by Moss Hart. Miss Garland had been absent from films for four years and it was hoped that *A Star Is Born,* which was to be produced by her husband, Sid Luft, for Warner Brothers, would prove to be an important comeback vehicle for her.

Work on the film for the song writers began officially when Moss Hart drove up to Beverly Hills on a Sunday in January 1953 to meet with Arlen and Gershwin at the latter's home on Roxbury Drive. Hart outlined the story, specifically noting the differences from the Janet Gaynor-Fredric March original, and suggested seven spots in the script for songs. The songs were discussed in terms of their place in the story as well as their psychological motivation in respect to the characters and the plot. Since Miss Garland would do all the singing, except for some incidental choral work, the songs were naturally projected with her in mind as the character she would portray in the film, a girl singer who makes good in Hollywood, while the man she marries, a onetime star, is on his way down. The latter was to be portrayed by James Mason.

From the first discussion Gershwin came out with a song outline:

1. Shrine Auditorium—Judy and band
2. *Dive Song*
3. Preparation in rehearsal (gay song) (Then at preview complete ※)
4. Song on sound stage (proposal with interruptions)
5. Motel song (probably one to reprise later)
6. Prop ※ Tour de force (in Malibu sings all parts & imitations)
7. Reprise of 5 probably

Using this breakdown by Gershwin as a guide, on the following Tuesday the lyricist and composer began working. Because Gershwin prefers working in the "Gershwin Plantation," Arlen would come around to Roxbury Drive about one in the afternoon (Gershwin habitually goes to bed late and does not awaken before noon). They started with the first song first; it took about two weeks resulting in "Gotta Have Me Go with You," which satisfied them. Whereupon, encouraged, they immediately decided to tackle the "Dive Song." This song Hart felt "was obligatory." It was important to a dramatic point he hoped to make that made it clear to Mason, and the audience, that Miss Garland was a fine singer with a flair for acting.

Arlen had an idea, in his usual jot form, which he played for Gershwin. "I know how Ira's ear works and was sure he would like the theme, one that I'd had for some time— an eight-bar phrase." Gershwin did like it, particularly the insistent movement of the rhythm; he listened a while and suggested as a possible title "The Man That Got Away." It was Arlen's turn to be impressed. "I like" was his simple indication of approval and work was begun on the so-called "Dive Song."

Interestingly, none of the music Arlen played for Gershwin is the accompaniment for the words of the title. What Gershwin heard was merely the introduction, the first four bars of mood setting music and the melody for which he devised:

> The night is bitter,
> The stars have lost their glitter,
> The winds grow colder
> And suddenly you're older . . .

By mid-February Gershwin was able to write to a friend, "Am busy with Arlen. We're at about the halfway mark," but he had sad news to report. "Our work has been somewhat delayed because of Arlen's father's illness and subsequent death— but Harold is taking it exceptionally well."

Samuel Arluck died in February 1953, and though Arlen did have to continue working he was deeply affected and distressed by this not unexpected blow. Always acknowledging his indebtedness to his father as his greatest musical influence, Arlen tried to lessen the bitterness of his father's death by working even harder.

Despite the delays Gershwin and Arlen continued their work, and by May 12 Gershwin, then preparing to come to New York for a revival of his *Of Thee I Sing*, was pleased to write that the *Star Is Born* songs had been completed "a couple of weeks ago." The songs they turned out, related to the original breakdown Gershwin had made were: the "gay song," a calypso commercial. Instead of using it in the preview spot another song was used instead, "Dancing Partner," which was discarded, to be replaced by the new "Green Light Ahead," also discarded and replaced by "I'm off the Downbeat," which remained, though shakily. As originally planned *A Star Is Born* was to have had an intermission and it was hoped that the number preceding it would be an especially rousing one.

The "song on sound stage" became "Here's What I'm Here for;" the "motel song," "It's a New World;" and the "tour de force," "Someone at Last." One additional song grew out of the work and was found usable and even remained in the final film, "Lose That Long Face."

Actual shooting of *A Star Is Born* did not go so rapidly as did the writing of the songs. A year after Arlen and Gershwin had begun their work Gershwin mentioned to a friend, "*Star Is Born* should be finished shooting by the end of this month [February 1954]. Almost like the Von Stroheim days—twenty or so weeks." Already finished with their part of the effort, Arlen and Gershwin had also completed another score for a Bing Crosby film that, Gershwin expected, "would shoot in March sometime. Not many technical problems on this one as its not really a musical—we had to do only four songs, only one of which has any production values and those are very simple."

With all delays out of the way *A Star Is Born* was finally ready by March 25 to be shown in rough-cut form. On seeing it Miss Garland called Gershwin the following morning, exclaiming, "Oh, Ira, I know you and Harold wrote every one of those songs just for me!" Which was true, of course. Some of the songs even contain subtle allusions to Miss Garland's personal life.

Gershwin's reaction to the rough-cut was also enthusiastic: "Everything about *Star Is Born* looks and sounds great. There's only one problem: what to do about a production number that's to wind up the first half (the showing is to have an intermission—the picture runs about three hours so far). Have no idea what's going to happen to this spot. Arlen and I wrote two songs for it ('Green Light Ahead' and 'I'm Off the Downbeat'), both good by anyone's standards, but it seems the choreographer couldn't get any production ideas. Could be they may even interpolate an outside number which would be a shame. However, there's still a chance that Arlen may be able to leave N.Y. for a week or so and we'll try to give them what they think they want."

Script changes called for further work in April 1954—the resulting song was "Lose That Long Face." But the composer and lyricist could not "give them what they think they want." Instead, a medley put together by Leonard Gershe, and called "Born in a Trunk," an obvious allusion to Miss Garland's triumph at the Palace Theater, was inserted. This was to be the big production number winding up the first half, but by the time the film was released the intermission was discarded.

Arlen had become seriously ill in New York, where he had gone to work on a musical, and could no longer make further contributions to *A Star Is Born*. Meanwhile the Crosby film had been shot on schedule, emerging as *The Country Girl*, and proved a dramatic triumph for both Crosby and Grace Kelly. The songs were secondary to the plot, though at least two were exceptional, "Dissertation on the State of Bliss" and "The Search Is Through," the first an almost cynical café-society blues and the second a fine ballad.

Though Arlen was assailed with production problems, delays, and changes, ill health, and the death of his father, his "wonderful spirit," in Ira Gershwin's phrase, saw him through those months remarkably well. Of course Arlen greatly enjoyed the work with Gershwin.

"It was wonderful," he has said. "We worked, we ate, watched television, played pool—all in great comfort and, I believe, in a spirit of calm and easiness and very little tension.

"I don't know any lyric writer who studies his work line for line, progressively for the ideas and for the rhymes, as Ira does. And I don't know any lyric writer who gets as much of a kick out of a song as Ira does when it's finished."

Though he has always labored long and hard over his work, Gershwin relaxes by enjoying what has given him trouble. He sings very easily and, for a nonprofessional vocalist, very well—on pitch, in tempo, and with a clarity that could be studied with profit by singers.

During the writing of the score an amusing incident occurred illustrating the relationship between Arlen and Ira Gershwin.

They had just completed "The Man That Got Away" and both were quite pleased. Arlen decided that, rather than work over the weekend, he would go down to Palm Springs to rest. Gershwin objected, for he sensed that once Arlen was there he would meet Moss Hart, the Lufts, who were also resting there, and someone would coax Arlen into performing what they had written up to that point. Somehow Gershwin felt that it was too early to let anyone hear what they had done, and a premature hearing would spoil everything. Besides he didn't want it known how quickly they had done the two numbers. Arlen promised, however, that he would not play anything for anyone, whereupon Gershwin felt that the trip would be all right.

On Saturday morning Arlen went over to the golf course, where he found the Lufts getting ready to play. He decided to walk around with them. At one point he unconsciously whistled a few bars of "The Man That Got Away." Until that moment not a word had been said of *A Star Is Born*. On hearing an unfamiliar phrase Miss Garland evidenced an interest. Noting this, Arlen decided to tease her and continued to whistle. Miss Garland finally asked what he was whistling.

"Oh, nothing," Arlen replied. Then he took to humming. "Is it something you've done for the picture?"

"No," Arlen told her, recalling his promise to Ira Gershwin.

Sid Luft had hit his golf ball into a sand trap, and while he was trying to extricate himself Miss Garland practically forced Arlen into the clubhouse, where they found a piano. Arlen attempted to get out of the trap he had got himself into, by telling her that it was a work still in progress and not yet in any shape to be heard, but she persisted. Arlen then played her the two completed songs, "Gotta Have Me Go With You" and "The Man That Got Away." She was delighted, called Luft to hear them too. Arlen was now completely in trouble, so he just enjoyed himself. They went over to the Harts', who were renting Frank Sinatra's home at the time, and because there was no piano in it had to go next door to the home of writer Norman Krasna where Arlen could demonstrate the song. By this time the songs had pretty well covered Palm Springs. It only remained for Moss Hart, in his innocence, to call Ira Gershwin to let him know how well the songs were going over "out of town." "Ira seemed terribly noncommittal," Hart noted, "but I attributed that to his inability to accept a compliment."

Gershwin had learned, though in a pleasing fashion, that composers betray. He was very happy with the reception of the songs, and when Arlen reported at the Gershwin Plantation on the next Monday, he was greeted with a rare and highly self-satisfied Gershwin smile.

A Star Is Born finally opened in New York at both the Paramount and Victoria theaters in October 1954 with appropriate fanfare, kleig lights, and the usual opening-night fuss. Bosley Crowther, of the *Times*, hailed it as "one of the greatest heartbreak dramas that has drenched the screen in years . . . they have fattened it up with musical numbers that are among the finest things in the show . . . Miss Garland is excellent in all things."

Variety reported that "The Harold Arlen-Ira Gershwin numbers are tailored for the plot and not the jukeboxes although
'The Man That Got Away' is on the road in that direction . . .
the new songs fit into the script like it was a one-man libretto."

Time put it even more colorfully when it stated that the
composers had given Miss Garland "six good songs—among
them one unforgettable lump in the throat, 'The Man That
Got Away.' Her big dark voice sobs, sighs, sulks, and socks
them out like a cross between Tara's harp and the late Bessie
Smith."

The staging and singing of "The Man That Got Away" were
unforgettably handled. Not only were they simply presented
with the unpretentious background of an empty cabaret, but
Miss Garland sang out in great voice. The mood and impact
were heightened by her almost balletic gestures and the imaginative camera technique. As with "Over the Rainbow" Judy
Garland introduced a song that not only was written for her
but has become identified with her ever since. When she made
a return appearance at the Palace, the audience called for the
song along with her other standards.

"The Man That Got Away," like so many of Harold Arlen's
"long-pull" songs, is of unusual structure (sixty-two bars) and
is in a sense a blues. The difference lies in the fact that it is
not a folklike blues such as "Blues in the Night" or "Stormy
Weather." In keeping with the character portrayed by Miss
Garland in the film the song springs from different roots, those
of the popular music business rather than the South. But whatever its structural uniqueness, or its base, it is one of the
great film songs, music and lyrics.

Another fine song from the score is the remarkably simple
yet extraordinarily complex "It's a New World." The simplicity
lies in the song's direct expression of emotion as carried by
the superb Gershwin lyric. But what is particularly curious
about the song is that the main theme, that is, the melodic
phrase for the words of the title, is never repeated throughout
the song once it has been used. In other words, the entire
song is one long-line melody. It is, of course, constructed of

variants of the theme, but always without actual quotation. What is interesting is that it is not a difficult song to learn but is a difficult one to sing. The melody is made up primarily of half notes (which require the ability to sustain tone), no easy feat for any singer. Miss Garland handled it beautifully in the film; the composer has made an affecting recording of it. "It's a New World" is a favorite of singers, though they rarely attempt to sing it, but it is an even greater favorite of composers, who recognize in the song an amazing creative virtuosity.

Ira Gershwin, in his book *Lyrics on Several Occasions,* set down his impression of Harold Arlen in this way: ". . . Arlen is no thirty-two bar man. As one of the most individual of American show-composers he is distinctive in melodic line and construction. Frequently when collaborating with him the lyricist —whether Koehler or Mercer or Harburg or myself—finds himself wondering if a resultant song isn't too long or too difficult or too mannered for popular consumption. But there's no cause for worry. Many Arlen songs take time to catch on, but when they do they join his impressive and lasting catalog."

CHAPTER 9

I Never Has Seen Snow

A Broadway friend of Harold Arlen habitually refers to the composer's two-decade residence in Hollywood in penalogical terms. This would ignore Arlen's occasional parole to do a Broadway musical, often as not something he was able to do on the money earned in Hollywood. Arlen had worked steadily, except for the two years he himself decided to take off, since 1935, but by 1953 he began to gravitate toward New York.

The far-from-stimulating atmosphere of the film capital, not to mention a steady stream of disappointing films, led to Arlen's decision to desert the land of eternal summer for the headier airs and paces of New York. He missed the stimulation of the complete immersion that comes from working on a show. But he was to learn that even the theater has its forbidding aspects.

In November 1953 he began his three-month stint on the songs for *The Country Girl;* the same month it was announced that he was to compose the music for *House of Flowers,* a musical based on a short story by Truman Capote.

Producer Arnold Saint Subber, who had gained valuable experience in the production of musicals with Cole Porter's *Kiss Me, Kate,* had produced Capote's arty though unsuccessful *The Grass Harp.* Saint Subber was sufficiently impressed with Capote's gifts to overlook the fate of *The Grass Harp* to sign him to another play commitment.

In 1948 Capote had lived in Haiti, settling for a time in Port-au-Prince. "If you want a drink there," he will complain, "you have to go to one of the boring hotels." To save himself such excrutiating boredom, Capote found, on a country road nearby, a string of bordellos where he went to spend the evenings, sitting on the porch, drinking and absorbing an enormous amount of local gossip from the girls who came more or less to adopt him. They also fully appreciated his bringing along supplies of American beer to share with them. Capote became the best-informed man in Port-au-Prince.

On returning to the United States he wrote down his impressions of Haiti, finding that those portions of his manuscript that most pleased him were those dealing with the colorful bordellos on the outskirts of town. Capote created a special little piece based on fact and fancy, "House of Flowers," a short story that received the O. Henry Award as one of the finest of 1950. He then set to work making a play of it for Saint Subber, deciding as he went along that the color, setting, and personalities seemed right for a musical play, instead. After completing his play script Capote went through it again, inserting tentative song lyrics wherever it seemed logical.

Saint Subber decided that so delicate a tale would require a sensitive musical gift and asked Harold Arlen to compose the score. Arlen read the script (then an exact rendering of the short story) and demurred, feeling that, as the play stood, it would receive a more fitting score from a composer such as Gian-Carlo Menotti.

But then he changed his mind. "I jumped at it because I really liked the story and, especially, because I admire Capote's work. I said yes, and don't regret it. I had a good time writing it." ·

By this time the peregrinating Capote was living in St. Moritz, where he received a telegram from Arlen confirming their collaboration. To Capote, Arlen's name then meant very little. Not until he learned that several of the songs he liked were Arlen's did he know his future collaborator's identity. At that, he still believed Arlen was a Negro.

To get the project under way, what with Capote in Switzerland and later in Rome, and with Arlen in Beverly Hills trying to complete the seemingly interminable *A Star Is Born*, the collaborators began to exchange ideas by mail. As they completed a lyric, Arlen would set it to music, make an acetate disc of it, and immediately ship it to Capote, wherever he happened to be. To Capote, for a long time, Arlen remained a disembodied phonographic voice with "a muddy-colored tone," Capote found, and his singing "warm, plaintive."

Capote moved to Paris and from there called Arlen in Hollywood. "He put the telephone on the piano and played for me for what seemed like hours," Capote recalls. The show's title song was written in this way, via transatlantic and transcontinental telephone.

Finally after three months of long-distance collaboration Arlen and Capote met in New York early in February 1954. It was then that Arlen became seriously ill with an ulcer.

They had completed three songs, "House of Flowers," "I Never Has Seen Snow," "A Sleepin' Bee," and had begun work on "Two Ladies in de Shade of de Banana Tree," when Arlen was rushed to Doctors Hospital. His old friend of the Croydon days, Dr. Elias, took charge of the case. On operating the doctor found bleeding so profuse that he felt there was little chance for Arlen. As he lost blood, more was almost literally pumped into him; he now refers to 1954 as "The Year of Transfusion." Close to three-dozen transfusions were given to Arlen; in the years he'd been practicing Dr. Elias had never seen a patient receive as many.

There were six doctors in constant attendance or on a round-the-clock call. When hemorrhaging began for a second time, the doctors used the Blakemore tube to stop it. They inserted the special plastic tube into Arlen's esophagus, inflated it, and thus exerted pressure upon the flowing capillaries and stopped the bleeding.

Dr. Elias looked down at his friend-patient one day, his mind half resigned to losing him, and said with rough compassion, "Harold, you poor bastard, you been took with an ugly spell."

But Arlen managed to hang on. He even insisted upon having Capote visit the hospital so that work could continue on *House of Flowers*. In his room they took up the uncom-

pleted "Two Ladies." Using a tin dinner tray and a couple
of spoons, Arlen tapped out the rhythm while he and Capote
worked on the lyric. As they completed a chorus they would
sing it out to Arlen's tapping; he was a little hampered, for
there was an intravenous tube in his arm. They kept this
up until nurses came in and put a stop to the racket.

Capote's constant and profound curiosity made for a daily
ritual. As soon as he came into the room, and before work
could begin, he had to read Arlen's letters and telegrams.
Arlen then took to hiding them under things, which rather
spoiled Capote's day. "Dads,—or Bunny—where are they?" he
would plead, rifling the drawers of the single table and chest
till he found what he sought. Among the morning's messages
he was apt to find one to himself from Arlen: "Aren't you
ashamed of yourself, you little bastard?"

They were having a fine time despite Arlen's illness—and
a twenty-year gap in their ages.

Finally released from the hospital, after what seemed to
be a miraculous though by no means yet complete recovery,
Arlen returned to his vast apartment at 375 Park Avenue,
where he and Capote could work more regularly. Living with
him were his mother and his brother Jerry, who had been
asked to conduct *House of Flowers*. Capote would appear
in his work clothes: T-shirt, khaki slacks, and sneakers—like
some small boy set for a day in the country. This gave rise to
a story that made the rounds for a while: one day Mother Arluck found a small boy raiding the refrigerator and slapped
his hands, only to learn that he was Truman Capote.

Capote would, Arlen recalls, "curl up on the couch; he
would do his thinking and make his little notes and I would
be making my large ones on a big drawing tablet." Thus
did Arlen and Capote collaborate on the lyrics for the *House
of Flowers*, only to have their work interrupted again when
Arlen had to return to the hospital. By now he was bored
with hospitalization, even if it did save his life.

A couple of days back and he began to beg for permission
to get out "just to see a movie or something" one evening.

The permission was granted, provided that he did not exert himself, adhered to his strict diet, and got back to bed early.

Dressed, and happy to be free of the monotony of his hospital room, Arlen left Doctors Hospital and instead of going to a movie, which would have enabled him to return by eleven o'clock, he decided to visit some of his friends. This led to making the rounds of a few clubs and talking into the night. Around five in the morning Arlen felt perhaps that it would be wise to get back to the hospital.

When he arrived he gave the elevator operator the floor number. The operator studied Arlen with curiosity; obviously he had not seen this man before—and it was an unusual time of the morning to be coming in—except for maternity cases. The perplexed man remained silent until they arrived at Arlen's floor, then inquired, "Doctor . . . ?"

"No, patient," Arlen informed him, and blithely went back to bed.

By the summer, when rehearsals began, Arlen was well enough to devote his full energies to *House of Flowers*. Once again he had collaborated on the lyrics, and this meant a great deal to him.

"The musical play is a medium that is full of technical things I didn't understand and I still don't understand," Capote stated after the show was completed. "I had thought that I was thinking in terms of pacing and variety when I was working alone on the lyrics, but I found that I really didn't know enough about it. When Arlen came in everything had to be changed except for the actual characters and lyrics for the title song. Even the story had to be changed.

"I had no understanding of song writing (and Lord knows, still do not). But Arlen, who I suppose had never worked with an amateur before, was tolerant and infinitely encouraging . . ." As they worked on "Turtle Song," a folkish ballad, Arlen acquired a volume on sea life to be sure that all references to fish in the song would be accurate. Capote, who spins his tales out of his own imagination, was surprised at this evidence of research.

There were other interruptions on *House of Flowers* besides Arlen's illness. Though Capote had a typical intellectual's contempt for television, he could not bring himself to avoid watching the gentle Boston lawyer Joseph N. Welch clashing with "Indian Fighter" Joseph McCarthy. The viewings went on throughout most of the collaboration on *House of Flowers*. Capote rightly attributed his devotion to the Welch-McCarthy "program" to the fact that it wasn't typical of television "show biz."

He was soon treated to other facets of show biz, hardly less deadly than the television altercation. Very early in the show's production his original story was greatly changed. The role of one of the madams, small in the story, was expanded to suit the talents of star Pearl Bailey. Eventually the entire second act was thrown out and a new one substituted, and the character of a grandmother, important in the short story, completely disappeared. *House of Flowers* was no longer an adaptation of Capote's prize-winning short story, but a Broadway musical with overtones of art.

"The action," Capote had explained to an informal preview group in Arlen's living room, "takes place in a house of ill-repute," a euphemism, as spoken by the boyish author, that led off to an especially entertaining evening. Capote's original concentrated upon the love story of a young, relatively innocent prostitute who married an equally young and innocent country boy. The early action takes place in the city, and the later action in the country, where the grandmother attempts to break up the marriage with spells. She is defeated by the girl who, one day, puts all the conjure objects (lizards, toads, etc.,) into the old woman's soup. After the grandmother enjoys the soup the girl informs her of its ingredients, whereupon the old woman conveniently dies. After an interlude, in which two of the girl's prostitute friends appear to try to get her to return to town, the story closes with a happy fade-out.

The musical turned its attention to the rivalry between two madams, Fleur (Pearl Bailey) and Tango (Juanita Hall); the boy-girl story became subsidiary. To keep her star attraction, Ottilie (the girl, enchantingly played by Diahann Carroll), Madam Fleur stoops to much skulduggery, but the play, too, manages to come to a happy conclusion. Between overture and finale the audience was treated to as sensual a musical as ever appeared on Broadway.

Capote had made up his mind to leave the show, even before the customary out-of-town problems arose in Philadelphia, but decided to stay with it because of Arlen's illness; Arlen himself felt that he was "living on protein and prayer."

George Balanchine gave up trying to conceive the choreography; Herbert Ross was called in to restage and redo the dances. Not only were the dances altered, but so were some of the characters, too. The part of the middle-aged planter in love with the girl was pared down to a minimum. So was that of the sea captain, whereupon that member left the cast (he had hoped to sing and his songs were taken away from him). The very nature of the show suffered a sea change in the short land voyage from the New York run-through to the Philadelphia tryout.

By this time Capote was ready to join the erstwhile sea captain. Arlen found him "staying out of trouble. He remained in his room working; nobody saw him, he never got involved with the show's problems. He was completely away from all heat." Since the book was no longer really his, Capote could not relate himself to the problem. And that problem lay in the book, which wavered between the boy-girl story and the rivalry between the madams. For "commercial" Broadway purposes it behooved the management and director Peter Brook to lean toward the latter emphasis, thereby missing completely the point of the original story.

House of Flowers opened to mixed notices in New York: some critics liked it and some didn't. Most interesting of the conflicting opinions were printed in the same paper, the bible of show biz, *Variety.* The Philadelphia reviewer (*Waters*) found Harold Arlen's score "top drawer," while the New York man (*Hobe*) found it "mediocre." In Philadelphia, Miss Bailey, it was felt, had "a part that's a natural . . . She also gives a sound and many faceted dramatic performance and she adds salty comedy touches." But in New York, according to *Hobe,* her "distinctive personality and style are quite limited, and she reveals only a dim idea of how to read lines. Under the circumstances unless she's singing her special brand of songs, she tends to become monotonous." In sum, *Waters* found that in Philadelphia, the "Capote-Arlen collaboration makes for an exciting theatrical evening." New York's no doubt less rube-ish *Hobe* decreed it to be "a dull thud."

Another dichotomy could be discerned in the pages of the *World-Telegram & Sun,* wherein the drama critic found *House of Flowers* "first-rate" and "Rabelaisian," while columnist Inez Robb found it only "dull and dirty" and even suggested that the city's authorities, who should be held responsible for the town's morality, had been "lulled into the belief that its subject matter treats of floriculture," at once intimating a monumental stupidity on the part of the officials and introducing a rare word into the columns of the paper.

The distinguished George Jean Nathan came to the musical's defense. The erudite, informed, and balanced critic agreed with some of the critics on their negative opinions but found that *House of Flowers* had provided "the most visually beautiful and in some respects the most exotically exciting evening I have encountered since I was last on the semi-tropical island where it is laid. Its alleged weaknesses, indeed, are the very things about it that fetch me. Quite aside from its unanimously admired lovely pastel settings by Oliver Messel, and its handsome and witty costumes also by Messel, its much criticized Harold Arlen score, reinforced here and there by a Trinidad steelband, is not only, it seems to me, richly atmospheric, but all the more appropriate because of its lack of the kind of tunes that convert their hearers into counterparts

of whistling roast peanut machines . . ." He even managed
to find some good in the remains of Capote's book, and
criticized the critics with a wise observation: "Anyway perfectly regulated plots in musical shows are for ploughboys
and are best forgotten."

John O'Hara sardonically described the opening night:
"There was Gloria Vanderbilt Di Cicco Stokowski sitting with
Frank Sinatra, first row on the aisle. In the same row a couple
of seats away, Mrs. Alfred Gwynne Vanderbilt without Mr.
Alfred Gwynne Vanderbilt watching a troupe of native dancers.
Out in the lobby there was a little man who was being
taken for Truman Capote, but wasn't. Oh, the place was full
of celebrities and that curious category of people who are
not celebrities but whom celebrities know, and who pretend not
to be impressed by celebrities (Boy, couldn't I give you a
bunch of names of *those*). There was an overabundance
of the Gay Boys in their '54–'55 uniform, which is the black
suit with the narrow pants; too, too Edwardian. There was
the English actress—a good one, too—giving a performance in
the aisle, much more professional, I must say, than the walk-
through given on stage by Pearl Bailey."

Mr. O'Hara's description might easily be applied to any
show's opening, which is as completely an artificial event as
occurs in our society. It is an "opening" by semantic stretching
only. Before the official première takes place, friends and
backers (and potential backers) have heard the songs many
times over; then come the rehearsals, followed by the New
York run-throughs: complete performances without costumes
or orchestra.

The out-of-town opening, supposedly functioning as a
polishing opportunity before a real audience, usually turns
out to be a boiling pot out of which comes the final stew,
and out of which many a personality comes stewing. A couple
weeks in Philadelphia, or Boston, or New Haven, and the
show is more or less (and most everyone thinks less) ready
to come to town. By this time the rumors from out of
town have been circulating among the knowing ones; such

rumors may even have a subconscious effect on the critics. A week of previews may precede the official opening night, a tension-laden, back-stabbing, vicious, tiring night of reckoning.

Not only are the critics present, so are the professional first-nighters, the celebrities, the near-celebrities, and the near-to-celebrities (whose names Mr. O'Hara did not mention). And there are the "friends," little claques sitting in clusters, and by their palm-pounding shall ye know them. One need only note who makes an on-stage entrance to a round of isolated applause to learn who gave out the free tickets.

These so-called "free" tickets, incidentally, are free only to the "friends," for the hapless donor must pay for them. An opening night can cost a composer, a lyricist, or a star a few hundred dollars even if he isn't interested in purchasing a claque. He is expected to furnish tickets—and woe to him if they are not for good seats—to powerful friends and even enemies. Very few regular theater-goers, the ones who actually pay for their seats and who keep the theater alive, attend an opening night. Tickets are generally not available to them.

Under these completely supercharged, phony, and often distracting (remember Mr. O'Hara's English actress in the aisle) conditions is the fate of a show determined. The peasants read the reviews the next day to decide whether they will want to see the show. And while the New York critics protest that they do not, as they have often been accused, make or break a show, it is possible that the menagerie attending a first night could. It is exciting, it is glamorous, and deadly.

But it was ever thus. The only quite recent innovation that has bred its own form of destructiveness is the theater party. Its practitioners, it has been intimated, hold the producers in thrall enough to determine the direction a show might take even before it is written. But more of that later.

For all its faults *House of Flowers* was a lovely show and even Walter Kerr, of the New York *Herald Tribune*, who was hard on it, found its score "tantalizing," taking wing "with the overture itself, a magical medley that begins with the

blast of a police whistle and ends in a cascade of drums."
Despite the critical contradictions the score was voted the
Critics' Award as the best of the year.

Time has proved the *House of Flowers* score one of the
finest of the decade; as Richard Rodgers has observed, "I
can't go to an audition without hearing 'A Sleepin' Bee,'
and it's always a pleasure." Rodgers feels strongly that the
score is "gravely misunderstood and underrated." While Arlen
composed *House of Flowers* primarily to please himself, the
recognition now coming to the score is hardly any consolation
for the failure of the show. Its Caribbean setting afforded
him an opportunity to write in a musical genre he had never
attempted before. The color of the West Indian instruments
could be mingled with conventional instruments of the pit
band; folk song would be blended with sophisticated song.

"A Sleepin' Bee" is a reference to a Haitian folk belief mentioned in Capote's short story. The melody itself dates back to
before *A Star Is Born,* for which it had been only momentarily
considered and discarded. In its *House of Flowers* form "A
Sleepin' Bee" is a sensuous, undulating melody that rises a
tenth and drops a fifth in a mere four bars. This swelling
and lowering give it its characteristic shape, an almost languid
personality of great melodic beauty. Capote's and Arlen's lyric
for the song, several versions of which exist in Capote's tiny,
precise script, was worked over many times before the right
words were found.

Possibly the most unusual song composed for the show
is "I Never Has Seen Snow." Dr. Elias's comment to the
ailing Arlen is preserved in the first line of the verse:

> I done lost my ugly spell,
> I am cheerful now.
> Got the warm all-overs a-smoothin' my worried brow.

Which with:

> Oh, the girl I used to be
> She ain't me no more,
> I closed the door on the girl I was before.
> Feelin' fine and full o' bliss,
> What I really wants to say is this:

Accompanying Risë Stevens on the "Ed Sullivan Show."

Lena Horne singing "Push de Button" in Jamaica.

Harold Arlen and Truman Capote caricature by Al Hirschfeld.

With Robert Breen in Minneapolis listening to André Kostelanetz conducting the first performance of the Blues Opera Suite.

The première of the Blues Opera Suite *was scheduled for performance in an outdoor stadium, but was rained out twice, thus the appropriate prop while conductor and composer discuss the* Suite.

Cantor Samuel Arluck (center) *conducting service in Temple Adath Yeshuron in Syracuse, N.Y. The composer's father frequently wove some of his son's best-known melodies into the music for the services.*

In Moscow: Leonard Lyons the columnist is standing beside Harold Arlen. Alexander Smallens, conductor of Porgy and Bess, *and Mrs. Smallens are in the right foreground.*

Two members of the Porgy and Bess *company are married in Russia: Helen Thigpen, on the left, watches as the minister congratulates the groom, Earl Jackson. To the left of the boy stand Warner Watson and, behind him, Robert Breen. Harold Arlen and Leonard Lyons observe from the stairs.*

Judy Garland at the Palace. Her inscription reads: "Harold—Let's always go 'Over the Rainbow' together—love, Judy."

Portrait taken in Russia, 1956, by Horace Sutton.

Ted Koehler.

Ira Gershwin.

Truman Capote.

Johnny Mercer.

E. Y. ("Yip") Harburg.

Jack Yellen.

Ralph Blane.

Leo Robin.

Dorothy Fields.

Jerome Kern, oil by George Gershwin.

Oil by Pierre Henry.

Oil by Gloria Vanderbilt.

Still life, oil by Harold Arlen.

Oil by Henry Botkin.

Scene from Free and Easy (Blues Opera), *Paris, 1960. Irene Williams, as "Della," is at the head of the staircase.*

Portrait, 1960, by Carl Van Vechten.

serves as the introduction of the song. What is lacking from this printed rendering is Arlen's wonderful musical intervals. For example, immediately after the word "brow," there is almost a bar of musical comment, as there is also following the word "before," a "slow and steady" preparation (it is marked so in the printed music) for the song proper. After the word "this," just before the chorus is to begin, there are almost four bars of developement of the "slow and steady" theme building to a climax of a complex, sustained chord (with a span of a tenth in the bass and an octave in the treble). The pause is most effective, then Ottilie goes into her song:

> I never has seen snow
> All the same I know,
> Snow ain't so beautiful,
> Cain't be so beautiful like my love is,
> Like my love is
> (musical interlude, two bars: "Lazy but steady")
> Nothin' do compare
> Nothin' anywhere with my love.
>
> A hundred things I see
> A twilight sky, that tree,
> But none so beautiful,
> Not one so beautiful, like my love is,
> Like my love is
> (musical interlude, two bars)
> Once you see his face
> None can take the place of my love.
>
> A stone rolled off my heart
> When I laid my eyes on that near-to-me-boy
>   with that faraway look,
> And right from the start,
> I saw a new horizon and a road to take me
>   where I wanted to be took,
> Needed to be took.
> (musical interlude)
> And though
> I never has seen snow
> All the same I know nothin' will ever be
> Nothin' can ever be
> Beautiful as my love is,
> Like my love is to me.

Ottilie's mood fluctuates from wonderment in the first part of the song to an almost defiant assertion in the second (on the words "Nothin' do compare . . ."), introduced by the powerful music in the accompaniment. After the "release" ("A stone rolled off my heart") the chorus returns and a marvelous inner unity is achieved, for Arlen has combined the stately build-up theme of the verse with the powerful music of the chorus. What results is a trio with the voice carrying the melody, and, under that, two countermelodies.

"I Never Has Seen Snow" violates all the rules of popular song writing, but then it never was designed to be a "popular song," nor has it become one. It is, however, one of the most distinctive and distinguished songs written for the theater, concert stage, or wherever.

The most often heard song from *House of Flowers* is "Two Ladies in de Shade of de Banana Tree," a calypso-like rhythm number that in the show was built into a stunning dance arranged and orchestrated by a bright young musician, Peter Matz. Matz also arranged the music for an exciting ballet that closed the first act. Into this dance Matz wove themes from some of the songs already heard plus an additional delicious tidbit composed by Arlen, a waltz.

Truman Capote, though a poet, found writing songs a new experience. Arlen often would ask, "Does it sing?" when Capote produced a lyric. For a song is different from a poem; it may have meter but it must also be singable; it must be able to move with the melody. Capote has said that Harold Arlen is "the only living artist in popular music. He is always courageous, intelligent, and incapable of cliché. His songs almost invariably contain some melodic surprise, some difficulty —which is one of the reasons he has not had the recognition he deserves."

For all their difference in outlook it is interesting that Arlen and Capote share the same attitude toward their work, one believing that it is a search for the "phrase that comes at the right moment out of nowhere" (Capote) and the other, Arlen, in finding "the unsought-for phrase." Neither speaks of inspiration. Arlen, in fact, even refers to his work as "this comfortable trap," into which he has fallen and that saved him from a career as a performer but has placed him in a position to do what he loves to do, and yet out of which he cannot escape. This is work, not inspiration. The ivory-tower composer could not exist in the less than romantic atmosphere that a Broadway show emanates. Working in this milieu, in fact, would actually seem inimicable to the production of anything approaching art. Yet it sometimes happens.

House of Flowers exemplifies that compromise between art and commerce that eventually succeeds only in almost canceling itself out. Unlike the completely successful work, which runs a long time, or the complete flop, which disappears quickly, *House of Flowers* continued to creak along for five months. It was no more loved in May than it had been in December, and on the night of May 22 the final curtain came down.

Magically, as it is in the paper-moon world of the theater, wounds were healed, feuds forgotten, all forgiven. After the performance the cast and audience remained for what the *News* described as "a ripsnorter of a wake that kept the capacity audience in its seats until the early hours." After several curtain calls Pearl Bailey, acting as spokesman for the cast, told the audience that all the family quarrels that had been afflicting the show had been settled. But not soon enough to have stopped the rumors that were hurting the show. Miss Bailey then called Harold Arlen to the stage and led a community sing in a medley of his songs. She was then joined by Juanita Hall in tossing roses to the audience.

It remained for Miss Hall, however, to sum up the emotions of the evening in a simple statement spoken as tears rolled down her cheeks. Looking out over the full theater, she said, "Where were all you people last week?"

CHAPTER 10

A Game of Poker

The *House of Flowers* post-partum blues that might have afflicted Harold Arlen were deflected by a concentrated rash of recording activity. When Columbia Records, happily, preserved the *House of Flowers* score on the Sunday following the opening, Arlen was there to observe, to enjoy himself, and even be heard here and there on the record. Though not by any means completely recovered, he managed by virtue of his "protein and prayer," plus an indomitable spirit and a will to work to give, at least, the show of health. "The only important thing is work," he said at the time, "and work is experiment, searching."

He became involved with two other recording projects, both devoted to his own interpretations of his own songs. Except for his one vocal on the original cast album of *Bloomer Girl*, Arlen had done no recording since 1937. The first album, recorded by a small independent company, Walden Records, was an ambitious attempt to cover Arlen's output up to 1955, with emphasis on the lesser-known songs. Capitol Records recorded Arlen in his better-known songs. As arranger Arlen chose Peter Matz, with whom he had worked for the first time on *House of Flowers*.

All sessions were carefully planned beforehand, with enough leeway left for spontaneous contributions that might just happen during the actual recording. The resulting tapes were later carefully auditioned and edited, with the composer mercilessly critical of himself. He even came to the dull, almost endless editing sessions, which were consuming both his time and energies. The resultant albums were exciting, though they never received the notice they deserved when released.

Another diversion was Arlen's trip to Moscow with Ira Gershwin in January 1956, to attend the opening of *Porgy and Bess*. Gershwin had chosen to ignore most of the international openings, but found the Moscow one intriguing. Arlen had returned to Hollywood—he and Yip Harburg had begun work on a film about Nellie Bly.

Gershwin has been called "the master of inertia," because he prefers to stay on the "Plantation," except for excursions to the tracks nearby. That he would willingly make so bizarre a journey was an earth-shaking developement that must have set Beverly Hills agog. On his part, Arlen could not resist the opportunity to make the trip. Both he and Gershwin were asked by director Robert Breen to come to Russia. Breen and Arlen had long before begun their relationship that resulted in *Blues Opera,* which Breen planned to produce after the *Porgy* tour.

Once the decision was made there were technicalities to attend to, such as visas, passports, and the necessary preparations before leaving the country.

One of the necessities was Arlen's passport, which was in Washington. Arlen put in a call to his friend Richard Coe, dramatic critic on the Washington *Post,* who took Arlen's passport to the airport and gave it to a friend of his, a pilot about to leave for Los Angeles. Plane, pilot and passport arrived there at six in the morning, where Gershwin's secretary, Peggy Martin, was waiting. Arlen and Gershwin were scheduled to take off that evening. But it was discovered, on checking Arlen's passport, that it lacked some official stamp or other and would be invalid without it. A double check found Gershwin's passport lacking the same stamp. That required a fast trip to San Francisco by their mutual friend Lawrence D. Stewart, who returned in time for the two song writers to board their plane for Stockholm.

Because of the spur-of-the-moment decision Arlen did not yet have his Russian visa, which was to be picked up in

Helsinki. They had dinner in Stockholm and were surprised to hear the little orchestra in the dining room of the Grand Hotel playing a medley of songs from *Can-Can*. "Let's send a wire to Cole," suggested Arlen; and they did, telling Porter that they had heard his songs, French songs, composed by an American, played in Sweden.

Not many hours later they arrived in Helsinki, where, to Arlen's dismay, he found that his visa was not awaiting him as he had been assured. "I said to Ira, 'You go on, Ira,' and he did! Leaving me all alone in Helsinki, without a visa, I couldn't speak the language, and didn't know what might happen. I went to the Russian Embassy, ended up at the Intourist section; no one seemed to know anything about my visa. I tried to get into their favor by telling them my wife was of Russian descent, but that meant nothing. I began to panic. I'd get on the phone and talk to Bob Breen, or Lenny Lyons, or Truman in Moscow, and they'd all tell me everything would be fine. I'd make the trip from my hotel to the Russian Embassy, tired, troubled, and all alone in the reception room—except for very large photographs of Lenin and Stalin. It was like a Warner B movie."

"Between the trips and the phone calls and the waiting, I began to wonder. Finally after what seemed like many hours, an official bustled into the reception room, gave me my visa, smiled and said, 'You see—no problem.' "

He managed to make the Russian air liner leaving Helsinki for Leningrad; it was, as described by Lawrence D. Stewart, "a beaten-up two-motor job . . . individualistic in the extreme: no life belts, no stupid instructions about not smoking or not walking around when the plane was landing or taking off . . . but it got them there."

On the bouncing plane Arlen recognized violinist David Oistrakh, whom he had heard play at Carnegie Hall not many weeks before. When they arrived in Leningrad for lunch, Arlen tried to open a conversation using the three Russian words he knew, with the great violinist, only to learn that Oistrakh's English vocabulary consisted of "Carnegie Hall, Es-

sex House, Russian Tea Room," which summed up the extent
of his horizons outside Russia.

Arlen was met at the airport in Moscow by Warner Watson,
a friend, and an associate of Robert Breen. There was no time
for any stop at the hotel except to drop off Arlen's luggage,
before they were on their way to the theater, where they
found Breen on-stage with Leonore and Ira Gershwin and an
interpreter. Arlen, exhausted, settled, he hoped unobtrusively,
into his seat, only to be thumped on the back by Truman
Capote, urging him to stand, for Breen had introduced him.
Arlen was little more mystified than the Russians, who, found
suddenly standing in their midst, a celebrity in a slept-in suit
and a two-day beard.

The Moscow visit was pleasantly spent sight-seeing, attending concerts and the ballet, visiting homes of celebrated
Russians, and appearing at a reception at the American Embassy given by Ambassador Bohlen. In his enthusiasm Arlen
called Anya in California; the thrill at being called from so
exotic a place made up for the fact that it was 6 A.M. in
Malibu. Cole Porter sent them simple instructions, in reply
to their Stockholm wire: "Have fun boys."

The return was not so hectic as the trip out; both song
writers were happy to be back in the warmer climate of California—Gershwin to his lackadaisical pace on the "Plantation,"
and Arlen back to work on the Nellie Bly picture.

He and Harburg had completed a song for that before
the project was called off. Roger Edens, who was to produce
it, was under contract to Paramount to do another film,
Funny Face. Since he couldn't do both, the Nellie Bly idea
was dropped. Arlen hadn't been terribly taken with it and was
happy to be out.

Yip Harburg then began to discuss an idea that he and
Fred Saidy had begun to think about, "a simple folk tale"
(Harburg's description) they called *Pigeon Island*. It was set
on a West Indian island and had been written with Harry
Belafonte in mind. Calypsos were very popular, and Belafonte
was the major purveyor of that special song.

Although he wanted very much to work again with Harburg and Saidy, Arlen hesitated, primarily because of the setting. He felt that with *House of Flowers* to his credit he had mined all possible musical material from the Caribbean. After completing extensive research, in his customary quest for the "authentic ring," Arlen found that he could work up little enthusiasm for calypso's limited form. "Calypsos never have a strong melodic nature," he decided. "The few that have drive are closely related to our own Negro spirituals and work songs. I think it's boring and repetitious, if done authentically. 'Marianne' and 'Jamaica Farewell' are delights and are interesting on records, or as given an exciting performance by an artist like Belafonte. Otherwise, calypsos are theatrically uninteresting; you couldn't build an entire show on them."

But the persuasive Harburg and Saidy persisted and Belafonte became interested. Belafonte was eager to appear in an Arlen show, for even as a youngster he first became attracted to popular music through songs by Harold Arlen. He can still remember the impression that "Over the Rainbow" made on him. And he remembered meeting Arlen in those casual meetings that occur among people connected with show business. "Harold Arlen was always warm and gracious," he recalls. "And he was just as warm and gracious *then* as he was when my career reached the point where I became a big name."

Arlen felt that he couldn't fill an evening with calypso, but forced himself to work. The "jots" flowed easier with the voice of Harry Belafonte in mind. It was during this early stage of the work on *Pigeon Island* that Belafonte came to know Arlen so well. What impressed him most of all about the composer, besides "his deep humanity," was his patience, his willingness to wait—for about the time that producer David Merrick was ready to announce the forthcoming musical Belafonte had developed a serious throat trouble, and a realization of the great responsibility of starring in a full-scale Broadway show. Though the two were not connected, the rumors that went about hinted that the throat trouble and the sense of responsibility were closely related.

Actually Belafonte required an operation, but then wanted to spend a year resting his throat and studying, acting as well as the songs, which by now he had come to love—both music and words. But the exigencies attending the economics of show business could not wait a year. Merrick announced his production in May 1956, which meant that he planned a 1958 opening. Of all concerned, Belafonte remembers, only "Harold Arlen was willing to wait. It was an unfortunate experience for me, for I wanted so badly to do the musical; and now it just seemed impossible. You see, I consider Harold Arlen one of the three great geniuses of American music—the other two, George Gershwin and Leonard Bernstein—and I wanted to do his show. It was so warm and relaxing to work with him. As my wife has said, 'Harold's just so easy to be with,' if there's any strain, or tension when he's around—*you've* brought it, not Harold!"

By February 1957, Belafonte "withdrew," from what was now being called *Jamaica*, a story about a simple island boy whose girl longed for the complexities of urban "civilization." To replace Belafonte an attempt was made to enlist Sidney Poitier in the role, but he too had his commitments.

Rather wistfully, early in the search for a "name" star (for few shows can exist on Broadway without a name), Arlen had mentioned the glittering name of Lena Horne.

Miss Horne had just completed a highly successful run at the Waldorf-Astoria. She had hoped for years to star in a Broadway show. In 1939 she had appeared in a short-lived *Blackbirds,* but had made no Broadway appearance since. Instead, except for a brief fling in Hollywood, Miss Horne had concentrated on the cabaret grind. In 1957 Lena Horne was an international favorite, an exciting song stylist, eager to star in a show.

Her friendship with Arlen went back many years—to the Cotton Club—and it fell to him to ask Miss Horne to star in *Jamaica*. She, of course, happily accepted and the year's work by Arlen and Harburg was not to be wasted, but would require more work since the dramatic emphasis was to shift from the male lead to the female. Harburg and Saidy set to work at this in their book.

Lena Horne had for years made Arlen songs a part of her repertoire, referring to them as "soul rewarding. Harold doesn't write the cheap commercial tripe that is always recorded. Harold writes a song, not a mood coloring for a scene—and his songs are singable away from the story. But, oh—their excruciating range!"

But the presence of a personality of the stature of Lena Horne did not solve all problems; a giant also introduces problems and Miss Horne is a giant. While she had kept aloof from Broadway, an aloofness not necessarily of her own making, the fact that she was now to make the plunge contained within it the seeds of tension, of a greater striving for perfection. An audience is rarely aware of the doubts, the hard work, the endless rehearsal that a star entertainer forces on himself before he—or she—feels that even the smallest bit of business is ready to be tried before an audience. The irony is that the special polish, acquired only after tears, even pain, is so taken for granted by the audience that it is hardly noticed. The over-all impression is all that is remembered, and its perfection, timing, surface effortlessness are what is called "professionalism," the most coveted quality of all. There are many stars who are not professionals. Miss Horne is a professional, Belafonte is a professional, Judy Garland is a professional—and so on. But these are much rarer than we think, and it comes from an almost fanatical dedication to their work.

Shortly after she had agreed to appear in *Jamaica*, Miss Horne appeared on the Ed Sullivan Show and announced that she would appear in the Harold Arlen-Yip Harburg musical, and within a few weeks the advance sales on tickets reached close to a million dollars.

David Merrick, the producer, is a smart young lawyer who had fled from the provincial confines of St. Louis. Merrick has, since his entry into the Broadway lists, proved himself a smart businessman-showman who can make a hit of a flop. Among his bag of tricks are cheap publicity stunts, which he sanctimoniously decries but cynically practices. During the run of the musical *Fanny* it just happened that a nude statue of one of the show's dancers appeared in Central Park; at one performance of *Look Back in Anger* a lady charged onto the stage out of the audience and slapped the villainous hero in the face. It was good for a few days' newspaper coverage—and good for business.

A producer has more to do than cook up publicity stunts. His major job is raising the capital necessary to a show's production. This is something Merrick is supposedly able to do with little more than a half-dozen phone calls. Once the money is raised, the producer must then see that it is wisely dispensed and protected after that. Merrick's reputation as a producer rests primarily on his ability to return an investment, with interest. The means hardly interest the investor. To some the production of a show is an investment, to others it is an excursion into art, to others entertainment, and to others just a job. The glamour of a show is what comes over the footlights, not what happens in the much less glamorous back-stage areas and the completely unglamorous box office.

The box office, ultimately, is the most important determinant of a show's fate. A musical requires an investment of several hundred thousand dollars, which makes the box office an important factor indeed. And a major force in the theater today, because of its relationship to the box office, is the fairly recent phenomena, "the theater party."

The advance sale to theater parties can assure a "hit" even before it becomes one—and even if it doesn't, can be used to protect the investors' money. Theater-party tickets are bought by groups, clubs, and charities as fund-raising devices. Tickets are bought in blocks and resold at a raised price "for charity," to club members or the social group.

Theater-party groups are hardly to be confused with theater-goers, and certainly not with lovers of the drama. What contributes to the sale of tickets to shows even before they are completed are the names—the celebrities who are to star in the proposed show. The majority of theater-party members are bored, celebrity-hunting housewives from the suburbs (those who frequent the Wednesday and Saturday matinees; equally bored husbands and wives attend the evening performances). They have all come to see Ethel Merman, or Mary Martin, or Lena Horne; they have paid a lot for their tickets and they want to be entertained with a vengeance.

If a show has received a poor critical reception, such audiences tend to be greatly influenced by the reviews and they frequently take it out on the performers by being inattentive, by talking to one another during the show, and walking out before the curtain. Such an audience has no real interest in the theater, has no background to fall back on, must depend upon what they read in the papers for their views. They cannot judge a vehicle on their own and can literally kill a performance. If the show happens to be an unqualified hit—that is, if the critics liked it—the theater party will respond accordingly, robot-like. Not only have they been told what play they are supposed to see, they have come prepared to like it or not as they have also been told.

There are, as always, exceptions, but on the whole theater parties behave as described. Arranging for these parties are a group of women, coincidentally, whose job it is to decide which shows will be made available to the theater-party groups. This handful has been for years determining the direction of the American theater—again with exception—downward. Straight dramas aren't as readily chosen for theater parties unless an important "name" may be found in the cast. The name of the dramatist is hardly important, unless he happens to be a sensationalist like Tennessee Williams. But his plays are hardly thought of as the proper entertaining fare for a theater party. Thus the musical has come to depend heavily on the theater party, and the musical demands a great deal of backing to produce.

But if you have the right star in an unproblematical vehicle, you can raise the money on the strength of those elements alone. You can begin with little else than the names: the star and the title of the show, and find yourself with a lot of promised cash on hand. With this assured your investors may even come in ex post facto, and you are in business, traveling onward and upward with the arts.

With Miss Horne as an important asset to *Jamaica*, Merrick naturally tended to slant the entire production in her direction, as did director Robert Lewis. Soon the work of librettists Harburg and Saidy was reshaped to fit the handsome form of the star. Staging was planned so that Miss Horne could stand and sing as she had done so successfully at the Waldorf. Songs that had been planned for others were given to her, and by the time *Jamaica* opened Miss Horne was literally singing half the show. This was, of course, fine for Arlen and Harburg, song writers, but not so good for Harburg and Saidy, librettists.

By the end of April the score was pretty much completed and Arlen was able to supply Philip Lang, who was to orchestrate, with piano copies of all the songs. Piano copies are the songs as they appear in sheet music—the vocal line and accompaniment. From these the arranger makes his arrangements and orchestrates, after the treatment has been agreed upon by the composer and arranger, and the songs have been blocked out relative to their function in the show, and the choreographer and director have had their say. Because of the nature of the songs Lang came up with what he felt were some "provocative thoughts" on the orchestration that he realized were a "departure from the staid conservative concept of a theater orchestra that has persisted for years. There are many who will object violently," he admitted, "however, I see no reason why we should not muster our allotment of musicians for the best results complementing the score, locale, style, etc. of *Jamaica*."

To his letter Lang appended a suggested instrumentation; his remarks for his departure illuminate a little-known aspect of the work that goes into constructing a musical:

"DRUMS: Obviously the usual allotment of one drummer is unthinkable. In addition to the ever present drums, timpani, etc., it is essential that we avail ourselves of the South American drums along with all the exotic traps that distinguish that kind of music. A marimba is also in order. Its warm, throbbing sound is delightful and could even be used for vocal backgrounds. GUITAR: The usual guitar plus the bass guitar seems a must. Also the banjo and the Spanish guitar are often used. REEDS: I would like to see a lot of reeds, as many as six or seven. They would play Flutes, Alto Flutes, Oboes, Clarinets, (including the Alto, Bass and Contra Bass, Piccolos, etc. Saxes do not seem to be in order. BRASS: Three trumpets (specializing in the florid South American style) and three trombones (one bass trombone) would do and give us sufficient impact for choreography. Horns are not necessary. PIANO: While not absolutely necessary would be an asset. He could double on celesta and an accordion would be an asset. STRINGS: I have left this to the last as they seldom appear in this style of music. I would like to suggest that we minimize the number of strings to say, 4 violins, a viola and cello. This group would satisfy us for soft vocal accompaniment and under-dialogue incidental music. Also cutting the number of string players enables us to indulge in the luxury of additional drummers, guitarists, reeds, etc."

For his suggested instrumentation Lang managed to keep under the accepted maximum of twenty-eight to thirty musicians in the standard pit band. His orchestration called for twenty-six. He then had about five weeks to orchestrate the shows' score.

Jamaica's problems had little to do with the orchestration, and they began in Philadelphia on September 16. As reported in the Philadelphia *Daily News:* "Last evening perhaps did not constitute a fair test for a musical première. The humidity was at drenching highs and at times the rustling of the program fanners in the audience drowned out the quieter passages of the theatricals. There are obviously numbers, we felt, which deserved better reception than they got under the unseasonable playgoing conditions."

The reviewer from the *Evening Bulletin,* Wayne Robinson,

found that "Lena Horne, making her debut in her first
major role on the stage, understandably put a lot of real
meaning into her song ('Push de Button') of an islander
wishing for life in Manhattan where a push of the button
could turn on an air conditioner," but he continues, "*Jamaica*
has three weeks to get ready for Broadway, and from the
evidence last night it is going to need every minute of this
time . . ." He found, too, that Miss Horne had "the flash
and fire of a truly professional performer. She never lets
her audience down, whether it be in a routine show tune
such as 'Ain't It the Truth,' or the more tuneful 'Cocoanut
Sweet,' but most particularly when she can coil herself around
the words of 'Take It Slow, Joe,' giving this sensuous meaning
beyond the lyrics."

Appearing opposite Miss Horne was Ricardo Montalban,
engagingly portraying the island boy happy with his lot.
He sang charmingly, if without great vocal powers, and
managed to bring a definite conviction to the part.

In Philadelphia, Arlen became ill seriously enough to be
hospitalized, which precluded his writing additional songs
for Lena Horne; she was by then asking for just two more
numbers. At an early stage Arlen and Harburg had polished
up a song originally written for Miss Horne to be sung in
the film *Cabin in the Sky;* it was cut from the film and
seemed too good to waste, so it was interpolated into the
Jamaica score. Another good idea was saved, though it went
back further, to *Hooray for What?* There was a song titled
"Napoleon" in the show that was heard for a short while
sung by June Clyde. For *Jamaica* Harburg and Arlen revived
the idea but discarded the original lyrics and music for a
completely new song. Its evolution is interesting, as might be
noted in the first stanzas of each:

Hooray for What? version:
> Napoleon's a pastry so fellah beware
> Louis the fourteenth is only a chair
> Here's the moral in black and white
> We may be sponge-cake over night.

Jamaica version:
> Napoleon's a pastry
> Bismarck is a herring
> Alexander's a creme de cocoa mixed with rum
> And Herbie Hoover is a vacuum.

The musical structure of the *Jamaica* version is so designed that there are musical interludes after each lyric line, so that if there should be the hoped-for laughs they would not cover the succeeding line. And, too, it provided a brief breathing space for the hard-working Miss Horne.

Completely tailored to her delivery was "Take It Slow, Joe," a song Miss Horne found to be most effective, though as used in *Jamaica* thought it to be mocking and satirical rather than romantic, as she hoped it would be. Miss Horne's projection of most songs is satirical, poking fun at the song and frequently at the audience. Her singing of "Take It Slow, Joe" depended upon her mood at the moment, and she would change it from performance to performance both in tempo and delivery, but almost always tongue in cheek. As a song representative of Arlen's versatility, "Take It Slow, Joe" has yet to be discovered.

Miss Horne was pleased, however, with her "lyric fun" songs—"Napoleon," "Push de Button," the trio, "I Don't Think I'll End It All Today"—but loved most of all the unusual lullaby, "Cocoanut Sweet." It was sung in the first act by "Grandma," portrayed by Adelaide Hall, who had introduced Arlen and Koehler's "Ill Wind" in the Cotton Club *Parade* in 1934. Miss Horne joined her to make it a duet, and later reprised it, solo, in the second act—most beautifully.

Because it was obvious that *Jamaica* "needed work" by the time it reached Boston, warring factions had sprung up and there were high winds indeed. Harburg, serving as spokesman for the authors, found himself and Fred Saidy locked out of the theater. Arlen, who had come up to Boston despite his illness, found it simplest to keep out of the melee, though he faithfully sided with the writers against the management and director, who Harburg felt were distorting the book to make it only a Lena Horne vehicle and a palpable Broadway hit. By the Boston opening on October 8 the die was cast, for any further libretto changes would only have added to the confusion. But it assured Harburg and Saidy the role of sitting ducks for the critics.

Wrote Eliot Norton in the *Boston Daily Record:* "Although the libretto is silly and the director has yet to harness properly the remarkable talents of Lena Horne, *Jamaica* is potentially a fine musical comedy." This view summed up the general Boston consensus. There was a nod in the direction of Harold Arlen's "entrancing," "highly inventive" score and a concentration on Miss Horne, who was described variously as "fascinating," "breath-taking," "hauntingly beautiful," and so on—but it was obvious that the total musical did not please everyone. Of course, this posed no great financial problem, for the entire three-week Boston run was sold out, and the New York advance sale, with the help of theater parties, was in excess of a million dollars.

This was fine for the producer, his backers, and for those performers who were well received (though the critical remarks tended to note that Robert Lewis's direction of Miss Horne consisted of little else than standing her up front and center, beautiful to see and hear—but not really in context with any plot). Thus did the show come into New York— a stunning vehicle for its star, but almost without a plot.

The morning after was hardest on authors Harburg and Saidy. Their tale, under the Philadelphia stress and strain, played second fiddle. *Jamaica* had become a diverting and even a reverberating evening. The emphasis on percussion obscured the delicacy of some of the songs, particularly in the sensitive "Savanna," but it did keep one's attention riveted in the direction of the stage, where a great deal went on. Needless to say, Lena Horne stopped the show several times on opening night, which resulted in a great personal triumph for her.

Brooks Atkinson, of the good, gray *Times*, provided the

most ecstatic appraisal: "*Jamaica* is as beautiful, jovial, old-fashioned musical comedy that has been produced and staged with taste and style." Mr. Atkinson had deplored the production of *House of Flowers,* but found the same setting—away from the bawdyhouses—much more to his taste.

Walter Kerr, however, didn't agree, except in his estimation of Miss Horne (the even more gallant Richard Watts, Jr., stated it simply: "Lena Horne is probably the most beautiful woman in the world"), but Kerr asked: ". . . can you make a whole show out of sheet music?" He found "Harold Arlen of considerable assistance in keeping this marathon going. He has hummed out a low, rolling, altogether affecting lullaby in 'Little Biscuit' [highly doubtful, for this song is a cynical duet; Mr. Kerr was probably referring to "Cocoanut Sweet"], a bittersweet ballad in 'Pity The Sunset,' and a couple of antically, breezy, engagingly light-footed didoes in 'What Good Does It Do?' and 'Napoleon.' "

Harburg the lyricist received deserved accolades for his stilettoed lines for such songs as "Leave the Atom Alone," "Push de Button," "Incompatibility," and "I Don't Think I'll End It All Today." There was some typical critical carping about some of the songs' "social significance," which Mr. Kerr found "stimulating in the thirties and . . . so uncomfortable now." Social events and political developments were not merely characteristic of the Thirties, of course, and the atom bomb that obviously concerned Mr. Harburg did not even exist in Mr. Kerr's Thirties. Like most critics, Mr. Kerr successfully missed the sardonic tone that did remain in the book.

Though the characters in *Jamaica* supposedly lived on the isolated Pigeon Island they were a singularly sophisticated and well-informed group. They carried on like calypso-singing "natives" only for the benefit of tourists. For all their simplicity the inhabitants of Pigeon Island proved to be intelligently satirical and wise. The thesis of the Harburg-Saidy book was much the same as Thoreau's in *Walden:* "Simplify, simplify, simplify." This hardly seems to be too much of a message to absorb, particularly when so entertainingly stated, by the average intelligent theater-goer, or even a critic. The complexities of civilization that *Jamaica*'s Savanna yearned for did not interest Koli (Montalban), who pointed out that tourists came to Pigeon Island to shed their tensions and their shoes. "I am here," he observed with disarming wisdom, "and my shoes are already off."

The so-called social significant songs were stated in clever, intricately rhymed lyrics and were a credit to anyone's intelligence.

As for Lena Horne, *Jamaica* provided a stimulating experience. "Cabaret audiences made me grateful for the captive audience in the theater," she will say somewhat pointedly. "I think it was good for me."

Though receiving much praise for his *Jamaica* score Arlen feels that it lacks the musical unity of *Bloomer Girl*, *St. Louis Woman*, or *House of Flowers*. He may admit that he has a fondness for individual songs, but feels that as a unit the *Jamaica* songs fell short of his mark. Of course the final product the public views is invariably the end result of tugging and the wounding of the opposing egos involved. The finished product cannot favor any one faction lest it become a choreographer's show, a composer's show, a librettist's show, a star's show, or even, as has happened, a set designer's show. When all these elements combine in perfect balanced whole, something close to art is the result. But when one of the elements predominates, a top-heavy show is the result, which is the case with *Jamaica*. But luckily there at the top was Lena Horne, and the show ran well over five-hundred performances—a fact that Arlen almost completely attributes to the presence of the star.

Interestingly, in December 1959 *Jamaica* was presented at the Karamu Theater in Cleveland in its original form, without a "name," and with the original, uncut score—including the deleted "Noah"—and ran much longer than its planned few weeks, in fact was extended for a couple of months.

After completing *Jamaica*, Arlen didn't touch music for over a year. He found nothing to interest him, so he simply did no writing—a mistake, he feels, "for we should always keep in trim by writing something every day." The short run of *House of Flowers* and the unpleasantness of *Jamaica*, despite its outward success, disappointed him, and, worse, discouraged him into a disinterest in work.

One morning in October 1958 the mail contained a letter from dramatist Paddy Chayefsky; enclosed was a poem for which he felt that he would like to have music written by Harold Arlen. The title was "In the Middle of the Night," then on Chayefsky's mind, for his play of the same title was about to be produced as a film. Possibly, he felt he and Arlen could collaborate on a theme song for the movie. Ordinarily Arlen ignores such unsolicited lyrics, even from a writer of Chayefsky's stature, but he was so touched by the sentiment as expressed in this lonely night song, that he found himself reading it through a few times; more importantly, the lyric "sang." Within a couple of days he had set the lyric with a melody of an elusive, haunting beauty. But when *In the Middle of the Night* was released, the song was not heard; arrangements between Arlen's representatives and the film studio had not worked out. The song remains unpublished.

Any disappointment Arlen may have felt because of that was completely overshadowed by his grief over the death of his mother in December 1958. He bore the loss as he did the death of his father, but it was something he carried with him silently. As he wrote friends, "I'll not go into the emotional end of this mysterious and final curtain."

He and Anya left the cold of New York for the more relaxing climate of California. Arlen was then considering two possibilities: a film score for a cartoon version of *A Christmas Carol* and a stage work. He chose to do the musical.

From its inception *Saratoga* was a mistake, and while its drawbacks were obvious (a ponderous story, unsympathetic characters) there was just that gambling possibility that it might be brought off. Arlen was banking on the great talent and reputation of Morton DaCosta, who had adapted the Edna Ferber novel *Saratoga Trunk* and would also direct.

DaCosta had enjoyed a run of hits for a period of about five years, beginning with the musical *Plain and Fancy* and running through *The Music Man*. DaCosta could, if anyone could, make something of an essentially old-fashioned book. The locales were tempting: Paris, New Orleans, Saratoga. So was the period, and even the characters: an Oklahoma cowboy, a young adventuress, her proud commanding duenna, and a dwarf servant.

Johnny Mercer was approached to do the lyrics, but he wasn't easily convinced. On the train from California he had read the book, and on arriving in New York greeted DaCosta with a typically soft-spoken speech that had little good to say about the book or the people in it. He devastatingly all but dismissed the idea as an obvious dated sequel to *Show Boat* that should have been done some thirty years before. But the lyricist was finally placated and he resigned himself to the job, having had his initial say: "I wasn't really keen on it, but I'm always doing jobs I don't want." He hoped, too, for some form of magic that just might make it all come off.

Early in 1959 the first announcements began to be made: most exciting to the theater-party groups was the intimation that Rock Hudson was willing to desert the screen for a fling at Broadway, but what promised to be a historical musical debut was spoiled by the Hollywood fathers, who kept Mr. Hudson in Hollywood. The columns, however, began documenting Hudson's vocal lessons etc., but he was out of the picture early.

In April the Arlens moved to California for an extended stay, hoping to avoid New York's summer heat in a place where Arlen and Mercer could work. They would have to return in September when *Saratoga*'s rehearsals were to begin.

DaCosta's first draft was used to develop the score; in it he had indicated song cues, even suggested titles. By March all the discussions were over and Mercer and Arlen began. The work went rapidly and in May the bulk of the songs were completed, enough so that Arlen could send a friend in New York a page of jots. Both DaCosta and producer Robert Fryer were exceptionally pleased with the songs; all was apparently going smoothly.

On June 16 Arlen was writing to his friend in New York: "If you don't believe my pen is to paper—neither do I—it's bad enough feeling guilty about not working when you're in the pool, let alone having wakeful hours with your [unanswered letter] staring me in the face——

"As you know from the lead jots I sent you John and I did an enormous amount of work up to that point but we've pulled in our reins and have been trotting slowly but surely down the back stretch——

"I can't determine its worth or dare guess what it will have out of the theater but I'm fairly certain it will work *in* the theater—that is if our principals are cast well——

"What does amaze and amuse me about the work is the difference in style from *Jamaica—Blues—Flowers*, etc. When I ponder about it it makes me stop in my tracks & wonder how long this can go on—I don't think an audience nor the critics realize (alas why should they) how much is taken from a writer every time he goes to bat——

"That is why I have always been a true lover of & might add slightly in awe of the Gershwins—Porter—Rodgers—Berlin —Hammerstein—Kern— The very few others with a smidgen of exceptions borrow well—at least well enough to blind the critics' ears—I think we've had enough of the above——

"As to my work with John—I have a hunch we might come down the finish line by the middle of July or thereabouts——

"We are taking Dr. Bunche & his wife & daughter to Ira's tonight—perhaps you shall hear from me soon . . . Anya sends her love to you both & the children."

In July, Arlen came into New York for a week of casting; at that time he would hardly have hesitated to say that the ingredients of *Saratoga* added up to a hit: Howard Keel and Carol Lawrence had been chosen to star; DaCosta was directing, among other chores, décor was to be by Cecil Beaton, songs by Arlen and Mercer, and Robert Fryer was producing.

But when rehearsals did get under way at the Central

Plaza in New York's lower East Side, there was something obviously wrong. On some days the different parts of *Saratoga* were rehearsed in various parts of the building, the dances in one, the book in another, the singing in another. When all were brought together for a run-through, it was obvious that the show would run too long. Also, it opened with a deadly prologue that contributed to the exposition but served even more efficiently to hold up the show for close to fifteen minutes. Most of the original dialogue, effective in the best-selling novel, sounded stilted coming from the stage.

The score was a full one—ranging from a French-like waltz, "The Parks of Paris" to atmospheric street cries and New Orleans work songs, an early jazz band tune, "Petticoat High," as well as the usual ballads and rhythm numbers.

One of the finest songs, "Goose Never Be a Peacock," was assigned to concert contralto Carol Brice; a lovely, fragile melody was sung by Odette Myrtil, a musical-comedy star of the Thirties (*Cat and the Fiddle* and *Roberta*) who left the security of running a business for *Saratoga*. Her song was "Love Held Lightly," which was devised to be sung in counterpoint to the cynical "A Game of Poker."

Two fine ballads were written, "You for Me" and "The Man in My Life," but the first was dropped along the way. An entire musical sequence of great imagination and invention was written for a scene in a New Orleans restaurant in which the cowboy is having his troubles with the French menu: its title was "Bon Appétit." Another number was an ingenious treatise on gossip, set to the rocking accompaniment of the singers on-stage sitting in rocking chairs. The lyric makes some illuminating observations:

> Have you heard?
> Too absurd!
> Her masseur!
> Bold as brass
> On the grass!
> By the pool—
> She's a fool!

All seemed to be working out during rehearsals. Both Miss Lawrence and Keel were in fine voice, each seeming to fit the roles perfectly. Word had even got around to "those in the know" that the hard-sell ticket would be *Saratoga;* the talk, too, was that the score was good, and some of its songs were already being heard at parties.

Inevitably Philadelphia came on October 26. The audience was bad. "It was disgraceful," in the opinion of veteran Dr. Albert Sirmay, a man who has been seeing musicals for the past three decades and who has served as musical editor for such composers as Gershwin, Rodgers, Porter, and Arlen. "The audience did not give much attention to what went on on the stage. They were not interested enough. And they were sometimes so noisy that you couldn't understand the songs."

Obviously *Saratoga* was being smothered under the weight of its own opulence. The costumes and sets by Beaton encouraged the oohs and ahs from the audience, but once these had been acknowledged attention was turned elsewhere. One production number, "Petticoat High," with choreography by Ralph Beaumont, sparked the first act (though the number itself ran too long) and captured the audience. But the inactivity that followed could not sustain the audience for the rest of the show until the imaginatively staged "Railroad Fight" (in slow motion) in the last act.

Instead of attempting to repair the book DaCosta responded to the critical reception by cutting five musical numbers, hoping perhaps that new songs would liven the show. The prologue was cut, which helped, but practically all of the book remained as it was. It devolved upon Arlen and Mercer to repair the show musically. They tried: they did "You or No One," "Countin' Our Chickens," and "I'm Headed for Big Things," of which the first two remained.

After a few days of constant work Arlen's health broke down. Without rest and under the tensions inevitable with a floundering production, he could do no more than bow out and suggest that they get another composer for any other songs that might be needed. He left for New York and within a few days was in Mt. Sinai Hospital getting the rest he desperately needed. But he was aware, too, of a terrible truth: *Saratoga* was a sure flop.

In Philadelphia the work continued; there would be changes from matinee to evening performances. The cast became confused, fatigued, and demoralized. But with the book as it was there was little that could be done without a vast revision.

One definite deficiency was the absence of laughter, and attempts were made to inject lightness by restaging some of the numbers and adding little bits of business and new songs.

At this stage in the shambles Johnny Mercer's personal affection for Arlen, by now quite ill, manifested itself in three songs for which he wrote both words and music: "Why Fight This?" "Gettin' a Man," and "The Men Who Run the Country." He did this without hesitation and did not even expect to receive credit for the work. He was surprised, in fact, when a friend let it be known that he knew the lyricist had written the three songs; Mercer assumed that only he and the arranger were aware of the authorship. Mercer accepted the work as part of the turn of fate and merely wanted to keep it within the professional family. Arlen, however, called the publisher when he learned of Mercer's work and insisted that the lyricist receive full credit for his songs.

Though out of the hospital by the time *Saratoga* opened Arlen was still too weak to attend; besides, he had lost all interest in the show. The expected happened: in Broadwayese, "It was bombed."

In retrospect it is doubtful that any show could have been as bad as the critics said *Saratoga* was. The reception was not uniformly bad, some critics even liked it, but those who considered it bad thought it to be very, very bad. "I'm sure," Walter Kerr began his comments in the *Herald Tribune* on a positive note, "all hearts lifted at the sound of the Harold Arlen overture at the Winter Garden last evening. I know mine did. While I don't remember just which tunes were threaded through it to give it that jubilant air, I solemnly swear to you that they were one and all good."

John McClain, of the *Journal-American,* was another critic
who enjoyed the score as "simply wonderful. It is singable,
whistleable and delightfully in the mood of Edna Ferber's
novel . . ." The other critics found it "lackluster" (Atkinson),
"nothing tuneful" (Aston), "bouncy but undistinguished"
(Coleman). Richard Watts, Jr., found all the songs pleasant
but summed up the critical opinions when he called *Saratoga*
"a pictorially beautiful bore."

"Everything's wild and the chips are down" is a line from
"A Game of Poker," and it was true of *Saratoga.* Morton
DaCosta received the worst of the critics' barbs. His book
was attacked in unison. The skill of his direction simply could
not lift up the show, and there it stood—or lay. It was possible, with heroic revisions, that *Saratoga* might have been re-
fashioned into an entertaining musical that might have enjoyed a comfortable run. But for some reason the required
work was not forthcoming. DaCosta, in fact, left for Europe
to attend to commitments made months before. Before he left,
however, he called all members of the cast and staff onstage
and manfully admitted that all responsibility for the show's
failure should fall on him.

The cast remained behind, however, to contend with the
theater-party crowds primed by the reviews. While *Saratoga*
remained a lovely show to see and hear—for Jerry Arlen
provided sensitive orchestral direction of his brother's score—
no one saw and no one listened; there were too many faults
untouched by expert hands and *Saratoga* collapsed after eighty
performances with an estimated loss of $390,000. The original
investment had been $400,000.

Late in February 1960, not many days after *Saratoga* collapsed, Arlen wrote to friends: "As you know the show closed
unfortunately, but that's the way of the theater and we will
have to take it in our stride." Unlike others, especially close
friends, Arlen could not agree with DaCosta in his accepting
the blame. "We were all to blame," Arlen would assert, "we
were all professionals, we should have recognized what was
wrong early. But that's in the past."

CHAPTER 11

I Wonder What Became of Me?

Of all the works of Harold Arlen undoubtedly the one with the most curious history is *Blues Opera.* It is one on which Arlen worked the longest, that has given him the most personal satisfaction and a consistent series of disappointments.

When Robert Breen, co-producer and director of the internationally celebrated *Porgy and Bess* company, was seeking companion pieces for the Gershwin opera—Breen was hoping to form a repertory company specializing in American musicals—he began by discussing the idea with conductor Alexander Smallens, who suggested commissioning a prominent "serious" composer, but Breen disagreed on that point. He felt that the kind of opera, or musical play, to be produced by his Everyman Opera Company, while it should not be written down to the public in any way, should on the other hand be accessible, literally, to every man. He based his dissent on the paucity of melodic appeal, the lack of singability, found in many contemporary works for the theater.

The sort of thing he had in mind, Breen explained, would have to be filled with memorable, rich, viable melodies. He expatiated on this point, even compiled a list of such songs as he would like to hear in the work he had in mind, one that could be alternated with *Porgy and Bess* and could be sung by the same company.

Breen showed his list to Cab Calloway, then appearing as Sportin' Life in the Gershwin opera, and was surprised when Calloway told him that all eight of the songs were composed by one man—Harold Arlen. Though he knew the name, Breen had not associated Arlen with all of the songs. Calloway had known the composer during the Cotton Club period but had lost track of him over the years, though he was fairly certain that Arlen had disappeared into the wilderness of Beverly Hills. Breen then wrote to Ira Gershwin, asking if he knew the whereabouts of Harold Arlen. Another coincidence: Arlen was with Gershwin, for they were then at work on *A Star Is Born;* this was late in 1953.

When Arlen came East to begin working on *House of Flowers,* he and Breen began their discussions on what kind of musical, or opera, might be done. Even while he was in the hospital Arlen continued his talks with Breen, between work sessions with Capote and transfusions from the doctors. While they talked, such possibilities as an adaptation of the John Henry folk tale came up, so did *The Madwoman of Chaillot, Mrs. McThing,* and other equally fanciful ideas.

Finally Betty Comden brought Breen's attention to the *St. Louis Woman* score. Like so many other song writers, Miss Comden had a great fondness for the score and hoped that something might be done to rescue it from undeserved obscurity. Breen, who had been executive director of ANTA at the time *St. Louis Woman* ran in New York, had never seen it. He had been so tied up in his own work, and besides he habitually saw the dramas first each season and saved the musicals for last. By the time he got around to musicals in 1946 *St. Louis Woman* was not to be seen. But he was able to hear some of the score on the highlights recorded by Capitol Records by the cast. He was immediately taken with the musical quality of the score and the poetry of Johnny Mercer's lyrics.

But this was not quite it, Breen felt. He hoped for a more fully developed work than a series of songs of a Broadway score. He suggested that the book be revised, the score filled out with other appropriate Arlen songs, new songs written, and even all the dialogue set to music.

This last suggestion did not immediately win Arlen. He felt that recitative might prove burdensome, pretentious, and not good showmanship. Breen was, as always, most persuasive and

Arlen changed his mind. They then took the basic *St. Louis Woman* score, restored all the songs that had been deleted on the road, and as the dialogue was rewritten began setting it to music. Because of his involvement with *House of Flowers*, and still dangerously ill, Arlen's time and stamina were terribly limited. Breen then called in Samuel Matlowsky, composer and conductor, educated at the Paris Conservatoire, to transcribe Arlen's melodies as he dictated them; Matlowsky also orchestrated the work.

Matlowsky began their initial session with, "Now, the first thing about *recitative*——" Which Arlen cut off with, "Don't tell me!" And Matlowsky didn't tell Arlen (who knew, of course, but wanted to handle this in his own way). Arlen is also sensitive about influences, even unconscious ones—as Breen observed, "When he's working on a score Harold won't even listen to Beethoven."

In a way this is true. Actually Arlen's interests away from his work rarely include music. If he does listen to the radio, he is an inveterate dial twirler, as he seeks to avoid the aural onslaught of today's popular music. If he does settle at one station on the dial, it would most likely be to hear a solo piano performing a work by one of the impressionists. As for Beethoven, Arlen naturally admires the music, though for his taste he feels it "is too grand, too imposing." He loves Bach's architecture. He admires the romantic richness of Rachmaninoff. But he does not listen to music very often; he would rather read—particularly about art and artists—or look at pictures.

A friend may call and get a polite and hasty brush-off with, "Sean O'Casey is on television now, I'll call you back; or he might be watching Carl Sandburg or Stravinsky.

Or a ball game. His doctor and friend Dr. Maurice Schachtel may come by for a visit and the two of them, composer and doctor, will sit watching the game, discussing the plays, the players, the records of the players for years back, and all other such esoterica associated with the game. Because his office is not far from the Arlens' apartment, Dr. Schachtel is apt to receive a daily visit from Arlen to exchange jokes, and to discuss yesterday's game. With the retirement of Dr. Elias, Dr. Schachtel keeps a close watch on Arlen's health. When he replaced Dr. Elias, the doctor's name sounded extremely familiar to Arlen. Dr. Schachtel turned out to be Murray Schachtel of Buffalo, whom he had known as a boy, and whose parents were very good friends of the Arlucks.

Dr. Schachtel became Arlen's personal physician during the period Arlen worked with Breen on *Blues Opera*. He allowed but one hour a day for that. Breen and his wife, Wilva, would come to Arlen's home to read from the revised libretto. The character and situation would be described; Breen would enact the scenes, in fact, portraying all the characters, describing the set, the color schemes, the very movements of all the characters. When a character was shot, Breen would fall to the floor; it was an exciting one-man performance.

With all this before him Arlen would be given a line or two of dialogue that, if he were not in bed, he would play for the Breens and Matlowksy, or he would sing the lines. Matlowsky, who would note it down, was most impressed with Arlen's natural feeling for sung dialogue, and Arlen, in turn, appreciated Matlowsky's muscianship and understanding of what they were trying to accomplish. Under these conditions Arlen composed sixteen extended recitatives—and when he heard them played months later did not even remember them!

Work continued in this precarious manner as Arlen's health and work on *House of Flowers* permitted. When he went back into the hospital in September 1954, enough work had been done on *Blues Opera* so that Breen felt he could announce a Paris production in December.

But in December there was no opening in Paris; instead M-G-M announced that it would film *St. Louis Woman* with Frank Sinatra, Ava Gardner, and Sammy Davis, Jr., as the leads. It took two years to clear up that situation. The film was never made, but M-G-M did have a claim to the original show. Finally an agreement running to 116 pages was drawn

up in November 1956 (already three years after Breen had
had his idea); all the legalities, rights, etc., were made turgidly
proper. *Blues Opera* was then announced for an April 1958
opening. In the meantime Arlen had collaborated with Yip
Harburg on *Jamaica* and continued to add songs to *Blues
Opera*.

The major factor now was the backing. Until the production
money was raised *Blues Opera* would not be presented. There
was a bright developement: Andre Kostelanetz had heard of
the work and asked to see the score. He liked it so much he
asked to have a suite drawn from it that he would introduce
in his popular concerts. Kostelanetz and Arlen chose about
twenty songs and themes that were woven together in sequence and orchestrated by Matlowsky into a suite lasting
about twenty-five minutes. *Blues Opera*, by this time, had
grown to a work of close to three hours of music.

The world première of the *Blues Opera Suite* took place in
Minneapolis; scheduled for Tuesday, August 27, 1957, in the
Bloomington Stadium, the concert was rained out. On
Wednesday, with the rains still falling on the outdoor stadium,
the concert was switched to the Minneapolis Auditorium. The
warm reception by the cheerfully displaced audience was gratefully acknowledged by Arlen, who had flown to Minneapolis
with the Breens.

On November 2, Kostelanetz played the *Blues Opera Suite*
for the first time in New York at Carnegie Hall with the New
York Philharmonic. On the same program were Berlioz's *Ro-
man Carnival Overture*, Prokofieff's *"Classical Symphony*, Villa
Lobos's *Memories of Youth*, and Rachmaninoff's *Vocalise*. The
suite closed the concert.

The suite again was received exceptionally well by the over-
flow audience. Kostelanetz gestured to Arlen, seated in a box.
The composer stood to an even greater hand, which he characteristically insisted upon sharing with Matlowsky and the conductor. For the composer it was naturally a thrilling experience, though his theatrical instincts cried out for vocals.

But this was more than compensated for by the brilliant interpretation by the Philharmonic.

The *Herald Tribune,* in commenting on the concert, observed that "Mr. Arlen's music was played in a suite effectively orchestrated by Samuel Matlowsky. Its series of well-turned tunes illustrated the composer's well-known fertile and copius melodic invention.

"A sense of individuality, however, was sometimes tempered by certain conventions which have been used by other noted contributors to the Broadway stage and song literature.

"While there was much color and some dramatic characterization, the music did not always seem to realize the locale and action outlined in the program notes, what with an occasional air of sophistication that could have been wider.

"A stage performance," was the conclusion, "might, indeed, modify this impression."

The Sidney Lumets (Gloria Vanderbilt) had a party in honor of the New York première. Accompanied by his cousins, the Earl Cranes, and their daughter, Arlen arrived at the Lumet home. While Bill Sweigart, a devoted collector of Arleniana, helped Mrs. Lumet choose recordings for the Arlen evening, the composer sat away from the hubbub talking with his friends, Fred Saidy, A. L. Berman, columnist Leonard Lyons. It was a pleasant, name-filled, tuneful evening, attended to by the dedicated Sweigart. Kostelanetz was pleased with the suite and its reception and decided to record it, unprecedented for an unproduced work.

But this was not the end of the story. Arlen continued to add new music to the score, such inventions as the remarkable "Flower Chant," with its almost startling accompaniment, "Many Kinds of Love," and "Della's Ballad," a song without words. Breen had been able to interest several producers—all impressed with the score, which Arlen had taped in part; other vocalists and Matlowsky had filled in the other parts. The dynamic, dedicated Breen had conceived *Blues Opera* as a single set, smoothly flowing work combining the elements of opera, ballet, and drama all fused into one.

Such songs, or more precisely, fragments of songs, as "Blues in the Night," "Ac-Cent-Tchu-Ate the Positive," and "One for My Baby" were woven into the fabric of the score, all so skillfully that there is no impression that they have been dragged in, but are integral to characterization and action. There are no planted, deliberate, show-stopping numbers—customary in a musical that must afflict itself with a big-name star—instead, there is a continuous, dynamic course of melody and rhythm.

As an example of such use of a mere melodic strain there is the song, "A Woman's Prerogative," which served as a Pearl Bailey show-stopper in *St. Louis Woman;* in *Blues Opera* it is heard only as a brief comment on some action in the story. "Blues in the Night" becomes a bitter declamation of a castoff woman, beginning parlando, as if spoken, and rising in intensity, developing into song, in a climax in which a piercing soprano is heard against an emotionally charged choral background.

Dramatically the entire opera abounds in such moments of high pitch balanced by moments of lighter musical touches and humor. Musical unity is further strengthened by employment of stylized movement and pantomime that is balletic. There are actual dances, too, as in the first act's imaginative and authentic cakewalks. The second act utilizes an inventive idea: the sound of a telegraph key is a part of the music, while a rapid flashing of lights (timed to the rhythm of the telegraph key) suggests the running of an off-stage race.

In March 1959 a change came into the history of *Blues Opera* when it was announced that Stanley Chase, young co-producer of the long-run off-Broadway hit, *The Threepenny Opera,* would produce *Blues Opera,* with Robert Breen attending to direction.

The original title was quickly dropped in favor of *Free and Easy* because it was felt that the word "opera" had unfortunate connotations for public and critics alike. "Free and Easy" was borrowed from the first line of "Anyplace I Hang My Hat Is Home" and was felt, at least by Chase, to be a

better title. Early in April 1959, Arlen wrote on the final page
of the score: "Now you take it from here, Bob," a message to
Breen, for Arlen had finished work on the opera and felt that
the rest was up to Breen. The copyist, thinking Arlen's joking
message to Breen was a stage direction, left it in the score.

Arlen was deep in work on *Saratoga* with Mercer when he
completed work on *Free and Easy*. Between songs for the
Ferber-DaCosta musical they completed two songs for the
opera, including lyrics for "Della's Ballad," now titled "Won't
Dat Be de Blessed Day." Both *Saratoga* and *Free and Easy*
rehearsed simultaneously. While Breen worked with the company, Chase and his staff made preparations for the scheduled
opening in Europe on December 7—coincidentally also the
opening date of *Saratoga*.

Irene Williams, strikingly beautiful daughter of composer
Clarence Williams, was chosen to sing the role of Della; it was
hoped that after *Free and Easy* had completed its "out-of-town"
European tour Sammy Davis, Jr., would join the company before its New York opening, in the role of the jockey, Augie.

In the *Times*, Lewis Funke reported the elaborate plans:
"Ten years in the making. Yet, to be sure, no man can tell
how long in the showing will be the destiny of Harold Arlen's
musical *Free and Easy*, for which Johnny Mercer provided the
lyrics. The future notwithstanding, in the offices of Stanley
Chase, producer, and Robert Breen, director, the project is
being laid out with a world view . . . men and women will
grow old in the service of *Free and Easy*, some even will marry
and have babies."

O brave new world, that has such people in't!

Mr. Funke followed his earlier dispatch with another about
a week later, announcing that jazz arranger-musician Quincy
Jones would completely reorchestrate *Free and Easy* in a
"completely new jazz idiom." Mr. Jones, who was to be assisted
by Bill Byers in his imposing task, is a representative of the
new school of jazz, a far cry from either the idiom of the
theater or even the blues. Mr. Jones was then quoted as saying,
"We're either going to rock the boat or sink it."

A further innovation was introduced when it was decided to use the musicians on-stage, purportedly to allow for the accompaniment to grow out of the drama, just as the orchestrations, it was hoped, would germinate out of the idiom of the music. The musicians on-stage would allow a more realistic, unobtrusive use of music, a closer relationship between score and accompaniment.

Thus with their plans laid and their future set the company boarded a chartered plane and left for Brussels on November 15, in time for further rehearsals before the set opening date. Arlen was too much involved in *Saratoga* to be able to get away to watch over the fortunes of his labor of love on which he had spent over half a decade of work.

But when the opening approached, *Free and Easy*, like *Saratoga*, was in floundering chaos. A week before its scheduled opening preview performances were presented, and the reception, especially by the press, was far from favorable. It was then decided to postpone the opening from the seventh to the fifteenth. Breen and Chase began having their differences. The former insisted that the show needed rewriting and more rehearsals, and the latter contended that the show was ready to open and that the cast was being overworked. The situation exploded into a series of charges and countercharges, with the ultimate result being the displacement of Breen, now titled "acting director," by his assistant, Donald McKayle. Critical reactions improved, though there were still serious reservations about the book. The cast and the score were always enthusiastically received. On opening night at the Theatre Carré in Amsterdam there were eight curtain calls.

The next month was devoted to tightening the book in preparation for the Paris opening. Just before Christmas *Variety* sent a man to look in on *Free and Easy* in Amsterdam. To his (Sall's) expert eye he found many excellent ingredients, though he held some minor reservations: "At first, this musical had a lot of action but no meaning. With already a full 15 minutes cut, and still lasting three hours, *Free* will gain by some more editing.

"The one set by Ballou . . . is a thing of beauty . . . Costumes by Jed Mace are wonderful. Irene Williams has a wonderful voice and enough allure to carry the role [of Della] . . . Scene stealer is Harold Nicholas [as Augie, the part he had in the original *St. Louis Woman*], not gifted with a good voice, but what he lacks as a singer he makes up in personality." Sall concluded with "*Free and Easy*, given time and rehearsals, can grow into an impressive musical."

The Amsterdam reviewers were critical though friendly. "Since yesterday evening," wrote the critic for *Algemeen Handelsbad*, "we know what the Americans mean by an 'out-of-town' opening, which is neither a dress rehearsal nor yet an opening. The charming and touching qualities of the show, which are already obvious, will undoubtedly be further developed." *Het Parool* found that "not much can be made of such a meagre story, and Breen could only show his great talent as director in the mass scenes." In *De Telegraaf*, Jan Spierdijk pointed out, "The setting was beautiful and practical, the costumes magnificent and colorful. The most striking factor, however, was the staging of Robert Breen."

According to Walter H. Waggoner, writing in Amsterdam for the New York *Times*, Breen "first came to grief . . . with the musicians. He was not only faced with a lot of free spirits unaccustomed to the firm hand of a director; he also had the task of dealing with a whole set of new problems.

"This was the first time, Breen said, that there had ever been a complete jazz orchestration for an entire musical. It was the first time that a jazz band had appeared on the stage not only as musicians doing their work in their own way, but also as characters in a play. And they had to memorize their scores. Finally, Breen had to adapt jazz orchestrations and the musicians in the art of accompaniment. Some of these free spirits, who represented the cream of jazz musicianship, found it hard to adjust to direction and Breen's directorial responsibility."

"I had to convince them," Breen is quoted as saying, "that when Della comes out with the statement about home being where she hangs her hat, it comes from her and not five trombones."

The next *Times* dispatch, date-lined Paris, January 15, 1960, announced that Paris had hailed *Free and Easy*. "Tonight's audience, which included Government officials, members of the diplomatic corps, and a considerable number of artistic personalities, showed their appreciation by way of a 'warm reception.' Among the artistic personalities were writer Françoise Sagan, whose only quoted comment applied to the audience ("bad"), and composer Francis Poulenc who stated enthusiastically that *he* was having a good time, and was almost "intoxicated with the rhythms."

Figaro described its reaction thus: "There is an opening fanfare and the brass orchestra led by trumpets and trombones files across the stage in New Orleans fashion. Then the musicians scatter themselves about the stage; one sits on the stairs, another on a table; and throughout the show they give the impression that they are improvising the accompaniment. In this lies the interest and originality of *Free and Easy*."

In *Paris Presse*, Émile Vuillermoz waxed intellectual: "This 'easy-going' title should not be taken literally. It hides a malicious irony. Certainly this extraordinary show seems to consist of nothing but continual improvisation where all is free and easy, but in fact this liberty and ease are achieved by a relentless discipline . . . Harold Arlen has treated his subject quite different from Gershwin. He has described it as a blues drama and in fact it is a systematic and methodical apotheosis of the blues in all their forces which we find in the score of this seemingly disordered show. Arlen seems to have wished to show us that the elastic and balanced rhythm of the blues can lend itself to the expression of all the human sentiments. In the completely intellectual period in which we live, an age of scientific and mathematical music and research directed toward the abstract and the ascetic, this score, in which all is sensitivity, passion and pathos, contains a mighty lesson for us. It is full of harmonic surprises of extraordinary refinement . . ."

Variety followed up with the news: *"Free and Easy* Musical Clicks On Paris Preem; Run May Be Extended." *Newsweek* headed a column with "They're Crazy for Jazz" and reported that "though the story may be thin, the score is not. It is a dazzling collection of torch songs, blues and such vintage Arlen-Mercer favorites as 'Accentuate The Positive' and 'Blues In The Night.'"

But ten days after, the New York *Times* headlined its column: "U. S. Musical Ends Abruptly In Paris." And that was that. Despite the opening-night excitement and the generally sympathetic press, business had fallen off rapidly after the first ten days and Chase was forced to close a week before the scheduled closing. Some members of the cast chartered a plane and returned home; others remained to make a concert tour. But as for *Free and Easy*, another chapter in its uncomplete history came to a bitter end.

In the feuding between Breen and Chase factors of some importance were simply overlooked, or even forgotten entirely, notably the Arlen-Mercer songs and, of course, the stranded cast.

During the period of bickering Arlen was too ill to be bothered with its details, which were wisely looked after by friend and attorney A. L. Berman. When he finally heard of the fate of *Free and Easy*, Arlen shrugged it off as readily as he had the closing of *Saratoga*. He was disappointed—not to mention a bit mystified—by *Free and Easy*'s sudden closing. But there are still many who have a great faith in the work and feel that Arlen poured some of his best into it, and that eventually, inevitably it will rise up out of the ashes to be recognized as one of his worthiest efforts. If not, however, Arlen himself feels there is other work to do.

Characteristically, Arlen began to work on a new idea. On his piano appeared a most interesting jot, which by early March had developed into a full-scale composition. Of unusual structure (of course) it is not in song form (though Arlen denies this), not even in a typically unconventional Arlen song form. Its harmonies are almost acrid, indigo, rather than blue. The composition is not a blues, but rather a study in a theme-and-variations style using unusual harmonic ideas: it opens in one key, ends in another.

When he played the new piece for his publishers, with Edwin H. Morris and Sidney Kornheiser present, they were immediately struck by the originality and strange beauty of this musical miniature. It was without lyrics and without a title, though for a short while it was called "Halfway Home," for Arlen planned to write a contrasting, lighter, and friskier piece to go with it.

A copyist from Harwin reported in at the composer's home so that Arlen could dictate the composition and attend to the "searching down colors" (his term for harmonies), and put it in its final shape. After checking the piece Arlen jokingly, in deference to its rather serious mood, wrote across the top of the manuscript, "Tennessee Arlen's Ode To The Deeper Side Of All Of Us." He was much surprised, a few days later when he received black-and-white photostatic copies, to find that his "title" was imprinted across the top.

He has since had the title corrected, though the designation of *Ode* seems to have stuck. It is a searching piece (one listener found in it a sense of protest, but the composer denies that, saying, "Let's just say it's not a tone poem"), almost brooding, and thoughtful. While his original title is an example of Arlen's characteristic lightheartedness, the impression of the little two-and-a-half-minute *Ode* is one of profound feeling.

Once the *Ode* was finished, Arlen began sketching ideas for a "bluette," a term he discovered while browsing through a recondite musical dictionary. As he sought for its happier contrasting sounds, Anya, as she had since the earlier, more carefree days at the Croydon, listened, and while Arlen played, she timed the uncompleted work. For she is his best and closest critic.

CHAPTER 12

Have You Heard?

The Arlens live in a comfortable duplex in New York's East Fifties, on one of those charming, rare streets shaded by trees. The walls of their apartment are decorated with a few of their paintings (some are still in California storage). In the living room, where Arlen works at a grand piano, are paintings by Dali (an excellent study of his sister), Gershwin (the portrait of Jerome Kern), Henry Botkin, Montañes (two canvases of his trademark, the urchins, and the Arlen portrait painted in Paris), and a large oil by Gloria Vanderbilt.

On the piano are photos inscribed to the Arlens by Irving Berlin, Cole Porter, Richard Rodgers, and Judy Garland. Also on the piano are manuscripts of works in progress.

More paintings decorate the walls of a hallway joining the living room with another interior room, among which is a fine still life by Arlen. The other artistic side of composers is well represented in Arlen's collection, for he owns besides the already-mentioned Jerome Kern portrait by George Gershwin, a self-portrait by Gershwin also; a drawing of Arlen by Ira Gershwin, and a portrait of Arlen by Ted Koehler. Among other paintings by Arlen himself are an interesting abstract of a seated woman, evidencing an unusual sense of color and design; there is also a study of a keyboard, and an amusing clown.

Arlen began to paint under Anya's direction, for she had long proved herself a gifted artist. She taught the composer principles of perspective, and a few other somewhat technical aspects of the art, and he took it from there. Painting was but one of Anya Arlen's gifts; she has also demonstrated an unusual flair for words. She came upon Arlen discussing a project with his friend Bob Wachsman—it may have been a radio program that Wachsman had hoped to produce in California—and the talk had become heated and excited, and possibly a little profane. Anya studied the two men briefly, then advised them, "Don't be so anxientious." She devised the title for the David Rose composition he had intended calling *Monotony for Strings* and for which she suggested the alternate *Holiday for Strings.* Her opinion of a lyric has always been important to Arlen, although Anya will not intrude into the work of collaborators.

Arlen's books reveal an affinity for art; he enjoys reading biographies of painters he admires: Dali, Picasso, Chagall, Matisse. He still prefers to read non-fiction, particularly those in which the creative process is explored.

For all his common-sense practicality, his denial of the need for inspiration, Arlen continues to approach his own creative process with a slightly mystical awe. As he sits at the piano hoping for the "unsought-for phrase," the only really inspired one, to drop from the sky, Arlen may give his search a rather practical side by saying that "the ideas are there, disorganized maybe—it's up to the creator to organize them."

The ideas are there, of course; they only need to be caught in Arlen's "comfortable trap," the scale. The material at his disposal, literally in black and white, in the seven white and five black keys of the piano's octave. From these twelve units of sound must come the thousands of songs by the Berlins, Rodgerses, Porters, Gershwins—and Arlens; all miraculously different.

Although the twelve tones of the major and minor scales sound delimiting, there are countless possible combinations—mathematically. But combinations do not make melodies. The composer must create a melodic idea that is at once original and sensible. The lyricist can help by giving the melody a title and a lyric that makes sense.

"A fine musical idea," Arlen maintains, "can lose itself because it doesn't happen to have the right frame, the happy wedding of lyric and music. For example, 'Black Magic.' That wanders melodically—a typical Arlen tapeworm—but Johnny's lyric sustains the idea, keeps up interest, and so the song comes off. I could say the same about 'Blues in the Night,' 'World on a String,' 'The Man That Got Away.' In fact, after Ira got to working on 'The Man,' I cut a few bars because I felt it lost its natural flow."

Watching Arlen in the act of creation almost substantiates the *mystique* idea about his work. He will close his eyes, cock his head, furrow his brow in deep concentration while his powerful yet sensitive fingers search among the seven white and five black keys for an idea worth keeping. And when he performs one of his songs, something many believe he does much better than anyone else, he becomes lost in the performance as he invests the lyrics with an almost impassioned delivery. It is obvious that those songs of his he likes—and he is completely honest in admitting that he loves several of his creations with that same detached yet involved affection that parents have for their children—he sings with great fervor. And for all his humor, certainly one of the richest aspects of his personality, he takes his work seriously and maintains a level of integrity rare in popular music. Irving Berlin put it best when he declared, "I don't know anyone who can wrap himself up so much in his work, who is as sincere a writer."

He is also the most approachable of men. Whatever may be brewing inside, Arlen always presents a completely relaxed and friendly aspect to an interviewer. He quickly places the interviewer at ease with his unaffected interest, disarming humor, and complete naturalness. He may smoke a pipe or a cigar.

The interviewer may begin with a question on Arlen's use of form in popular music, *Is it an attempt on your part to be different?*

I don't think I'm trying to be different. Sometimes I get into trouble; in order to get out of trouble I break the form: I start twisting and turning, get into another key or go sixteen extra bars in order to resolve the song. And often as not,

I'm happier with the extension than I would have been trying to keep the song in regular form.

Whatever the reason, it always seems effective; wouldn't you feel this is a rather intellectual way of composing?

Well, if you want to call it that, but getting out of trouble isn't intellectual—it's just being shifty.

Would you say that your early piano lessons were of value to you as a composer?

The value of piano lessons would have been to add to skill. The more skillful you are at the keyboard the more combinations you are apt to find. While imagination is an important factor, technique helps you to find—even by accident—melodic springboards and colors you might not have found otherwise.

Do you remember anything today from your early lessons?

I remember my first teacher's hands—that is, Miss Faller—her shiny, creamed hands, I felt were the reason she played so well—remember, I was about nine then. Also I remember "Good Deeds Are Ever Bearing Fruits," and "Fat Boys Eat Apple Dumplings Generally."

What?

The "Good Deeds" sentence was a device for remembering the sharp-key signatures: If the key were G sharp there would be one sharp on the staff; if D sharp, two sharp symbols, and so on through "Fruits"—F sharp, with six sharps. The "Fat Boys" was the same system for flats. And I remember F-A-C-E, for the spaces and Every Good Boy Deserves Fudge, E-G-B-D-F, for the lines of the treble staff. It's been a long time but I still remember them.

How long did you study the piano?

About four years.

You mean that after only four years of study, you were ready to become a professional pianist?

My professional piano was a kind of attempt at aping what jazz I heard at the time and superimposing on that my own ideas—which led to orchestrating and my beginnings. When I look back on it now—though I didn't realize it then—the orchestrations showed an enormous amount of melodic invention, even though it was limited to hot solos. It never rambled the way they do today, it was always fluid, round, the rhythms were precise.

Do you enjoy working in the theater more than in films?

They are two different mediums and require two different approaches. I guess I enjoy the firsthand involvement that a theater score requires. You can follow your work through rehearsals and all the inevitable changes that come in the preparatory stages. Of course, a little of your flesh is taken away during this time. You've got to compromise—you can't don a goatee and smock and start strutting around. The song's function in the show takes on significance now. Does it work theatrically? Does it motivate action? Is the song, in a sense, part of the dialogue? Does the music capture character without getting out of the framework of the show? And lyrics should not be sacrificed to the music: actually, melody and lyric should be a single unit—and, in a truly good song, inseparable.

I won't ask you which comes first, but can you give some specific example of how you might collaborate and how the work might progress?

Each lyricist is an individual and I have to work with each in his own way, but take for example Yip and our work on *Jamaica*. About 90 per cent of the songs began with an idea or a title. We'd jump around a lot, begin a song, leave it, begin another. That is how we worked for a year and a half without getting too bored with any one number. Once we'd set the mood and point of the song, we knew what we still had to do when the time came. In fact, we knew we were home even though we were still 75 per cent incomplete.

What would you say the theater needs, say, to continue developing?

A new kind of producer—and a more healthy relationship between the producer and creator. This business of believing that only the producer can get the stars and the theater is old hat. The star of any intelligence isn't swayed by the producer, but by the script. The material is what really counts. Likewise the theater. The only way to get a theater is to have a property people believe in—and, of course, to have a theater available. If one isn't available, a producer can't get one anyhow. The rest is up to the businessman: bargaining about salaries, publicity, and so on. But it all begins with the creators. With certain exceptions, the theater has only a few creative producers—just as in Hollywood there are only a few creative directors. I think the relationship was very well put by Walter Kerr when he wrote "Plays themselves are not absolutely written, or absolutely produced, but gradually "found," in a group effort that is partly a game and partly a dead-serious treasure hunt." And the treasure hunt began long before the producer entered the picture.

What would you consider one of the less pleasant aspects of working in the theater?

Backers' auditions. I don't believe any writer, producer, or director of proven worth should be put through the rigors of such trials. If an individual is interested in backing a show, he should have enough confidence in the people who create it and produce it to offer backing on the basis of past performances of these theater people. Most potential angels who listen to a score are rarely equipped to judge its merit. The crushing line composer after composer hears from these would-be financial wingspreads is: "I don't know anything about music . . ." They then go on to guess what may or may not be a hit. If most of these backers knew as much about money as they claim to be sounding boards for the general public on music, they'd be financial bankrupts.

How about critics?

While critics are very competent, generally, in evaluating a conventional play, they are at a loss if the play is musically scored. To begin with, the critics seem to evidence little knowledge of what has gone before—that is, there is a lack of a historical sense so far as the musical is concerned. Nor do they recognize individual development in a writer. But give them, say, a play by Tennessee Williams and they'll wring it dry with analysis, evaluation, and exploration of its meaning. Not that a musical should be approached in the same manner as a serious drama, but the critic could surely come up with better terminology than "integrated," or do better than to refer to a score as "hummable," or indicate that the "tunes are bright and gay." Occasionally they may note that a musical is "un-hackneyed," which is something. Of course a dramatist can get fine actors, but the choice is quite limited in a musical. You might get someone who can act but not sing. Or the reverse. Likewise the dancers. You must find a personality with ex-citement and a voice. Many good songs suffer for lack of talent. Why does a song languish in a show for a long time and then suddenly come to life? It may have been that the inherent quality of the song was obscured by an inferior interpretation, or the wrong one. No other art—and the American musical is an art—takes such a beating and survives.

It is interesting that you use the term "art" in connection with a form springing from so disreputable a place as Tin Pan Alley—which of course doesn't exist except as a symbol of something cheap and inferior. What do you mean by "Art"?

I like to think about art in terms of something special, highly individual, poetic. When we say art we naturally think of big canvases by great painters. You can't exclude songs be-cause they're in cameo form. Stephen Foster's work is art.

I like Vaughan Williams' definition: "Art is the means by which one man communicates spiritually with another . . ."

Would you say that art is a form of combining materials in near perfection?

We get back to the wedding of the two—words and music. If they come off well the art is widely recognized. But that doesn't necessarily mean that a song that hasn't a wide appeal isn't artistically written (But isn't it always healthy to have found a large audience?). Now, are we talking about art songs, which is something else, or of the man who wrote them as an artist?

Are there songs, written by so-called popular composers, you feel are artfully conceived, even though conceived on a small scale?

I am not one to look down on song writing. Just because it

happens to be thirty-two bars—or more, and less than a tone poem—doesn't mean a song doesn't belong to the arts. The fact that so many magnificent songs take such a battering, and continue to live, is a sure sign of their tremendous impact and universality.

What songs, for example?

Berlin's "Alexander's Ragtime Band," and I could cite dozens of others, "Say It with Music." I could go on with Berlin for an hour. Porter's "Night and Day"; Schwartz and Dietz's "Dancing in the Dark," Dick Rodgers' "My Heart Stood Still," or take "Shall We Dance?" from *The King and I*: it has great joy—it's one of my great favorites! Or "Oh, What a Beautiful Morning," there's a little one—with great power, and worthy of Schubert. How about the juicy creations that George and Ira did. Like doing an engraving rather than an oil.

What creations?

All of 'em!'

I suppose you've been asked this many times, but what do you feel is your own favorite score—and why?

The Wizard of Oz. Because it was written for a children's classic and we happened to capture it perfectly. Now you can always find weaknesses even in a score that excites you, but not in *The Wizard of Oz.* Though it is not a big score, everything it says it says well lyrically and musically. As for why, I think William K. Zinsser sums it up in his *Harper's* article: ". . . it was the score that set and sustained the mood. Even so, M-G-M had its worries. 'This score is above the heads of children,' one executive told Harburg. He was wrong, needless to say, though it is true that the music and lyrics are more sophisticated than they seem. 'If I Only Had a Brain,' for example, is no simple nursery rhyme. At any rate, Arlen and Harburg had the satisfaction of appealing to children without talking down to them."

What does a composer think about when he isn't composing?

"Why am I not writing?"

What do you feel is the most satisfying kind of recognition?

Any recognition or applause you might get from your colleagues is terribly important.

How could that be done?

Maybe ASCAP could give an award for the outstanding musical contribution of the year from whatever origin—musical, film, or a song not written for any production. Or they might, as has been suggested by Howard Dietz, set up a song writer's Hall of Fame. I'm all for seeing that the men who deserve it get all their laurels now. George M. Cohan has a statue now; they might have given it to him while he was still around.

What would you say characterizes a good song musically?

It must capture a melodic turn that's interesting.

How would you define melody?

That isn't easy. I suppose a melody might be the main theme of a song. Or [laughing] anything in the upper staff of a piano copy is a melody [laughing again]—though not necessarily good.

It is said that contemporary "serious" American music, though it draws upon the same sources—blues, jazz, folk song— as popular music, lacks melodic distinction. Would you agree?

Just call me a fringe student of contemporary music. All I can say of the little I've heard—and the reason I've heard so little is that I don't find what I've heard terribly interesting— is that there is no doubt that these composers have a fine musical education and great technique, but to my mind what they lack, with all their knowledge of how to put things down correctly, is the natural gift that no amount of schooling can make up for. I always feel that as soon as they get an idea—let's say a theme—that is about ready to capture you, they run like hell to avoid the natural resolution of it. Their thematic material lacks emotion; it lacks love. Love can have a twinkle, love can be moving. As far as they're concerned, it may not exist.

Possibly that's a reflection of the times. Do you feel that this—political events, for example—has any effect on the writer?

It would be false to think that the state of the world we

live in and its push-button madness is conducive to high spirits. It is my belief that it is more desirable for a writer to be in good health and a cheerful state of mind when he is creating. Tensions from the outside certainly don't help the free flow of ideas. As for what we just witnessed [*the reference is to the breakup of the Paris summit meeting and the U-2 "spy plane" incident*], my guess would be this civilization is going to have to—and I stress the "have to"—coexist with madmen. This has nothing to do with the peoples of the iron countries, but with their schizophrenic leaders. And my hunch is that, though it hasn't been bandied about much, Khrushchev's threat that our children's children will live in a communist society, is going to backfire. I believe they'll change more to our way of life than we to theirs.

Let's return to the idea of a good song—how would you judge a song?

By the freshness of its theme, how it's developed and re-solved—and most of all the happy wedding of music and lyrics.

And a good song writer?

To my mind a fine writer is one who can tackle any style and be interesting. Almost everybody has tried his hand at writing a song, but it's getting the melodic design and the right colors together that makes great song writers like Gershwin, Berlin, Porter, Rodgers, Kern, Schwartz, and others. But there is one other important factor.

What's that?

A good lyric writer is the composer's best friend.

THE WORKS OF HAROLD ARLEN

The following is a complete and, it is hoped, accurate listing of the compositions of Harold Arlen, both published and unpublished, including those published under the name of Harold Arluck. Published songs are indicated with an asterisk (°). This listing has been compiled with the assistance of William Sweigart from original playbills, from the U.S. copyright records, and from the files of the American Society of Composers, Authors and Publishers. The composer himself was most helpful in digging back into the past for copies of songs he had long forgotten; his lyricists, too, very willingly helped to make this list both complete and accurate.

1924
My Gal, My Pal (lyric: Hyman Cheiffetz)
I Never Knew What Love Could Do (lyric: Hyman Cheiffetz)

1925
Easy Strain (lyric: Phil Shapiro)
I Want Your Kisses If You Want My Kisses (lyric: Phil Shapiro)

1926
° *Minor Gaff* (*Blues Fantasy*), instrumental by Harold Arluck and Dick George

1927
° *Buffalo Rhythm,* instrumental by Harold Arluck, Ivan Beaty, Marvin Smolev

1928
° *Rhythmic Moments,* for solo piano
Jungaleena (lyric: Herb Magidson and James Cavanaugh)

1929
° The Album of My Dreams (lyric: Lou Davis)
Can't Be Bothered (lyric: Charles Tobias)
Heap o' Misery (lyric: Ted Koehler)
° Rising Moon (lyric: Jack Ellis)

That's What I Call Love (lyric: Jack Ellis)
* Gladly (lyric: Ted Koehler)
Who Could Say No? (lyric: Ted Koehler)
Bring Him Back Here (lyric: Lou Davis)

1930

NINE-FIFTEEN REVUE

Lyrics by Ted Koehler; sketches by Ring Lardner, Paul Gerard Smith, Eddie Cantor, Anita Loos and John Emerson, Geoffrey Kerr, H. W. Hanemann, Robert Riskin and Adorian Otovos; songs also by Kay Swift and Paul James, George and Ira Gershwin, Vincent Youmans and Edward Eliscu, Rudolf Friml, Ralph Rainger, Richard Myers, *et al.* Produced by Ruth Selwyn at the George M. Cohan Theater, February 11, 1930—seven performances. In the cast were Ruth Etting, Harry McNaughton, Fred Keating, Oscar Ragland, Paul Kelly, and Earl Oxford.

* Get Happy
Gee It's So Good, It's Too Bad
* You Wanted Me, I Wanted You

EARL CARROLL VANITIES (eighth edition)

Lyrics by Ted Koehler; sketches by Eddie Welch and Eugene Conrad; songs also by Jay Gorney and E. Y. Harburg. Produced by Earl Carroll at the New Amsterdam Theater, July 1, 1930—215 performances. In the cast: Jimmy Savo, Jack Benny, Patsy Kelly, Faith Bacon, Harry Stockwell, Herb Williams, and Eddie Harrison.

* Hittin' the Bottle
* Contagious Rhythm
* One Love
* The March of Time
* Out of a Clear Blue Sky

BROWN SUGAR

Lyrics by Ted Koehler; produced by Dan Healy at the Cotton Club, 1930
* Linda
* Song of the Gigolo

1931

YOU SAID IT

Lyrics by Jack Yellen; book by Sid Silvers and Jack Yellen; Staged by John Harwood. Produced by Lou Holtz and Jack

Yellen at the Forty-sixth Street Theater, January 19, 1931—
168 performances. Cast: Lou Holtz, Lyda Roberti, Benny Baker,
Henry Slate, Oscar Grogan, Syd Slate, Jack Slate, Allan
D'Sylva, Mary Lawler, Stanley Smith, Betty Bernier, and
Hughie Clark

What'd We Come to College For?
* You Said It
They Learn about Women from Me
* While You Are Young
* It's Different with Me
* Learn to Croon
* Sweet and Hot
* If He Really Loves Me
* What Do We Care?
* You'll Do

Ha-Ha-Ha (Gang Song) (lyric: Ted Koehler)
* Tell Me with a Love Song (lyric: Ted Koehler)

RHYTHMANIA

Lyrics by Ted Koehler; produced and staged by Dan Healy
at the Cotton Club, 1931
* Between the Devil And The Deep Blue Sea
* Kickin' the Gong Around
* I Love a Parade
Trickeration
* Without Rhythm
* Get Up, Get Out, Get under the Sun
* 'Neath the Pale Cuban Moon
* Breakfast Dance

1932
*The Song That Makes Me Blue (lyric: Jack Yellen)
* I Forgive You (lyric: Jack Yellen)
* Y' Got Me, Baby (lyric: Jack Yellen)
* Stepping into Love (lyric: Ted Koehler)
* Music, Music, Everywhere (lyric: Ted Koehler)
* Another Night Alone (lyric: Ted Koehler)

EARL CARROLL'S VANITIES

Lyrics by Ted Koehler; additional songs by Richard Myers,
Edward Heyman, Charles and Henry Tobias, others. Sketches
by Earl Carroll and Jack MacGowan. Produced by Earl Carroll
at the Broadway Theater, September 27, 1932—eighty-seven

performances. Cast: Will Fyffe, Milton Berle, Helen Broderick, Harriet Hoctor, and Lillian Shade.
* Rockin' in Rhythm
* I Gotta Right to Sing the Blues

AMERICANA

A revue with music mostly by Jay Gorney and Vernon Duke, lyrics by E. Y. Harburg; book by J. P. McEvoy. Produced by J. P. McEvoy (for the Shuberts) at the Shubert Theater, October 5, 1932—seventy-seven performances. Cast: George Givot, Albert Carroll, Francetta Malloy, Georgie Tapps, Lloyd Nolan, The Musketeers, and the Doris Humphrey Dancers.
* Satan's Li'l Lamb (lyric: E. Y. Harburg and John Mercer)

COTTON CLUB PARADE

Lyrics by Ted Koehler; staged and produced by Dan Healy at the Cotton Club, October 23, 1932. Cast: Leitha Hall, the Nicholas Brothers, Aida Ward, Swan and Lee, Carolynne Snowden, Roy Atkins, Cab Calloway and his orchestra.
* I've Got the World on a String
* Minnie the Moocher's Wedding Day
* Harlem Holiday
* You Gave Me Ev'rything but Love
* That's What I Hate about Love
* The Wail of the Reefer Man
* In the Silence of the Night
* New Kind of Rhythm

GEORGE WHITE'S MUSIC HALL VARIETIES

A revue with songs by Cliff Friend and Herbert Magidson, Sammy Stept, Carmen Lombardo, Herman Hupfield, and others. Book by George White and William K. Wells. Produced by George White at the Casino Theater, November 22, 1932—forty-eight performances, and January 2, 1933—twenty-four performances. Cast: Bert Lahr, Harry Richman, Lili Damita, Eleanor Powell, the Loomis Sisters, and others.
Cabin in the Cotton (lyric: Irving Caesar and George White)
* Two Feet in Two Four Time (lyric: Irving Caesar)

THE GREAT MAGOO

A play by Ben Hecht and Gene Fowler, produced by Billy Rose at the Selwyn Theater, December 2, 1932—eleven performances.
* It's Only a Paper Moon (lyric: Billy Rose and E. Y. Harburg).

1933
COTTON CLUB PARADE
   Lyrics by Ted Koehler; staged and produced by Dan Healy
   at the Cotton Club, April 6, 1933. Cast: Ethel Waters, George
   Dewey Washington, Duke Ellington and his orchestra.
* Happy as the Day Is Long
* Stormy Weather
* Raisin' the Rent
* Get Yourself a New Broom
* Calico Days
* Muggin' Lightly

* Shame on You (lyric: Edward Heyman)

LET'S FALL IN LOVE
   Lyrics by Ted Koehler; screen play by Herbert Fields; directed
   by David Burton; produced by Columbia Pictures, released in
   January 1934. Cast: Edmund Lowe, Ann Sothern, Gregory
   Ratoff, Betty Furness, Arthur Jarrett, Miriam Jordon, Greta
   Meyer, others.
* Let's Fall in Love
* Love Is Love Anywhere
* This Is Only the Beginning
   Breakfast Ball (not used)
   She's Not the Type (not used)

1934
COTTON CLUB PARADE
   Lyrics by Ted Koehler; staged and produced by Dan Healy
   at the Cotton Club, March 23, 1934. Cast: Adelaide Hall,
   Juano Hernandez, Pops and Louie, Jimmy Lunceford and
   his orchestra.
* As Long as I Live
* Ill Wind
* Breakfast Ball
* Primitive Prima Donna
* Here Goes

LIFE BEGINS AT 8:40
   Lyrics by Ira Gershwin and E. Y. Harburg; sketches by David
   Freedman, devised and staged by John Murray Anderson.
   Produced by the Shuberts at the Winter Garden, August 27,
   1934—237 performances. Cast: Ray Bolger, Bert Lahr, Luella
   Gear, Frances Williams, Brian Donlevy, Dixie Dunbar, Charles
   Weidman Dancers, and others.

Life Begins
Spring Fever
* Shoein' the Mare
* You're a Builder Upper
I'm Not Myself
* Fun to Be Fooled
Quartet Erotica
C'est la Vie
My Paramount-Publix-Roxy Rose
* What Can You Say in a Love Song?
* Let's Take a Walk around the Block
Things
The Elks and the Masons
I Couldn't Hold My Man
It Was Long Ago
Will You Love Me Monday Morning (Weekend Cruise)
Life Begins At City Hall
I Knew Him When
I'm a Collector of Moonbeams

1935

Mood in Six Minutes, for orchestra (orchestrated by Robert Russell Bennett). Composed for the *General Motors Symphony Hour,* Dr. Frank Black, conductor.

* Last Night When We Were Young (lyric: E. Y. Harburg)

STRIKE ME PINK
Lyrics by Lew Brown; screen play by Frank Butler, Francis Martin, and Walter DeLeon; directed by Norman Taurog. Produced by Samuel Goldwyn, released by United Artists, January 1936. Cast: Eddie Cantor, Sally Eilers, Ethel Merman, Parkyakarkus (Harry Parke), William Frawley, others.
* The Lady Dances
* Calabash Pipe
* Shake It Off (with Rhythm)
* First You Have Me High (Then You Have Me Low)

THE SINGING KID
Lyrics by E. Y. Harburg; screen play by Warren Duff and Pat C. Flick; directed by William Keighley. Produced by Warner Brothers and released in April 1936. Cast: Al Jolson, Sybil Jason, Edward Everett Horton, Allen Jenkins, Claire Dodd, Lyle Talbot, the Yacht Club Boys, and Cab Calloway and orchestra.

* You're the Cure for What Ails Me
* I Love to Sing-a
* Save Me, Sister
  Here's Looking at You

1936
STAGE STRUCK
Lyrics by E. Y. Harburg; screen play by Tom Buckingham and Pat C. Flick; directed by Busby Berkeley. Produced by Warner Brothers and released by First National Pictures in September 1936. Cast: Dick Powell, Joan Blondell, Warren William, Frank McHugh, Jeanne Madden, others.
* In Your Own Quiet Way
* Fancy Meeting You
  You're Kinda Grandish
  The New Parade

GOLD DIGGERS OF 1937
Lyrics by E. Y. Harburg; screen play by Warren Duff; directed by Lloyd Bacon. Produced by Warner Brothers and released December 1936. Cast: Dick Powell, Joan Blondell, Victor Moore, Lee Dixon, Glenda Farrell, others. Additional songs by Harry Warren and Al Dubin.
* Speaking of the Weather
* Let's Put Our Heads Together
  Life Insurance Song
  Hush Ma Mouth

THE SHOW IS ON
A revue with sketches by Moss Hart and David Freedman; conceived, staged, and designed by Vincente Minnelli; additional songs by Vernon Duke, Hoagy Carmichael, George and Ira Gershwin, Arthur Schwartz and Howard Dietz, Richard Rodgers and Lorenz Hart, others. Produced by the Shuberts at the Winter Garden, December 25, 1936—237 performances. Cast: Beatrice Lillie, Bert Lahr, Reginald Gardiner, Paul Haakon, Vera Ellen, others.
Song of the Woodman (lyric: E. Y. Harburg)

How's by you? (lyric: E. Y. Harburg)
I'll Thank You to Stay Out of My Dreams (lyric: E. Y. Harburg)

1937
ARTISTS AND MODELS
Film with composite score; screen play by Walter DeLeon and Francis Martin; directed by Raoul Walsh. Produced by Para-

mount Pictures, released August, 1937. Songs by Burton Lane and Ted Koehler, Ralph Rainger and Leo Robin, Frederick Hollander, Victor Young. Cast: Jack Benny, Ida Lupino, Richard Arlen, Gail Patrick, Ben Blue, Judy Canova, others, including Martha Raye, Louis Armstrong, Connie Boswell.

* Public Melody Number One (lyric: Ted Koehler)

It's a Long Way to Broadway (lyric: E. Y. Harburg)
When the Wind Blows South (lyric: E. Y. Harburg)

HOORAY FOR WHAT?

Lyrics by E. Y. Harburg; book by Howard Lindsay and Russel Crouse, conceived by E. Y. Harburg. Staged and supervised by Vincente Minnelli. Produced by the Shuberts at the Winter Garden, December 1, 1937—two hundred performances. Cast: Ed Wynn, June Clyde, Jack Whiting, Leo Chalzel, Gracie Reilly, Paul Haakon, others.

Hooray for What?
* God's Country
* I've Gone Romantic on You
* Moanin' in the Mornin'
Vive for Geneva
* Life's a Dance
Napoleon's a Pastry
* Down with Love
A Fashion Girl
That Night of the Embassy Ball
* In the Shade of the New Apple Tree
Hero Ballet—(orchestrated by Don Walker)
* Buds Won't Bud
I Click the Heel and I Kiss the Hand

1938
* Love's a Necessary Thing (lyric: Ted Koehler)

LOVE AFFAIR

Film starring Irene Dunne, Charles Boyer, and Maria Ouspenskaya. Produced and directed by Leo McCarey. Released by RKO Radio Pictures March 1939.

* Sing My Heart (lyric: Ted Koehler)

THE WIZARD OF OZ

Lyrics by E. Y. Harburg; screen play by Noel Langley, Florence Ryerson and Edgar Allan Wolff; directed by Victor Fleming. Produced by Mervyn LeRoy and released by Merto-Goldwyn-

Mayer, August 1939. Cast: Judy Garland, Frank Morgan, Bert Lahr, Ray Bolger, Jack Haley, Billie Burke, Margaret Hamilton, Charley Grapewin, and Clara Blandick.
* Over the Rainbow
* Ding-Dong! The Witch Is Dead
  Munchkinland
  Follow the Yellow Brick Road
* We're Off to See the Wizard
* If I Only Had a Brain (a Heart; the Nerve)
  Optimistic Voices
* The Jitterbug
  Gates of Emerald City
* The Merry Old Land of Oz
  If I Were King of the Forest
  Renovation Sequence

1939

AT THE CIRCUS
Lyrics by E. Y. Harburg; screen play by Irving Brecher; directed by Edward Buzzell. Produced by Mervyn LeRoy, released by Metro-Goldwyn-Mayer, November 1939. Cast: the Marx Brothers, Kenny Baker, Florence Rice, Eve Arden, Margaret Dumont, Nat Pendleton, others.
Step Up and Take a Bow
* Two Blind Loves
* Lydia, The Tattooed Lady
  Swingali

* Let's Hit the Nail on the Head (lyric: Ted Koehler)

* American Minuet, instrumental. Composed for Good News radio program, Meredith Willson, conductor.
  I'll Supply the Music If You Supply the Words
  (lyric: Ira Gershwin)

1940

* Americanegro Suite, for voices and piano; lyrics by Ted Koehler
  Reverend Johnson's Dream
  Little Ace o' Spades
  I'm Here Lawd
  I Got Dat Feelin'
  Where Is Dis Road A-leadin' Me to?
  Big Time Comin'

1941

* When the Sun Comes Out (lyric: Ted Koehler)
BLUES IN THE NIGHT
Lyrics by Johnny Mercer; screen play by Robert Rossen; di-

rected by Anatole Litvak. Produced by Harry Blanke and released by Warner Brothers, December 1941. Cast: Priscilla Lane, Betty Field, Richard Whorf, Lloyd Nolan, Jack Carson, Elia Kazan, Wallace Ford, Billy Hallop, Howard da Silva, Jimmy Lunceford and orchestra, Will Osborne and orchestra.
* Blues in the Night
* Hang Onto Your Lids, Kids
* This Time the Dream's on Me
* Says Who, Says You, Says I!

CAPTAINS OF THE CLOUDS
Film starring James Cagney, Dennis Morgan, Brenda Marshall. Released by Warner Brothers, February 1942.
* Captains of the Clouds (lyric: Johnny Mercer)

1942
* The Moment I Laid Eyes on You (lyric: Ted Koehler)
* Life Could Be a Cakewalk with You (lyric: Ted Koehler)

RIO RITA
Lyrics by E. Y. Harburg; screen play by Richard Connell and Gladys Lehman; directed by S. Sylvan Simon. Produced by Pandro S. Berman, released by Metro-Goldwyn-Mayer, May, 1942. Cast: Bud Abbott and Lou Costello, John Carroll, Kathryn Grayson, others.
* Long before You Came Along
Poor Whippoorwill
A Couple of Caballeros

Most Unusual Weather (lyric: E. Y. Harburg)

STAR SPANGLED RHYTHM
Lyrics by Johnny Mercer; screen play by Harry Tugend; directed by George Marshall. Released by Paramount, December, 1942. Cast: Victor Moore, Betty Hutton, Eddie Bracken, Walter Abel, Cass Daley—and Bing Crosby, Bob Hope, Mary Martin, Paulette Goddard, Veronica Lake, Dorothy Lamour, Eddie (Rochester) Anderson, Dick Powell, the Golden Gate Quartet, *et al.*
* That Old Black Magic
* Hit the Road to Dreamland
* Old Glory
* A Sweater, a Sarong, and a Peekaboo Bang
* Sharp as a Tack
* I'm Doing It for Defense

* On the Swing Shift
He Loved Me Till the All-Clear Came

CABIN IN THE SKY
 Lyrics by E. Y. Harburg; other songs by Vernon Duke, Ted
Fetter, and John La Touche. Screen play by Joseph Schrank;
directed by Vincente Minnelli. Produced by Arthur Freed, re-
leased by Metro-Goldwyn-Mayer, May, 1943. Cast: Ethel
Waters, Eddie (Rochester) Anderson, Lena Horne, Rex Ingram,
Louis Armstrong, Buck and Bubbles, Kenneth Spencer, the
Hall Johnson Choir, Duke Ellington and orchestra, others.
 Li'l Black Sheep
* Life's Full of Consequence
* Happiness Is a Thing Called Joe
* Ain't It de Truth
 Some Folks Work (Is You Man or Mule?)

1943
If This Be Propaganda (lyric: Ira Gershwin)

THE SKY'S THE LIMIT
 Lyrics by Johnny Mercer; screen play by Frank Fenton and
Lynn Root; directed by Edward H. Griffith. Produced by David
Hempstead, released by RKO Radio Pictures September, 1943.
Cast: Fred Astaire, Joan Leslie, Robert Benchley, Robert Ryan,
Freddie Slack and orchestra, others.
* A Lot in Common with You
* My Shining Hour
* One for My Baby (and One More for the Road)
 Harvey, The Victory Garden Man
 Hangin' On to You

THEY GOT ME COVERED
 Film starring Bob Hope and Dorothy Lamour. Produced by
Samuel Goldwyn, released by RKO Radio Pictures March, 1943.
* Palsy Walsy (lyric: Johnny Mercer)

UP IN ARMS
 Lyrics by Ted Koehler; screen play by Don Hartman, Allen
Boretz and Robert Pirosh; directed by Elliot Nugent. Produced
by Samuel Goldwyn, released by RKO Radio Pictures March,
1944. Cast: Danny Kaye, Dinah Shore, Dana Andrews, Con-
stance Dowling, Louis Calhern, Kenny Baker, others.
* Now I Know

* Tess's Torch Song
* All Out for Freedom (*Dedicated to Anya*)

1944

KISMET

>   Lyrics by E. Y. Harburg; screen play by John Meehan; directed by William Dieterle. Produced by Everett Riskin, released by Metro-Goldwyn-Mayer August, 1944. Cast: Marlene Dietrich, Ronald Colman, Edward Arnold, James Craig, Joy Ann Page.
>   * Willow in the Wind
>   * Tell Me, Tell Me Evening Star

BLOOMER GIRL

>   Lyrics by E. Y. Harburg; book by Fred Saidy and Sig Herzig, dances by Agnes de Mille, staged by E. Y. Harburg, book direction by William Schorr. Produced by John C. Wilson in association with Nat Goldstone at the Shubert Theater, October 5, 1944–654 performances. Cast: Celeste Holm, David Brooks, Joan McCracken, Dooley Wilson, Richard Huey, Mabel Taliaferro, Matt Briggs, others.
>   * When the Boys Come Home
>   * Evelina
>   Welcome Hinges
>   Farmer's Daughter
>   It was Good Enough for Grandma
>   * The Eagle and Me
>   * Right as the Rain
>   * T'morra', T'morra'
>   The Rakish Young Man with the Whiskers
>   Pretty as a Picture
>   Sunday in Cicero Falls
>   * I Got a Song
>   Lullaby (Satin Gown and Silver Shoe)
>   Simon Legree
>   Liza Crossing the Ice
>   I Never Was Born
>   Man for Sale
>   Civil War Ballet

HERE COME THE WAVES

>   Lyrics by Johnny Mercer; screen play by Allan Scott, Ken Englund, and Zion Myers. Produced and directed by Mark Sandrich, released by Paramount Pictures December, 1944. Cast: Bing Crosby, Betty Hutton, Sonny Tufts, Ann Doran, Noel Neill, others.

* I Promise You
* There's A Fella Waitin' in Poughkeepsie
* My Mamma Thinks I'm a Star
* Let's Take the Long Way Home
* Ac-cent-tchu-ate the Positive
* Navy Song
* Here Come the Waves

1945
OUT OF THIS WORLD

Lyrics by Johnny Mercer; additional songs by Sam Coslow, Bernie Wayne, Ben Raleigh, Eddie Chekose and Felix Bernard. Screen play by Walter DeLeon and Arthur Phillips; directed by Hal Walker. Produced by Sam Coslow, released by Paramount Pictures June, 1945. Cast: Eddie Bracken, Diana Lynn, Veronica Lake, Cass Daley, others.

* Out of This World
* June Comes Around Every Year

1946
ST. LOUIS WOMAN

Lyrics by Johnny Mercer; book by Arna Bontemps and Countee Cullen; directed by Rouben Mamoulian. Produced By Edward Gross at the Martin Beck Theater March 30, 1946 —113 Performances. Cast: The Nicholas Brothers, Ruby Hill, June Hawkins, Rex Ingram, Juanita Hall, Pearl Bailey, Robert Pope, others.

Li'l Augie Is a Natural Man
* Any Place I Hang My Hat Is Home
I Feel My Luck Comin' Down
* I Had Myself a True Love
* Legalize My Name
* Cakewalk Your Lady
* Come Rain or Come Shine
Chinquapin Bush
We Shall Meet to Part, No Never
Lullaby
Sleep Peaceful, Mr. Used-to-Be
Leavin' Time
* I Wonder What Became of Me?
* A Woman's Prerogative
* Ridin' on the Moon
Least That's My Opinion
Racin' Form

Come On, Li'l Augie

Not used: High, Low, Jack and the Game; A Man's Gotta Fight; Somethin' You Gotta Find Out Yourself; Sow the Seed and Reap the Harvest; Lim'ricks.

1947
* After All (lyric: Ted Koehler)
* Got to Wear You Off My Wary Mind (lyric: Johnny Mercer)

1948
CASBAH

Lyrics by Leo Robin; screen play by L. Bush-Fekete and Arnold Manoff; directed by John Berry. Produced by Nat C. Goldstone, released by Universal-International Pictures May 1948. Cast: Tony Martin, Yvonne DeCarlo, Marta Toren, Peter Lorre, Katherine Dunham and her dancers.
* It Was Written in the Stars
* What's Good about Goodbye?
* For Every Man There's a Woman
* Hooray for Love
  The Monkey Sat in the Cocoanut Tree

1949
Tell Me in Your Own Sweet Way (lyric: Bob Hilliard)

MY BLUE HEAVEN

Lyrics by Ralph Blane and Harold Arlen; screen play by Lamar Trotti and Claude Binyon; directed by Henry Koster. Produced by Sol C. Siegel, released by Twentieth Century-Fox September 1950. Cast: Betty Grable, Dan Dailey, David Wayne, Jane Wyatt, Mitzi Gaynor, Una Merkel.
* Live Hard, Work Hard, Love Hard
* The Friendly Islands
* It's Deductible
* Hallowe'en
* Don't Rock the Boat, Dear
* I Love a New Yorker
  Cosmo Cosmetics
  What a Man!

1950
THE PETTY GIRL

Lyrics by Johnny Mercer; screen play by Nat Perrin; directed by Henry Levin. Produced by Nat Perrin, released by Columbia

Pictures, August, 1950. Cast: Robert Cummings, Joan Caulfield, Elsa Lanchester, Melville Cooper, Audrey Long.
* Calypso Song
* Ah Loves Ya
* Fancy Free
The Petty Girl

1950–51
DOWN AMONG THE SHELTERING PALMS
Lyrics by Ralph Blane and Harold Arlen; screen play by Claude Binyon, Albert Lewin, and Burt Styler; directed by Edmund Goulding. Produced by Fred Kohlmar, released by Twentieth Century-Fox, June 1953. Cast: William Lundigan, Jane Greer, Mitzi Gaynor, David Wayne, Gloria DeHaven, Jack Paar, Lyle Talbot, Billy Gilbert.
I'm a Ruler of a South Sea Island
* Who Will It Be When the Time Comes?
* What Make de Difference?
Twenty-seven Elm Street
When You're in Love
Inspection
The Opposite Sex
Back Where I Came From

1951
MR. IMPERIUM
Lyrics by Dorothy Fields; screen play by Don Hartman and Edwin H. Knopf; directed by Don Hartman. Produced by Edwin H. Knopf, released by Metro-Goldwyn-Mayer October 1951. Cast: Lana Turner, Ezio Pinza, Marjorie Main, Barry Sullivan, Sir Cedric Hardwicke, Debbie Reynolds, Ann Godee.
* Let Me Look at You
* Andiamo
* My Love an' My Mule

1952
THE FARMER TAKES A WIFE
Lyrics by Dorothy Fields; screen play by Walter Bullock, Sally Benson and Joseph Fields; directed by Henry Levin. Produced by Frank P. Rosenberg, released by Twentieth Century-Fox June 1953. Cast: Betty Grable, Dale Robertson, Thelma Ritter, John Carroll, Eddie Foy, Jr., Charlotte Austin.
* Somethin' Real Special
* We're in Business

* With the Sun Warm upon Me
* Today I Love Ev'rybody
* On the Erie Canal
* Can You Spell Schenectady?
* We're Doin' It for the Natives in Jamaica
* When I Close My Door
  I Could Cook
  Look Who's Been Dreaming

1953

A STAR IS BORN

Lyrics by Ira Gershwin; screen play by Moss Hart; directed by George Cukor. Produced by Sid Luft, released by Warner Brothers, October, 1954. Cast: Judy Garland, James Mason, Jack Carson, Charles Bickford, Tommy Noonan.

* Gotta Have Me Go with You
* The Man That Got Away
* Someone at Last
* Lose That Long Face
* It's a New World
* Here's What I'm Here for
  TV Commercial
  Green Light Ahead
  I'm Off the Downbeat
  Dancing Partner

There's No Substitute for a Man (lyric: Howard Dietz)

1954

THE COUNTRY GIRL

Lyrics by Ira Gershwin; screen play and direction by George Seaton. Produced by William Perlberg, released by Paramount Pictures, December, 1954. Cast: Bing Crosby, Grace Kelly, William Holden, Anthony Ross, Gene Reynolds, Jacqueline Fountaine.

* The Search Is Through
  The Land around Us
* Dissertation on the State of Bliss (Love and Learn)
  It's Mine, It's Yours (The Pitchman)
  Commercial

HOUSE OF FLOWERS

Lyrics by Truman Capote and Harold Arlen; book by Truman Capote; direction by Peter Brook. Produced by Arnold Saint

Subber at the Alvin Theater, December 30, 1954—165 perform-
ances. Cast: Pearl Bailey, Diahann Carroll, Rawn Spearman,
Juanita Hall, Ray Walston, Geoffrey Holder, Don Redman,
Dino DiLuca, Frederick O'Neal, Dolores Harper, Ada Moore,
Enid Mosier, Miriam Burton.
Waitin'
One Man Ain't Quite Enough
Madame Tango's Tango
* A Sleepin' Bee
* Smellin' of Vanilla (Bamboo Cage)
* House of Flowers
* Two Ladies in de Shade of de Banana Tree
What Is a Friend for?
Mardi Gras
* I Never Has Seen Snow
Can I Leave Off Wearin' My Shoes?
Has I Let You Down?
Slide, Boy, Slide
Don't Like Goodbyes
Turtle Song
Indoor Girl (Lyric: Michael Brown)
What a Man Won't Do for a Woman
House of Flowers Waltz
Monday through Sunday
Love's No Stranger to Me

1956
Stay Out of My Dreams (lyric: E. Y. Harburg; written for
unproduced film *Nellie Bly*).

1956–57
JAMAICA
Lyrics by E. Y. Harburg; book by E. Y. Harburg and Fred
Saidy; direction by Robert Lewis. Produced by David Merrick
at the Imperial Theater October 31, 1957—557 performances.
Cast: Lena Horne, Ricardo Montalban, Adelaide Hall, Jose-
phine Premice, Ossie Davis, Erik Rhodes, Hugh Dilworth, Ethel
Ayler.
* Savanna
Savanna's Wedding Day
* Pretty to Walk with
* Push de Button
* Little Biscuit

Sweet Wind Blowin' My Way
* Incompatibility
Monkey in the Mango Tree
* Cocoanut Sweet
* Take It Slow, Joe
* Napoleon
* What Good Does It Do?
Leave The Atom Alone
* I Don't Think I'll End It All Today
* Ain't It de Truth
Whippoorwill
For Every Fish There's a Little Bigger Fish
Pity de Sunset
Workin' for the Yankee Dollar
What Did Noah Do (When the Big Wind Came)?

1958

In the Middle of the Night (Lyric: Paddy Chayefsky)

1959

SARATOGA

Lyrics by Johnny Mercer; book and direction by Morton Da-
Costa. Produced by Robert Fryer at the Winter Garden
December 7, 1959—eighty performances. Cast: Howard Keel,
Carol Lawrence, Odette Myrtil, Carol Brice, Tun Tun, Truman
Gaige, Edith King, Warde Donovan, James Millhollin. Richard
Graham, Augie Rios.

Reading the News
I'll Be Respectable
Work Songs
One Step, Two Step
Lessons in Love
* Goose Never Be a Peàcock
Promenade (Street Cries)
Petticoat High
Bon Appétit
Dog Eat Dog
* Love Held Lightly
* A Game of Poker
* Saratoga
Have You Heard? (Gossip Song)
You for Me
The Cure

Al Fresco
The Parks of Paris
° The Man in My Life
You or No One
Countin' Our Chickens
NOTE: Johnny Mercer wrote both words and music to Why
Fight This? Gettin' a Man, The Men Who Run the
Country.

FREE AND EASY, a blues opera
Lyrics by Johnny Mercer, with additional lyrics by Ted Koehler;
direction by Robert Breen. Produced by Stanley Chase at the
Carré Theatre, Amsterdam, December 17, 1959, and at the
Alhambra, Paris, January 15, 1960. Cast: Irene Williams, Harold
Nicholas, Moses LaMarr, Martha Flowers, Irving Barnes, Paul
Harris, James Randolph, Ruby Green, Elijah Hodges, and
Quincy Jones and his orchestra.
ACT I: *Overture;* Conjure Man; Cake Song; Live Hard, Work
Hard, Love Hard; Blind Man; Natchul Man; I Ain't Afraid;
Della's Entrance (Whatcha Sayin', Della?) Wheel 'em and
Deal 'em; Sweetnin' Water; Least That's My Opinion; Ladies
'n' Gentlemen; Bees 'n' Flowers; Second Wind; Free and
Easy (Any Place I Hang My Hat Is Home); I Gotta Right to
Sing the Blues; Blues in the Night; Streak o' Lightnin'; Like
Clouds up in the Sky; *Dressing Up Sequence* (Ridin' on the
Moon); Lookin' fo' Somebody; Rainbow; Black Magic;
Toastin' Sequence; Lumpin'; A Woman's Prerogative; *First
March; Second March; Third March;* Cakewalk Your Lady;
Cakewalk Turns: *Soft Shoe, Sword Dance; Tambourine;
Genteel Bastard; Boogie; Tangissimo; Blues; Waltz, Dixie-
land; Pandemonium; Minuet.*
ACT II: *Overture;* Ya Pushin' Ya Luck; Whatcha Sayin'?;
Higher den de Moon; Dis Is de Day; Legalize My Name;
Lullaby; Killing Sequence; Curse; Sleep Peaceful, Mr. Used-
to-be; *Elegy;* Fix Yo'self Up; *Dissolves;* I Had Myself a True
Love; Reap the Harvest; Ill Wind; Racin' Forms; Bettin' Calls;
Look What a Hole You're In; Easy Street; Race; Champagne
fo' de Lady; High, Low, Jack and The Game; Dis Little
While; I Wonder What Became of Me?; Somethin' Ya Gotta
Find Out Yo'self; One for the Road; Leavin' Time; A Baby's
Born; Come Rain or Come Shine. *Additional songs:* Many
Kinds of Love; Then Suddenly; Flower Vendor; De Right

Answer; Won't Dat Be de Blessed Day; News Chant; Blow de Whistle; Snake Eyes.

1960

Ode, for solo piano
Bon-Bon, for solo piano

SUPPLEMENTARY LIST OF THE WORKS OF HAROLD ARLEN

Published songs are indicated with an asterisk (*).

1961

GAY PURR-EE

Lyrics by E. Y. Harburg; written by Dorothy and Chuck Jones; directed by Abe Levitow, produced by Harry G. Saperstein and released by Warner Brothers, October 1962. This full-length cartoon employed the voices of Judy Garland, Robert Goulet, Red Buttons, Hermione Gingold and Paul Frees.

*Newsette
*Little Drops of Rain
*The Money Cat
*Take My Hand Paree
*Paris is a Lonely Town
*Bubbles
*Roses Red, Violets Blue
*The Horse Won't Talk
*Free at Last

*Happy With the Blues (Lyric: Peggy Lee)

1962

Abstractions, solo piano

*I Could Go on Singin' (Lyric: E. Y. Harburg; title song for Judy Garland film)
*The Morning After (Lyric: Dory Langdon)
Like a Straw in the Wind (Lyric: Ted Koehler; written, but not published, ca. 1940-41)

1963

You're Impossible (Lyric: Dory Langdon)
*So Long, Big Time! (Lyric: Dory Langdon)
The Silent Spring (Lyric: E. Y. Harburg)

1964

Hurt But Happy (Lyric: Dory Langdon)
I Could be Good for You (Lyric: Martin Charnin)
Night After Night (lyric: Dory Langdon)

1964-65

Summer in Brooklyn (Lyric: Martin Charnin)
This Ol' World (Lyric: Martin Charnin)

SOFTLY

Lyrics by Martin Charnin; unproduced musical with book by Hugh Wheeler, based on a story by Santha Rama Rau.
Once I Wore Ribbons Here
Spring Has Me Out on a Limb
Been a Hell of an Evening
Temples
The More You See of It
Baby San
Pacific
Come On, Midnight
My Lady Fair
Momma Knows Best
You're Not Fully Dressed Without a Smile
Yellow Rain
Happy Any Day
Little Travel Bug
The Brush Off
Suddenly the Sunrise
A Girl's Entitled
Hello
You Are Tomorrow
Don't Say "Love"—I've Been There and Back
I Will
We Were Always to be Married
Why Do You Make Me Like You?
Shoulda Stood in Bed
Fish Go Higher Than Tigers

1965
Fine Kind of Freedom (Lyrics: Martin Charnin)

1973
CLIPPITY CLOP AND CLEMENTINE
Lyrics by Harold Arlen; one-hour mini-musical (not produced); book by Leonard Melfi.
I Had a Love Once
Is What It's All About
A Happy Recipe
This Way or No Way at All
Dreamin' Suits Me Just Fine
Clippity Clop
Ridin' Through the Park in a Hansom Cab
Organic Food

1976
Looks Like the End of a Beautiful Friendship (Lyric: E. Y. Harburg)
Promise Me Not to Love Me (Lyric: E. Y. Harburg)

Songs without Dates
Little Lady on the Cameo (lyric: Ted Koehler)
Is the Curtain Up? (lyric: Harold Arlen)

SELECTED DISCOGRAPHY

The following is not an exhaustive listing of the recordings of songs with music by Harold Arlen. Since each month brings forth about two dozen new recordings of songs in various interpretations, any complete listing would become unwieldy. In selecting the following recordings a well-rounded survey of the composer's output has been the major principle whereby the choices have been made; recordings either of historical importance or of outstanding performance—even if not widely available—have been listed in the hopes that a new demand may lead to their reissuance. The mania for "high fidelity" has caused the too early deletion of records that might be of great interest or value. Such records as once existed on long-playing discs, but that may no longer be readily available, are marked with an asterisk (*).

The discography falls into five sections: the first is devoted to collections devoted exclusively to Arlen music; these are medleys and are often repetitiously overlapping in the choice of material. Since there are instrumental and vocal medleys, the instrumentals will be listed first, and the vocals second.

The next group covers the film scores, often in the form of sound tracks by the original performers. The third group lists the show scores, again as performed by the so-called "original casts." In connection with recent scores, the practice of also issuing satellite recordings from the scores has sprung up; these are usually instrumentals but will not be listed in the first group; it would seem more useful to list them and to comment upon them in conjunction with their source scores.

The fourth section is given over to a listing of individual performances that are for some reason or other outstanding but that, if they are to be owned, entail the purchase of a complete recording for the single Arlen song. In some instances the rendition of the song may not be so important as the fact that it represents the only available recording of that particular song. But this, as the discography itself, is not an exhaustive list and is meant only as a guide for anyone seriously interested in exploring the Harold Arlen lists of works as fully as it deserves. As is the case with all our great popular composers, the music of Harold Arlen as reflected by recordings is limited generally to the same old standards; many fine songs have never been recorded. Finally, there is a listing of titles of vocal recordings made by Harold Arlen in the Thirties; these are historical but doubtless unprocurable.

1. COLLECTIONS—Instrumental

Blues-Opera Suite
Opening, Act I; Cake Song; Conjure Man; Augie's Entrance; Whatcha Sayin', Della?; Streak o' Lightnin'; A Woman's Prerogative; Cakewalk Turns: Soft Shoe, Boogie, Blues: Minuet; Opening, Act II; I Had Myself a True Love; Champagne fo' de Lady; Dis Little While; I Wonder What Became of Me?; One for My Baby; Leavin' Time; Come Rain or Come Shine. (Side 2 of the record contains Out of This World, That Old Black Magic, Stormy Weather, and Blues in the Night). Andre Kostelanetz and his orchestra .... Columbia CL 1099

Kostelanetz gives the *Suite* a good straightforward interpretation, though the Matlowsky orchestration at times echoes the pseudo-jazz of the Paul Whiteman-Ferde Grofé era. The songs filling out the record are also well done, particularly "Out of This World," which is done as Arlen originally conceived it, interludes and all.

Oscar Peterson Plays the Harold Arlen Song Book
Happiness Is a Thing Called Joe; Stormy Weather; Over the Rainbow; The Man That Got Away; Ill Wind; Let's Fall in Love; As Long as I Live; Come Rain or Come Shine; Ac-cent-tchu-ate the Positive; Between the Devil and the Deep Blue Sea; I've Got the World on a String; That Old Black Magic. Oscar Peterson, pianist...........................Verve 6091

Peterson plays beautifully subdued, moody piano interpretations of these songs. He does not stray far from the original melodies and yet infuses them with his own ideas. "Stormy Weather" is especially well played.

* *The Melodies of Harold Arlen*
Blues in the Night; Ill Wind; Over the Rainbow; Come Rain or Come Shine; Stormy Weather; One for My Baby; Between the Devil and the Deep Blue Sea; I Gotta a Right to Sing the Blues. Ellis Larkins, pianist .... Decca DL 5391
Larkins is an unusually gifted, sensitive pianist whose style is particularly suited to interpreting Arlen's music. In fact, this is one of the composer's favorite albums. Because it was issued as a ten-inch record, Decca has since withdrawn it, though it is possible that a new one will eventually be made.

The Music of Harold Arlen
I've Got the World on a String; Come Rain or Come Shine;
It's Only a Paper Moon; Happiness Is a Thing Called Joe; Last
Night When We Were Young; Stormy Weather; What's Good
about Goodbye?; Over the Rainbow; Let's Fall in Love; Ill
Wind; That Old Black Magic; Blues in the Night.

David Rose and his orchestra . . . . M-G-M E-3101

This is an excellent, richly romantic playing in the Rose manner
of several of the best-known Arlen songs, plus a few not so well
known. In all instances the harmonies and tempos are true to the
composer's intentions. Rose's good taste, musically, brings fine interpretations to "Come Rain or Come Shine," "Last Night When We
Were Young," and "What's Good about Goodbye?" among others.

The Music of Harold Arlen
That Old Black Magic; Stormy Weather; I've Got the World on
a String; Come Rain or Come Shine; Over the Rainbow; Happiness Is a Thing Called Joe. (Side 2: *The Music of Richard
Rodgers.*)
Raoul Polakin, chorus, and orchestra . . . . Everest 5066
Though recorded more recently than the David Rose album,
this set is not as extensive a coverage of Arlen's catalogue nor as
adventurous a one. An added attraction, besides the fine sound, is
the occasional vocalizing of the chorus.

COLLECTIONS—Vocal

* *Harold Arlen and His Songs*
I've Got the World on a String; Ac-cent-tchu-ate the Positive;
Come Rain or Come Shine; Let's Fall in Love; One for My
Baby; It's only a Paper Moon; Blues in the Night; Over the
Rainbow; That Old Black Magic; The Gal That Got Away; Two
Ladies in de Shade of de Banana Tree; Stormy Weather.
Harold Arlen with orchestra conducted by Peter Matz . . . .
Capitol T 635
This is one of the two albums made by the composer in 1954;
this set made with a large orchestra is a fine collection with
emphasis on the standards. Although Arlen concentrates on sing-
ing in this album, he does play a most sensitive piano solo in "Let's
Fall in Love."

* *Composers at Play*
Stormy Weather; Let's Fall in Love; as Long as I Live; Happy

as the Day Is Long; This Is Only The Beginning (Side 2: *Cole Porter Plays and Sings*).

Harold Arlen with Arthur Schutt; with the Leo Reisman Orchestra .... "X" LVA-1003

This fine collector's record brought together several of the sides Arlen made in 1932–34, including the famous interpretation of "Stormy Weather." The recording quality is hardly "high fidelity," but the songs are of sufficient interest, as are their renditions, to merit this album's reissue by RCA Victor (the "X" label no longer exists). Cole Porter singing and playing his own songs on the reverse of the record makes it doubly valuable.

The Music of Harold Arlen
I: Hit the Road To Dreamland; Moanin' in the Mornin'; Minuet; You're the Cure for What Ails Me; It's a New World; Buds Won't Bud; I Never Has Seen Snow; Evelina; Last Night When We Were Young; T'morra', T'morra'; House of Flowers Waltz; Hooray for Love.
Harold Arlen, vocals and piano solos, with orchestra conducted by Peter Matz.
II: I Love a New Yorker; My Shining Hour; Come Rain or Come Shine; Let's Take a Walk around the Block; I Wonder What Became of Me?; Can I Leave Off Wearin' My Shoes?; I Had Myself a True Love; Fun to Be Fooled; Happiness Is a Thing Called Joe; Hallowe'en; Right as the Rain; One for My Baby.
Louise Carlyle; Bob Shaver; Warren Galjour; June Ericson, and Miriam Burton, with orchestra conducted by Peter Matz ...... Walden 306/307

This two-record set was made about the same time as the Capitol record and might be considered a companion set. The Walden record attempts to present a comprehensive collection without repeating too many of the obvious standards. In this set Arlen plays the piano, solo and as accompaniment for many of the songs, most notably "Last Night When We Were Young," and "It's a New World;" he joins Peter Matz in a charming piano duet in "Evelina." Even after several years the album holds up very well and features much fine singing by Arlen as well as the other vocalists.

Tony Bennett Sings a String of Harold Arlen
When the Sun Comes Out; Over the Rainbow; House of Flowers; Come Rain or Come Shine; For Every Man There's a Woman; Let's Fall in Love; Right as the Rain; It Was Written in the

Stars; What Good Does It Do?; Fun to Be Fooled; This Time
the Dream's on Me; I've Got the World on a String.
Tony Bennett with orchestra conducted by Frank DeVol ....
Columbia CL 1559

Bennett does his usual fervent, exciting work on this album which
combines a refreshing number of lesser known songs along with the
usual standards. Long an admirer of Arlen, Tony Bennett proves it
in this outstanding album. He does "When the Sun Comes Out"
especially well.

* *Diahann Carroll Sings Harold Arlen Songs*
It's Only a Paper Moon; What's Good about Goodbye?; A
Sleepin' Bee; My Shining Hour; Hit the Road to Dreamland;
Over the Rainbow; Come Rain or Come Shine; You're a Builder
Upper; Out of This World; I Wonder What's Become of Me?;
Down with Love; Let's Take the Long Way Home.
Diahann Carroll with orchestra conducted by Ralph Burns
.... RCA Victor LPM 1467

Miss Carroll made her debut in *House of Flowers*; this was her
first album made after she had appeared in that show. Her delivery
in this set is simpler than it has since become, and the album is
very good.

Ella Fitzgerald Sings the Harold Arlen Song Book
Thirty two songs on 2-12" Lp's. *Verve*

In preparation for release in 1961.

2. FILM SCORES

The Wizard of Oz (lyrics by E. Y. Harburg)—1938
Over the Rainbow; The Jitterbug; Munchkinland; If I Only
Had a Brain, A Heart, The Nerve; The Merry Old Land of Oz;
We're Off to See the Wizard (Side 2: *Pinocchio*).
Judy Garland, the Ken Darby Singers, Victor Young and his
Orchestra .... Decca 8387

Not a sound-track recording, but a special album made soon
after the completion of the film. It has the only recording of the
interesting "The Jitterbug."

The Wizard of Oz
Over the Rainbow; If I Only Had a Brain, A Heart, The Nerve;
Ding-Dong! The Witch Is Dead; We're Off to See the Wizard;
If I Were King of the Forest; The Merry Old Land of Oz.
Judy Garland, Bert Lahr, Ray Bolger, Jack Haley, Frank Morgan,

Margaret Hamilton, Billie Burke, and the Munchkins ....
M-G-M E 3464 ST
This record contains virtually the complete score of the film as taken from the sound track. Some of the dialogue is retained to fulfill a narrative function. A fine preservation of a classic film score.

° *Mr. Imperium* (lyrics by Dorothy Fields)—1951
Andiamo, My Love an' My Mule, Let Me Look at You (and other songs) Ezio Pinza, Fran Warren and orchestra conducted by Johnny Green .... RCA Victor LM 61
Since ten-inch longplaying records have become obsolete, this recording was withdrawn early. Pinza does a superb job on the splendid "Let Me Look At You," and it is possible that one day these songs could be reissued on another record.

A Star Is Born (lyrics by Ira Gershwin)—1954
Here's What I'm Here for; It's a New World; Someone at Last; Lose That Long Face; Gotta Have Me Go with You; The Man That Got Away (and "Born in a Trunk," a song medley).
Judy Garland, chorus and orchestra conducted by Ray Heindorf .... Columbia CL 1101
A dubbing of the complete score direct from the sound track. Little else need be said about it.

° *The Country Girl* (lyrics by Ira Gershwin)—1954
It's Mine, It's Yours (The Pitchman); The Search Is Through; Dissertation on the State of Bliss (Love and Learn); The Land around Us (Side 2: songs from *Little Boy Lost*)
Bing Crosby, Patty Andrews with chorus and orchestra under Joseph J. Lilley .... Decca DL 5556
Decca recorded all the Arlen-Gershwin songs from *The Country Girl*, but because it was released on a ten-inch record it has long since gone out of print. Miss Andrews joins Crosby in "Dissertation," but these accomplished singers don't get out of the songs what they might have; perhaps a new recording will give it better treatment.

3. *SHOW SCORES*
Bloomer Girl (lyrics by E. Y. Harburg)—1944
When the Boys Come Home; Evelina; Welcome Hinges; The Farmer's Daughter; It Was Good Enough for Grandma; The Eagle and Me; Right as the Rain; T'morra' T'morra'; The Rakish Young Man with the Whiskers; Sunday in Cicero Falls; I Got

a Song; Satin Gown and Silver Shoe; Liza Crossing the Ice; I
Never Was Born; Man for Sale; Finale.
Celeste Holm, David Brooks, Richard Huey, Joan McCracken,
Dooley Wilson, Toni Hart, Mabel Taliaferro, Harold Arlen and
the chorus and orchestra conducted by Leon Leonardi . . . .
Decca DL 8015
Though originally recorded for release on 78 rpm records, this
album has been refurbished and reissued on long-play. It has the
advantages of having members of the original Broadway cast singing the songs, though some were a little lacking in the vocal department. Also, for the record, Arlen sang "Man for Sale." Until the
score is rerecorded this one is an excellent record to have. The
sound has been improved, and most of the music is on the disc,
though not always as well projected as one might wish it to be. One
of the classic scores of the American musical theater, however.

° *St. Louis Woman* (lyrics by Johnny Mercer)—1948
Li'l Augie Is a Natural Man; Any Place I Hang My Hat Is
Home; I Had Myself a True Love; Legalize My Name; Cakewalk
Your Lady; Come Rain or Come Shine; Lullaby; Sleep Peaceful,
Mr. Used-to-Be; Leavin' Time; It's a Woman's Prerogative; Ridin'
on the Moon.
Ruby Hill, Harold Nicholas, June Hawkins, Pearl Bailey, Robert
Pope, with chorus and orchestra conducted by Leon Leonardi
. . . . Capitol H 355
This ten-inch record, no longer available, dubbed from shellacs,
contains some of the most beautifully written and sung music ever
heard in the theater. Though recorded several years ago the sound
is still fine, pointing up the lovely orchestrations. This rare disc has
fallen into the Collector's item class and may now and then be
found but at a rather steep price. It is worth it. Or possibly it will
be reissued.

House of Flowers (lyrics by Truman Capote and Harold Arlen)—
1954
Overture; Waitin'; One Man Ain't Quite Enough; A Sleepin' Bee;
Bamboo Cage; House of Flowers; Two Ladies in de Shade of de
Banana Tree; What Is a Friend for? Slide, Boy, Slide; I'm Gonna
Leave Off Wearin' My Shoes; Has I Let You Down?; I Never
Has Seen Snow; Turtle Song; Don't Like Goodbyes; Mardi
Gras.
Pearl Bailey, Diahann Carroll, Juanita Hall, Rawn Spearman,
Ada Moore, Enid Mosier, Dolores Harper, Miriam Burton, chorus

and orchestra conducted by Jerry Arlen .... Columbia
ML 4969

Though short-lived as a show, the score to *House of Flowers*
has grown with the years, and Columbia wisely keeps it available.
Under the supervision of show-astute Goddard Lieberson the entire
flavor of the score is wonderfully captured on the recording, including the exciting overture. The ballet music to "Mardi Gras" is also
included. A fine album.

House of Flowers
House of Flowers; I'm Gonna Leave Off Wearin' My Shoes;
Waitin'; Slide, Boy, Slide; Don't Like Goodbyes; Two Ladies in
de Shade of de Banana Tree; One Man Ain't Quite Enough; I
Never Has Seen Snow; What Is a Friend for?; A Sleepin' Bee;
Mardi Gras Waltz; Smellin' of Vanilla (Bamboo Cage).
Percy Faith and his orchestra .... Columbia CL 640
Beautifully atmospheric orchestral interpretations of some of the
songs; the "Mardi Gras Waltz" is the same as "House of Flowers
Waltz," although it is not heard in the original cast album. Faith
invests the score with a proper lush sound.

Jamaica (lyrics by E. Y. Harburg)—1957
Savanna; Savanna's Wedding Day; Pretty to Walk with; Push
de Button; Incompatibility; Little Biscuit; Cocoanut Sweet; Pity
the Sunset; Take It Slow, Joe; Yankee Dollar; Monkey in the
Mango Tree; Ain't It de Truth; What Good Does It Do?; Leave
the Atom Alone; Napoleon; For Every Little Fish; I Don't
Think I'll End It All Today; Finale.
Lena Horne, Ricardo Montalban, Josephine Premice, Ossie Davis,
Adelaide Hall, Augustine Rios, chorus and orchestra conducted
by Lehman Engel .... RCA Victor LOC 1036
Probably some of her best singing was done by Lena Horne for
this cast recording. Montalban records well, as do Josephine Premice
and Ossie Davis. Although the "feel" of the theater is not present
in this album as it is in the *House of Flowers* album above, it does
contain some fine songs.

Jamaica
Savanna, Cocoanut Sweet; Little Biscuit; Take It Slow, Joe;
Push de Button; I Don't Think I'll End It All Today; Monkey
in the Mango Tree; Pretty to Walk with; What Good Does It
Do?; Napoleon.
David Rose and his orchestra .... M-G-M E 3612
The beauty of Arlen's melodies and harmonies comes through in

Rose's interpretations so well that it would be tempting to recommend it over the cast album, but that would deprive one of the masterful Harburg lyrics, and the marvelous interpretations by the cast. The Rose album, however, is pure Arlen—if anyone is interested in comparing what he originally conceived and what finally came out in the theater.

Saratoga (lyrics by Johnny Mercer)—1959
One Step, Two Step; I'll Be Respectable; Gettin' a Man; Why Fight This?; Petticoat High; A Game of Poker; Love Held Lightly; Duet: A Game of Poker/Love Held Lightly; Saratoga; Countin' Our Chickens; You or No One; The Cure; The Man in My Life; The Men Who Run the Country; Goose Never Be a Peacock; Dog Eat Dog; The Railroad Fight; Finale.
Carol Lawrence; Howard Keel; Odette Myrtil, Carol Brice, with chorus and orchestra conducted by Jerry Arlen .... RCA Victor LOC 1051

In reviewing this album in *The Saturday Review* Irving Kolodin quite rightly stated that "Few shows of recent years have had as many fine, tuneful ideas as this one (half a dozen, at least, belong with the best of Arlen's sizable collection), but their effect is lessened rather than enhanced by the performance of the original cast." Unfortunately, however, it is all that exists of the songs sung. There are some fine moments and the album is worth having even if one is not an Arlen collector. Unfortunately RCA again misses some of the theater qualities that would have helped; and some cuts have been made—the Work Songs and Street Cries are eliminated, as is a second chorus of "The Man in My Life." The composer's brother, at least knew what the score was all about and does manage to infuse it with excitement and beauty.

Saratoga
Petticoat High; Goose Never Be a Peacock; A Game of Poker; The Parks of Paris; Saratoga; Love Held Lightly; The Man in My Life; You for Me; Dog Eat Dog.
The Paul Smith Trio (Paul Smith, Rolly Bundock, Jack Sperling) ...... Imperial LP 9095

Not only are the songs tastefully played by the piano-bass-drums group, but a couple of songs that turned out to be out-of-town casualties are included: "The Parks of Paris" and "You for Me." In most of the songs even the composer's harmonies are respected. "Love Held Lightly," certainly one of Arlen's most exquisite creations, is sensitively played by the trio.

Saratoga
Duet: A Game of Poker/Love Held Lightly; One Step, Two Step;
The Man in My Life; The Cure; Goose Never Be a Peacock;
Saratoga; Have You Heard?; Parks of Paris; A Game of Poker;
You For Me; Love Held Lightly; Petticoat High.
Larry Elgart and his orchestra .... RCA Victor LPM 2166
Arranged-jazz interpretations by a finely disciplined band. "Goose
Never Be a Peacock" is given an imaginative rendition. Tempos
are sometimes too fast for some songs, which seem perfunctorily
rendered, but because these are modern dance-band arrangements
it might just as well be excused. Highly interesting most of the
time.

4. OUTSTANDING SINGLE SONG INTERPRETATIONS
Get Happy (lyric, Ted Koehler)—1930
Judy Garland in *Judy Garland*—M-G-M 3149

Between the Devil and the Deep Blue Sea (lyric, Ted Koehler)
—1931
Ella Fitzgerald in *Sweet and Hot*, Decca 8155

I Gotta Right to Sing the Blues (lyric, Ted Koehler)—1932
Judy Garland in *Alone*, Capitol T 835

I've Got the World on a String (lyric, Ted Koehler)—1932
Frank Sinatra in *This Is Sinatra!* Capitol T-768

It's Only a Paper Moon (lyric, E. Y. Harburg and Billy Rose)
—1932
Nat "King" Cole in *Vocal Classics* Capitol T-591

Stormy Weather (lyric, Ted Koehler)—1933
Lena Horne in *Stormy Weather* RCA victor LPM 1375
Frank Sinatra in *The Frank Sinatra Story in Music*,
Columbia C2L-6

Ill Wind (lyric, Ted Koehler)—1934
Margie Rayburn in *Margie*, Liberty 3126

Fun to Be Fooled (lyric, Ira Gershwin and E. Y. Harburg)—1934
Anita Ellis in *The World in My Arms*, Elektra 179

Last Night When We Were Young (lyric, E. Y. Harburg)—1935
Judy Garland in *Judy*, Capitol T-734

Fancy Meeting You (lyric, E. Y. Harburg)—1936
Dick Powell in *The Dick Powell Song Book*, Decca 8837

Lydia, The Tattooed Lady (lyric, E. Y. Harburg)—1939
Bobby Short in *Sing Me a Swing Song,* Atlantic 1285

Where Is Dis Road A-Leadin' Me To? (lyric, Ted Koehler)—1940
Eileen Farrell in *Songs and Ballads,* Angel 35608

Happiness Is a Thing Called Joe (lyric, E. Y. Harburg)—1943
Judy Garland in *Miss Show Business,* Capitol W-676

One for My Baby (lyric, Johnny Mercer)—1943
Fred Astaire in *Now,* Kapp 1165
Harry Belafonte in *Belafonte Sings the Blues* RCA Victor
LOP 1006

Now I Know (lyric, Ted Koehler)—1944
Dinah Shore in *Moments Like These,* RCA Victor LPM 1719

I Wonder What Became of Me? (lyric, Johnny Mercer)—1946
Anita Ellis in *I Wonder What Became of Me?* Epic LN 3280
Lena Horne in *Stormy Weather,* RCA Victor LPM 1375

I Had Myself a True Love (lyric, Johnny Mercer)—1946
Felicia Sanders in *That Certain Feeling* Decca 8762

Hooray for Love and For Every Man There's a Woman (lyrics,
Leo Robin)
Jane Powell in *Can't We Be Friends?* Verve 2023

Today I Love Ev'rybody (lyric, Dorothy Fields)
Lena Horne in *At the Waldorf,* RCA Victor LOC 1028

5. EARLY RECORDINGS BY HAROLD ARLEN

1930-Linda (from *Brown Sugar,* lyric by Ted Koehler), with the
Red Nichols Band, Brunswick Records.
1931-You Said It/Sweet and Hot (both from *You Said It* lyrics by
Jack Yellen), with the Red Nichols Band on Brunswick
Records.
1932-Stepping into Love (lyric, Ted Koehler), with Leo Reisman's
orchestra—RCA Victor.
1933-Stormy Weather (lyric, Ted Koehler), with Leo Reisman's
orchestra—RCA Victor.
Happy as the Day Is Long (lyric, Ted Koehler), with Leo
Reisman's orchestra—RCA Victor.
1934-Let's Fall in Love/This Is Only the Beginning (both from
Let's Fall in Love, lyrics by Ted Koehler), with Leo Reisman's
orchestra—RCA Victor.
Ill Wind/As Long as I Live (lyric, Ted Koehler), with Leo
Reisman's orchestra—RCA Victor.

Ill Wind/As Long as I Live (lyric, Ted Koehler), with Eddy Duchin and orchestra—RCA Victor.

Shoein' the Mare/Fun to Be Fooled (from *Life Begins at 8:40*, lyrics by Ira Gershwin and E. Y. Harburg), with Leo Reisman's orchestra—Brunswick Records.

You're A Builder Upper/What Can You Say In A Love Song? (from *Life Begins at 8:40*, lyrics by Ira Gershwin and E. Y. Harburg), with Leo Reisman's orchestra—Brunswick Records.

1937-In the Shade of the New Apple Tree/God's Country (from *Horray for What?* lyrics by E. Y. Harburg), with Leo Reisman's orchestra—RCA Victor.

Note: In the late Twenties, Harold Arlen recorded with The Buffalodians for Majestic Records, but it is doubtful* that these recordings still exist. He recorded "Pardon Me, Pretty Baby" with the Blue Four (Joe Venuti, Jimmy Dorsey, Frank Signorelli and Eddie Lang) which was issued on the Harmony label in 1931. With a similar group, the same year, he sang on "There's No Other Girl," "Now That I Need You" on a Columbia Record. Columbia Records plans to reissue the original recording by Fletcher Henderson, "That's Dynamite," which was arranged by Harold Arlen.

A DISCOGRAPHICAL NOTE FOR THE DA CAPO EDITION

The original sound tracks to *The Wizard of Oz* (originally Decca, reissued on MCA Records) and *A Star is Born*, reissued on Columbia's Harmony label) are still around. So is "Harold Sings Arlen (with Friend) (Columbia OS 2920), although it might require special ordering outside the larger cities.

A fine survey of Arlen's output, sung by the composer, who sometimes also provides his own piano accompaniment, is "Harold Arlen Sings" (Mark 56 Records 683; address: P.O. Box One, Anaheim, California 92805).

Time-Life Records, in its "American Musicals "series, has prepared an Arlen album consisting of three LP records devoted to the original cast albums of *Bloomer Girl, House of Flowers*, and *Jamaica*. Entitled "Harold Arlen," the set number is STL-A11. Information about it may be obtained by writing to Reader Information, Time-Life Records, 541 North Fairbanks Court, Chicago, Illinois 60611. It is not necessary to subscribe to the entire series; individual sets can be purchased (ca. $25.00)—although the complete series is excellent and worth having.

Index